ELECTRONIC TEXT

Electronic Text

Investigations in Method and Theory

Edited by
Kathryn Sutherland

CLARENDON PRESS · OXFORD
1997

Oxford University Press, Great Clarendon Street, Oxford OX2 6DP

Oxford New York
Athens Auckland Bangkok Bogota Bombay
Buenos Aires Calcutta Cape Town Dar es Salaam
Delhi Florence Hong Kong Istanbul Karachi
Kuala Lumpur Madras Madrid Melbourne
Mexico City Nairobi Paris Singapore
Taipei Tokyo Toronto Warsaw
and associated companies in
Berlin Ibadan

Oxford is a trade mark of Oxford University Press

Published in the United States
by Oxford University Press Inc., New York

British Library Cataloguing in Publication Data
Data available

Library of Congress Cataloging in Publication Data
Electronic text : investigations in method and theory
edited by Kathryn Sutherland.
Includes bibliographical references.
1. English literature—Criticism, Textual—Data processing.
2. American literature—Criticism, Textual—Data processing.
3. Manuscripts, American—Editing—Data processing.   4. Manuscripts,
English—Editing—Data processing.   5. Transmission of texts—Data
processing.   6. Text processing (Computer science)   7. Electronic
publishing.   I. Sutherland, Kathryn.
PR21.E44   1997   820.9—DC21   97–18776
ISBN 0–19–823663–8

10 9 8 7 6 5 4 3 2 1

Typeset by Graphicraft Typesetters Ltd., Hong Kong
Printed in Great Britain on acid-free paper by
Bookcraft (Bath) Ltd., Midsomer Norton

ACKNOWLEDGEMENTS

My thanks go to Stuart Lee for technical expertise and the generous giving of his time, also to Frances Morphy, our commissioning editor at OUP, for encouraging the project, and especially to Marilyn Deegan whose ideas and energy helped to shape the collection in its earlier stages. I owe a particular thanks to the contributors for their enthusiasm, patience, and support throughout, not least for their cheerful co-operation in the undermining strategy of turning their electronic text into printed book.

K. S.

St Anne's College
Oxford

CONTENTS

NOTES ON CONTRIBUTORS

Patrick W. Conner is Eberly College Centennial Professor in the Department of English at West Virginia University. Founder and editor of ANSAXNET, an electronic discussion list dedicated to the early medieval period, he has written on Old English poetry and on the application of computers to problems practical and theoretic in early medieval literature and in modern American literature. He is currently working on two studies—*A Computer-Assisted Approach to Problems in Early English Literary History* and *Hypertext, Ideology, and the American Canon*.

Peter S. Donaldson is Ann Fetter Friedlander Professor of Humanities at Massachusetts Institute of Technology. He is the author of studies of Machiavelli and of *Shakespearean Films/Shakespearean Directors*. In 1991 he founded with Larry Friedlander and Janet H. Murray the Shakespeare Electronic Archive whose work includes the construction of a text-image-video archive for installation at the Folger Shakespeare Library and the production of CD-ROM editions of multiple text facsimiles of individual plays, beginning with *Hamlet*.

Julia Flanders is the Textbase Editor at the Brown University Women Writers Project where she is responsible for supervising and documenting the Project's transcription and encoding procedures. She holds degrees from Harvard and Cambridge Universities, and is currently a doctoral candidate in the English Department at Brown, where her research addresses the development of nineteenth-century theories of art, the book, and the body.

David Greetham is Distinguished Professor of English and Interdisciplinary Studies at the City University of New York Graduate School. Founder of the Society for Textual Scholarship, he is author of *Textual Scholarship: An Introduction*, *Theories of the Text*, and *Textual Transgressions*. He is currently working on a hypermedia archive of citation in the humanities and on a digitized study of textual morphology.

Claire Lamont is Senior Lecturer in English at the University of Newcastle and writes on English and Scottish Literature of the eighteenth and early nineteenth centuries. Her edition of Walter Scott's *Waverley* won the British Academy's Rose Mary Crawshay prize in 1983. She is a General Editor of the Edinburgh Edition of the Waverley Novels, and editor of Scott's

Chronicles of the Canongate in that edition. She recently acted as Textual Adviser to the new Penguin Edition of the Novels of Jane Austen.

JEROME J. MCGANN is John Stewart Bryan Professor of English at the University of Virginia. His many books on literary and textual theory include *A Critique of Modern Textual Criticism*, *The Textual Condition*, and *Black Riders: The Visible Language of Modernism*. He is the editor of Byron's *Complete Poetical Works* in seven volumes and of the one-volume Oxford Authors *Byron*. He is currently engaged in assembling 'The Complete Writings and Pictures of Dante Gabriel Rossetti: A Hypermedia Research Archive'.

ALLEN RENEAR, a philosopher specializing in epistemology and philosophy of science, is Director of the Brown University Scholarly Technology Group. His publications and current research are focused on the interplay between technology, methodology, and theory in the humanities.

PETER M. W. ROBINSON of the International Institute for Electronic Library Research, De Montfort University, is a medievalist by training. Joint general editor for the *Canterbury Tales* Project and developer of the widely used computer collation program *Collate*, he has published on textual criticism, electronic editing, and the digitization and encoding of textual materials. He is the editor of the electronic Wife of Bath's Prologue (Cambridge, 1996).

KATHRYN SUTHERLAND is Reader in Bibliography and Textual Crticism at the University of Oxford and a Fellow of St Anne's College. She has written on Romantic Literature and literature of the Scottish Enlightenment, on economic discourses, and on the theoretical and cultural implications of Literature in the electronic environment. Her editions, in traditional paper format, include works by Walter Scott, Adam Smith, and Jane Austen. As Director of Project Electra, an electronic full-text database of Women's Writings 1780–1830, she is planning paper and electronic publications from the assembled materials.

1

Introduction

KATHRYN SUTHERLAND

Why is the computer storage and dissemination of text causing such controversy and such diverse (even contradictory) assertions as to its significance for the representation and transmission of knowledge? The challenge posed by electronic technology to the technology of the printed book, which has dominated Western textual practices since the end of the fifteenth century, is voiced by enthusiasts and critics alike in extravagant, even apocalyptic terms. Both camps take it for granted that the shift is monumental, involving a reconsideration of such large and difficult issues as the nature and extent of authorial property, the stability/fluidity of text and its relation to material forms, the globalization or dis-/relocation of knowledge, and the threat to or likely changes in reading practices. Whatever interpretation we decide to put on these issues, the shared assumption is that the boundaries of what we know and how we possess what we know are changed for ever. To the enthusiast, the future looks rosy: '[t]he democratic thrust of information technologies derives from their diffusing information and the power that such diffusion can produce', George Landow confidently asserts; '[t]he electronic word democratizes the world of arts and letters', proclaims Richard Lanham.[1] But to the critic, the impact of electronic technologies on changing cultural practices is malign and regressive: in George Steiner's nightmare vision, computers contribute to 'the crisis of the word' and partake of the 'nihilistic logic and consequent extremity of the after-Word'; and Sven Birkerts's impassioned lament is for the loss of wisdom in the pursuit of data. His question is '[w]ill our narratives—historical, literary, classical—be able to withstand the data explosion?' and if they will not, 'then what will be the new face of understanding?'[2] The plangent title of Birkerts's study, *The Gutenberg Elegies: The Fate of Reading in an Electronic Age*, predetermines his answer. In this latter view (a view for those times which Gérard Genette in another context has suggested may be 'the last days of the book'[3]) it appears that, rather than expanding the reach of knowledge, electronic storage and retrieval ensures that what we know remains external, information merely, to be manipulated, as opposed to knowledge to be absorbed. It is as if the unfixing of text from its printed fixity destroys its traditionally valued capacity to enter and transform (unfix) the reader. Now such transformations are restricted to the level of external practices—commands given to the computer—whereby the changeable electronic text loses what Steiner calls its 'implosive powers within the echo chambers of the self'.[4]

Opposed as the positions of Landow and Lanham, on the one hand, and Steiner and Birkerts, on the other, are, both represent moral views and both are undoubtedly political views, pitting the (potential) access of the many against the (possible) enrichment of the few. As such, neither position is subject to substantiation or alteration by proof; neither view can be shown to be correct or false, though we will each undoubtedly be drawn (depending on our own political-cultural assumptions about what we think texts *should* do) to one side of the case or the other as to what we believe electronic text does do. This obvious point is worth pondering, because it alerts us to the nature of the current vigorous debate over electronic technology and to the terms within which much of the argument is being conducted. Electronic technology is, we are told, good/bad for us because: it liberates more of us (to know more)/it diminishes the knowledge (the need to know) we each have. More specifically in the arguments of Landow and Lanham and Steiner and Birkerts, it appears as if the technology itself acts upon text in certain ways, and that in itself this is good/bad for us, liberates/limits knowledge.[5] Among the assumptions at work here, assumptions to do with the power of technology as autonomous actor, is the assumption that there is a simple and simply congruent relation between a text and its production—that, to misquote Marshall McLuhan, 'the medium is the only message'. To question this congruence is not to deny what is powerfully true, that technologies are themselves meaning constitutive within texts, whether by technology we imply the chiselling of shapes on stone, the impression of inked metal type on paper, or the storing of a string of binary data (noughts and ones) on the hard disk or the CD-ROM to be translated at need into a 'readable' display on the computer screen. Unless we are determined to think of texts as no more than their linguistic codes (words with only an accidental relation to their material means of presentation), we will recognize the contribution of technology to meaning. But there is a reverse reasoning at work among enthusiasts and critics alike of electronic technology who assume that the method of production and the text exist in exactly the same real and theoretical space. More than this, that the technology *is* the text, and that what the one may or may not enable the other exclusively communicates. Why, after all, should an electronic version of *Hamlet* or *Paradise Lost* (setting aside the economics of the project, which in fact tell a less 'democratic' story) in itself denote either a 'democratization' within 'the world of art and letters', as Lanham suggests, or the 'consequent extremity of the after-Word', as Steiner prophesies? Why do we assume such powerful agency in this particular technology? Or to ask the question another way—what is it that we believe texts *should* give us access to and why does their electronic representation enhance, compromise, or betray this?

We are in the West living through a period of enormous transformation. Just as a mass literature market was shaped in late eighteenth-century Britain by the consumer demands and commercial relations of a proto-industrial society, so in our own age literary dissemination and the explanatory modes of postmodern aesthetics reflect transformations in our methods of production and communication generally. The electronic age is the age of globally dispersed capitalist economies, of trans-national corporations, of complexly mediated and hybridized cultural experiences, and, above all, of distance—telephone, television, teleconferencing, telecommunications generally—presented as proximity. Our cultural relations, how we represent to ourselves what we value in art, music, and literature, are themselves renewed through and implicated in these changes. In recognizing this, Steiner on the one hand and Lanham on the other are rehearsing in terms appropriate to our own times the élitist and populist positions ('can it be literature if it is/is not available to the many?') familiar to us from that earlier period in the debate between the romantic aestheticians and their critics. Just as that moment around 1800 which saw the invention of the iron-frame hand-press with its *mechanical* power to increase the rate of print production for the first time since Gutenberg and Caxton also saw an anxious debate over the *cultural* power of the disseminated book, almost regardless of its contents, so we are in the late twentieth century living through another such destabilizing crisis in the world of production and meaning.

Why the debate about the electronic representation of text is so vital has less to do with what electronic technology *really does* (as if the technology is an agent in its own right) and more to do with the fact that it furthers the impossibility of textual, literary, and cultural critics assuming and defending the separateness of their activities: electronic representation enacts the inclusiveness of text. The *fact* of electronic text is necessarily part of that renewed interest in what text is which has characterized cultural and literary debate at least since the 1950s when Roland Barthes re-expressed the formalist ideal of an open-ended literature. Text, textuality, textness, texture, intertext—from a variety of causes we have become sensitive to these terms and to the nuanced relations between them. For Barthes, 'text' (as opposed to 'work') signifies a redistribution of control from the object to the activity, from what is displayed ('a piece of merchandise') to a 'methodological field'; and from the author/writer to the reader. For the 'text' as opposed to the 'work' exists in the activity of its reception: 'the work is held in the hand, the text is held in language'.

'Text', proclaims Barthes, 'is a magnanimous word.'[6] Text is irreducibly plural, suggested in its etymology (from the Latin *texere*, 'to weave'), which points to its entwined (textile), or combinatory state, the interlacing of its materials. Hence Barthes's distinction that if the 'image' of a work is 'an organism', 'the metaphor of the Text is that of the *network*'.[7] 'Network' is the preferred translation into English of Barthes's term *réseau*, 'web', 'tracery', which has a natural as well as mechanical application. For Barthes and for Michel Foucault, whose sustained cultural criticism has decisively effected the work-to-text shift, 'text' is adversary, generous, liberal, polysemous, and above all *situated*—within the complex of cultural practices, among the networks of social power. In part characterized by a disavowal of the authorized and of authority (for Foucault, the 'author-function' exists as a brake upon the proliferation of meaning[8]), of received valuations, and of the canonical, and in part by a delight in the marginal, the subversive, and the unestablished, the shift from work to text would be democratic, except that the act of suspending conventional valuation (which is implied in the uncovering of the textual) and unpicking accepted classifications requires a special discrimination that seeks out the unfamiliar within the familiar.

For Julia Kristeva, whose coinage 'intertextuality' is, the writings of Bakhtin provide insight into the way in which the 'literary word' is always 'an *intersection of textual surfaces* rather than a *point* (a fixed meaning)'. As such, the text is both produced within history and itself the only producer of history: 'History and morality are written and read within the infrastructure of texts.' Within the three coordinates of textual space—writing subject, addressee, and exterior text—where all exists, the 'notion of *intertextuality* replaces that of intersubjectivity'.[9] As in the dynamic usage of 'text' by Barthes and Foucault, Kristeva's 'intertext' extends the properties of text to codes which are social and not necessarily written or printed. What is woven as text can be material *and* ideological across a wide range. Text, then, can refer to many kinds of practices which demonstrate the primary and secondary features of 'textness' (the qualities of text) which we have conventionally applied narrowly to written records only. That is to say, practices which: 1. are considered the result of what Barthes calls 'a combinatory systematic'[10] (the network, the web); and 2. are amenable to analysis or close reading as though they were a written record. Obviously, visual, oral, and numeric data (film, music, recorded sound, prints, photographs), will be included; but also buildings, clothing, dance, rituals of various kinds, those codes of influence which are inscribed at a farther remove from the world of writing or print.

Even if for the purposes of an investigation we choose to limit ourselves to a definition of text that excludes many of its wider practices, after Barthes, Foucault, and Kristeva, the term 'text' carries with it a vast range of unsettling meanings which, above all, imply the relativity of structures. 'Textuality', like the intensified '*inter*textuality', requires that we consider the unfixity of text, the promiscuity as opposed to integrity of its identity in an age when text has a diverse non-book existence, its mobility and openness to change across time and place, and the relation of text to other social structures, its permeability. As Kristeva puts it: 'any text is at once under the jurisdiction of some other discourses which impose upon it a context: what it has to do is transform that context' ('tout texte est d'emblée sous la juridiction des autres discours qui lui imposent un univers: il s'agira de le transformer').[11]

What is the contribution of electronic technology to these now widely deployed insights about text made over the last half-century? In general, textual critics came late to the debate over the relation of printed text to other forms of social discourse: until within the last ten years, textual criticism and the various positions within poststructuralist criticism have not had much to say to one another, with many textual critics doing their best work within a literary and cultural perspective which might be broadly defined as New Critical. So much so that their understandings of terms can appear starkly opposed to those adopted in the critical world immediately around them: against the *textile* or woven web of literary and social discourse, the already-written into which Barthesian and Kristevan writing inserts itself, the textual critic would set the *textus* (as in *textus receptus*, the received text of Scriptural authority), with its assumptions of at least an ideal fixity and point of origin, and, in the modern period, an author-derived identity. Most obviously, the Barthesian distinction between 'work' (limited, 'the imaginary tail of the 'Text', the text's false embodiment) and 'text' (plural, immaterial, allusive) is disputed in traditional textual criticism, where the material text is the physical (and imperfect) instantiation of the (ideal) literary work. For the textual critic, *contra* Barthes, it is the work which is held in imagination and the text in the hand. But with the coming of the computer to the arts faculties of the university campus, and, more particularly, with the arrival of the micro-computer on the scholar's desk, the textual critic in her/his manifestation as editor has perforce entered an environment of permeable boundaries, of fluid text, of non-bookishness, an environment in which these traditional assumptions no longer appear to hold true.

The first to go is the text/work distinction which was already under pressure from those sociologically minded bibliographers and text critics (D. F. McKenzie and Jerome McGann, in the English-speaking world)[12] who have argued that if the work is not confined to the historically contingent and the particular, it is nevertheless only in its expressive textual form that we encounter it, and material conditions determine meanings. While this is an argument against the notion that the physical book is

the disposable container, it is also an argument in favour of the significance of the text as a situated act or event, and therefore, under the conditions of its reproduction, necessarily multiple. Further, by an interesting
coincidence the computer's own history affirms the *textile* identity of its
products: the Jacquard loom, built in 1801, revolutionized weaving in the
early nineteenth century; it is also the acknowledged antecedent of the
early computer. In Jacquard's loom perforated cards controlled the movement of the warp threads and guaranteed the patterns of complicated figured fabrics. It was from Jacquard's invention that the computer punched
card was developed in the late nineteenth century. Allen Renear's three
theories of textuality, outlined in his essay in this volume, suggest a philosophical framework within which to define and encode the structures of
text in ways that bring the insights of the information technologist to bear
on the concerns of the textual and literary critic. For Renear, many key
epistemological issues involved in the identification of textual features are
highlighted by the procedures of electronic encoding, and these may help
us to recover from extravagant postmodernism a more rigorous account
of the semiotics of textuality.

In its functions as multi-text storer and in its capacity to weave,
unweave, and reweave text, the computer is at the service of a variety of
late twentieth-century theoretic and cultural practices, from the decompos-
ing strategies of deconstructive criticism to the data-dense contextualism
of the highly positioned cultural criticisms of postmodernism—new historicism, cultural anthropology, post-Marxism. What the practitioners of
these diverse approaches have in common is that all are engaged in processes of feigning (from the Derridean *jeux* of the deconstructionist to the
closely bit-mapped reproductions of the cultural critic) that the computer
as complex simulator can appear to make real. Because of its sophisticated modelling capacity, there is a dangerous tendency among enthusiasts and critics alike to declare the computer something more than the
technologically advanced moron that gives texture to our desires. There
are those who embrace electronic text with a messianic fervour and who
tend to read the signs and tokens of past and present—the print-based
typographical experiments of modernism and the bisected and otherwise
fractured pages of postmodernism—as evidences of electronic longing, as
anticipations of non-linear permeations. With George Landow and J. Hillis
Miller, they would argue the 'prescience' (Landow's word) of contemporary critical theory, as formulated by Derrida or Barthes, on the grounds
that electronic hypertext does the same things. But surely this is to mistake the point—that the electronic technology, and the uses to which it
is put, develop within the same dynamic field of cultural production and
cultural assumptions to which Barthes and Derrida contribute. Here is
Landow:

In making available these points, hypertext has much in common with some major points of contemporary literary and semiological theory, particularly with Derrida's emphasis on de-centering and with Barthes's conception of the readerly versus the writerly text. In fact, hypertext creates an almost embarrassingly literal embodiment of both concepts, one that in turn raises questions about them and their interesting combination of prescience and historical relations (or embeddedness).[13]

How can we seriously argue that this 'convergence' (Landow's term) is anything other than predictable, especially when we are reminded of the origin in non-print based technologies (in the radio text and screen text or image) of many of the insights of Barthes and Derrida?

By the same argument, Hillis Miller is guilty of a curious reductivism, not to mention sombre pedantry, in his misunderstanding of Derridean *jeu* when he argues that 'a hypertext linked textbase on CD-ROM' would be a 'much more useful' way of presenting *Glas* and *Glassary*.[14] Derrida's book-bound anti-bookishness belongs to a long tradition of bookish wit (and intentional obscurity) that scribes and printers in the Middle Ages knew how to manipulate in the service of a polylogically decentred text. The fact that *Glas* (1984) and the personal computer share a historical moment is worth attending to, as are Derrida's pronouncements on the end or death of the book, but not as prophetic utterances. Importantly, neither Barthes's poststructuralist distinction between 'work' and 'text' nor Derrida's project to break down the divisions between kinds of writing are ways of thinking about writing or print awaiting or dependent on the possibilities of electronic technology. That indeterminacy and instability, the perpetual field of production, which Barthes and Derrida point to as contextualizing all writing, are not brought any nearer, nor are they rendered less problematic, by electronic technology; they are always there, part of the conditions under which writing *is*. To assume otherwise is to mistake the theoretical enquiry into the book as a principle and locus of comprehensiveness, and writing as its resistance, for a search for an empirical resolution to this tension.

One way of thinking about the electronic environment is to see it as consisting of a set of supplementary possibilities which model those concerns voiced by theorists and practitioners in another medium, the book. In this sense the technology allows us to resituate aspects of text which, it has been considered, are in some way hampered by the sequential, or hierarchical, or other structural determinants not of writing and not of text but of that traditional container of writing and text, the book. This is not, of course, the same as saying that the electronic environment liberates text or that this is a good thing, since it recognizes that text has always been created in the *contexts* of a set of liberational fields. Several of the essays in this volume point in various ways to the adapted and unadapted conditions of bookishness with relation to literary kinds: the novel, Patrick Conner and Claire Lamont both argue, flourishes in terms of a vital contradictory dynamic, whereby it accommodates *and* resists its book-bound condition; the drama, as Peter Donaldson shows, is the least book-adapted form; and, as McGann argues, when it comes to the critiquing of information as communicated by books, when, for example, it is a matter of scholarly editing (the embedding of one book within the critical apparatus that, as it were, forms another), or when it is a matter of presenting the text in a holistic environment, then the book may not be the best scientific instrument (as in instrument 'of knowledge') or machine for that task. Of course, such thinking still requires that we set aside the claims on our attention of the book as something other than an expressive tool.

Another way of thinking about the new technology is to argue that its representational capacity does have implications for the formulation of knowledge and the reformulation of the discursive space: that, after all, McLuhan is right, and the medium *is* the message. Not a contradiction but an extension of the previous point, this is an argument which recognizes that computers like books are containers of knowledge, information, ideas, and as such are instruments of power shaped in the context of cultures and themselves communicators of cultures: changes in the media of communication map larger changes in culture and consciousness; and in this sense the computer provides simple clues to more profound changes, changes which its uses in turn promote and guarantee. It is in terms of changes in 'the material conditions of the production of text' that Conner distinguishes cybernetic from printed hypertext, and he enforces his argument with support from Raymond Williams. Williams argued in 1977 that changes occurring in the twentieth century in the 'electronic transmission and recording of speech and of writing for speech, and the chemical and electronic composition and transmission of images' are 'always more than new technologies, in the limited sense'. They are themselves '*means of production*, developed in direct if complex relations with profoundly changing and extending social and cultural relationships'.[15]

A pertinent rehearsal of some of the textual issues implied in the cultural production of technological production lies in the quality *v.* quantity debate which has raged for some time around electronic text and which has another equally significant manifestation in the presence *v.* absence debate. Stated crudely, electronic technology (the computer, the CD-ROM, the Internet) gives us access to more—to *more* texts (*all* the manuscripts of Chaucer's *Canterbury Tales*, multiply integrated print and film versions of a Shakespeare play), to *more* information about texts (transcripts, variant forms, digital facsimiles), to *more* ways of manipulating that information (rapid collation programs, spelling databases, search-engines of various kinds, image-enhancement tools), and it gives it all *more* quickly. As the essays in this volume by Donaldson and Peter Robinson suggest, electronic technology is transforming our understanding of the scholarly edition, that monument to a nineteenth-century model of disciplinarity and specialist knowledge. The edition or 'archive', as it is more often and more properly described in its electronic assemblage, no longer depends upon the coded features and scientific structures of the book refined to their highest application, the hierarchical layering of information on the page, from reading text at the top to the humblest variant in the smallest fount-size at the bottom, the complex appendices that need to be consulted in one place while one reads in another, and the shorthand ingenuities of typographic presentation—several sizes and styles of type, several kinds of bracket, deletion linings, superimpositions, etc. Instead, the electronic edition is itself an analogue computer, capable of constituting text in multiple forms. But is this shift, this vast assemblage of *more* achieved at a price? Will we use electronic editions differently from book-bound editions and will the difference amount to a loss as well as a gain?

Certainly, the potential for including so much more in an electronic edition means a rethinking of where we draw the bounds for inclusion: in the electronic medium critical discrimination is more likely to be concerned with what to leave out than with what to include (which is the dominant issue in the paper medium). It means a rethinking, too, of what is data; there is, for instance, a shift in the electronic environment to viewing source materials as data, which has implications for the conception and establishment of notions of origin (do texts have a beginning?); and a shift, too, in favour of assembling the 'raw' ingredients rather than presenting the 'cooked' product, based on the interpretation of a particular witness. Such a diffusion of information is not new to the computerized edition; it has steadily grown upon paperbound editing practice in the twentieth century, with its expanding pages of textual notes, glossaries, bibliographies, and, as Lamont points out in her essay, the 'increased quantity of annotation', which we have come to expect even for the more accessible literary forms, like the nineteenth-century novel. Editorial expansiveness is not new, then; but presentation in computerized form makes it easier to accomplish, and in making certain things easier, it makes the outcome different. Here is a small instance of the cultural pressure upon technological production which might extend and change cultural relationships or the ways in which we perceive our cultural inheritance and our own relations to it. To invoke a now outmoded set of terms and values, we have in the electronic medium the disassembled 'texts' but not the reassembled 'work'. The clear outlines of the 'work', a deception though we now accept them to have been, become blurred as its textual and extratextual boundaries expand. This obviously means a reconsideration of what processes now constitute editing and how the rapid interactivity between editor, reader, and data reformulates the role of the reader in the

editing process. Julia Flanders suggests below that the resulting 'caco-
phany of data' is not the creation of the electronic archive but itself 'the
true realm of textuality from which, through the traditional edition, we
seek to protect ourselves'. It is easy to establish the contradiction between
the computer's quantitative rendition of text as data and the qualitative
way we have traditionally thought of texts as shaped and discriminative
cultural artefacts. But what might the qualitative differences of the electronic environment be?

Techniques for reproduction, forms of reproduction (inked shapes on
paper, electronic impulses on a screen), and modes of understanding are
complexly related. We are already, *via* cinema and television, skilled at
absorbing meanings from a screen in ways which we would differentiate
from the communications of reading; the relation between the work of
eye and brain, we know, is different in each. (The visual cortex is a faster
processor of information than that area of the brain that reads words.)
Ingesting information from the computer screen is somewhere in between
the seductions of the eye and the activity of the brain. Does this change
of medium require us to reconsider our relation to what Derrida famously
declared is itself the 'transformational' act of reading?[16] If the reading
subject is itself constituted, as Derrida and others claim, in the act of reading, then what effects might the different media of screen and book contribute to that constitution?

There is the threatening possibility that in its display of instantly accessible and multiply manipulable data, the computer screen will deliver
information from the constraints of understanding. Herein lies the great
challenge of the electronic environment to those expert divisions of knowledge established in the Western world in the course of the nineteenth
century as the best means of advancing learning in a productivity-based
industrial society. And if the computer merely displays information to a
post-productive society, what might this imply for our ability to generate
new as opposed to retrieving and recycling old knowledge? Is there a real
danger that the scholar-worker, toiling for years in the remote regions of
the library stacks in the hope of becoming expert in one small field, will
be transformed by the computer into the technician, the nerdy navigator
able to locate, transfer, and appropriate at an ever faster rate expert entries
from larger sets of information that he/she no longer needs or desires to
understand? May it even be the case that the real subject of enquiry will
shift to the growing array of skills required to master the electronic environment itself? In a world whose primary law is that there is always *more
of everything* (and therefore less of everything), there will be a direct relation between the expanding freedom of those who have this mastery and
the shrinking possibilities of the disqualified, and this may have much
to do with the reshaping of the traditional account of what knowledge

is. (In this case the so-called 'democracy' of the electronic environment would quickly turn to repression.) Already we are faced with the fact of a large technological underclass, variously determined by age, economics (national and international), and geographical situation.

Looked at another way, if as Foucault argues, the 'author-function' is 'characteristic of the mode of existence, circulation, and functioning of certain discourses within a society' at a particular moment in that society's development, part of a wider system of ownership, of the individual patenting of property, and the strict control of meaning (of 'thrift');[17] then we might agree that, computers are instruments of a redistributed model of ownership in a world of deregulated signification and proliferating information bases, and that electronic communications are helping us to relocate meaning not in the 'author-function' but in the 'reader-function'. Donaldson urges a strong and optimistic argument in his essay below, based on his experience of assembling the Shakespeare Electronic Archive, that the electronic environment is adjusting our notion of reading from that of the willing absorption of one set of ideas (assembled under the 'author-function') and from a continuous activity in one cognitive space to an exercise in comparison and critical juxtaposition across several spaces; and he claims for this a new combinatory power, one that blends the 'coherence, context, and sequence' which distinguish 'what we now know as reading' with something more immediate and participatory. It is a reconfiguration of the work of brain and eye, and one which opens the way for fresh ways of knowing.

This capacity of the computer to transmute what it transmits is best represented in the structures of hypertext and hypermedia which situate the postmodern condition of knowledge in the interactive practices of linked, uncentred, deconstructed text, graphics, aural and visual data. As the principles of assembly of the Shakespeare Archive and the *Canterbury Tales* Project imply, there can be in the electronic medium a redistribution of controls to the reader which in turn demands that he/she be more skilled in the work of textual discrimination than the traditional book-edition would require. One immediate consequence of this redistribution of control (from author/editor to reader and from authorized version to 'fractalized' examples) is the discrediting of universal truths in favour of the relative and the indeterminate.

In their further articulation as the presence *v.* absence debate the issues surrounding electronic text yield other reflections. One significant aspect of the feigning properties of computerized text is its textlessness. For the very terms we have devised for locating electronic text deny this textlessness: for example, 'full-text database' or 'textbase', which, among other connotations of a reassuringly material nature, suggest a kind of repository or 'home' for text, as though we might point to a disk or a CD-ROM or even a hard drive and say 'this is a textbase' in much the same way as we might point to a book. But the term disguises the huge conceptual leap we need to make to understand electronic text.[18] Perhaps the place where the e-text seems really to reside is on the screen; and the early development of monitors which created black text on white background (now more likely to be in a range of colours, simulating an electronic illuminated book), a wide choice of type founts, and the general appearance of the printed page foster this illusion. (Some early electronic 'books' even simulated the sound of turning pages.) But it *is* all illusion, and the screen-page has, in fact, only the most fragile of existences; it is not one in a series of pages (as the pages of the printed book are) but the only page; and unlike the pages of a book it is not reassuringly available to us during the time that we are reading some other page. This availability as matter (as accumulating and dwindling stocks of paper) is one of the aspects of its bookish condition that the nineteenth-century realist novel delights to exploit.

On the contrary, the screen-page has to be constituted afresh from the encoded data string each time we as readers return to it. Further, this data string is not *inside* the monitor but held elsewhere in the form of a series of electronic impulses. These impulses have only two states, *on* and *off*, usually represented 1 and 0, but so complex are the patterns that can be constructed by them that all texts in all known languages can be 'written' in them. The internal machine representation of text as electronic signal can be 'read' only by machine, and the electronic text exists as text only during the time that it is re-created by the machine. This re-creation occurs anew whenever the machine is switched on and the appropriate commands given. It is in this precise and even physical sense that electronic text can be said to have no continuous existence or location. Even the locations that it does have in its existence as data string are diverse in kind and also in their relation to the machine from whose monitor we might read it: an internal hard disk, an insertable CD-ROM, or a database accessed remotely from the other side of the world. But it is this very dispersion of location, identity, and appearance which are so significant to the contribution that electronic text is making to our understanding of textuality. We have become so used to the book as textual mediator that for the most part we scarcely notice its artefactual state and how it imposes its 'machinery' on what we read; we accept a kind of synonymity between text and book. There is some sense in this, since the book (individually as well as generically) has proved a robust machine for text dissemination, while one of the current anxieties about electronic storage media is their rapid obsolescence.

Given this precarious and illusory immanence of electronic text, our increasing dependence on computers as assemblers of complex cultural data is an issue of some concern. The concern lies not merely in the fragility or limited shelf-life of a particular aspect of the technology but in what this technological dependence says about the cultural position from which we are attempting to understand culture. Reviewing the burgeoning field of cultural studies, Hillis Miller has recently asked the question (*pace* Walter Benjamin) '[W]hat is the place of cultural studies in this age not of mechanical but of digital reproduction?' Cultural studies, he answers, has the declared aim of 'politicizing' art, of embedding it in a particular language and class structure, in particular modes of production and consumption; that is, its aim is to localize art. But, he continues, developments in the twentieth century, in art and in technology, have conspired together to uproot 'art and popular culture from their local origins'.[19] Art and our modes of consumption in the twentieth century have become progressively international; and this internationalization (which includes blue jeans, tee-shirts, video-cassettes, fax machines, and computers) is what delivers to us those projects of localization.

For Miller the computer accelerates the deconstructive possibilities inherent in postmodern ways of knowing. As an archiving tool of immense power the computer stores and gives access to particulars. It works in the service of postmodern detailism and the micro-contexts of knowledge, and against the great meta-narratives of science, politics, or social relations. In their place it puts the closely bit-mapped context, a data-rich saturation so minute (even mundane) that the illusion of proximity is achieved. Computers model and accelerate this process, but it informs the current fashion for detail-dependent projects of cultural history and anthropology in their non-computerized forms. The danger is, however, that the very sameness of the procedures for assembling and interrogating these particulars will themselves level the cultural distinctions they seek to preserve. This is what Alan Liu has referred to as 'an increasingly generic discourse of contextualism'.[20] In the case of the electronic medium, there is also the irony that, in making available through international networks such a dense localization of meaning, its very particularity is eroded in the medium of its production and dissemination. Within computer culture, the local is a function of the global, and the network is conceived as a patchwork of interests.

The essays by McGann, Donaldson, and Robinson all assume the enriching potential of the electronically stored text as simulated artefact—the scanned images of Emily Dickinson's original fascicles declaring the handicraft nature of her poetry, the digitized photofacsimiles of the Shakespeare First Folio and the ephemeral but substantiating evidence of playbills, etchings, and photographs, and one thousand page images for the surviving fifty-four manuscripts of Chaucer's Wife of Bath's Prologue. Through the computer's mediation, we appear to have access to authentic forms, an authenticity previously denied to us in many cases by the constrictions of the print medium. But this authenticity is a fragile illusion whereby the electronic medium celebrates and eradicates presence simultaneously. Within the museum case of the computer screen the simulacrum of the authentic object may have newly attached search facilities, but its 'presence' is constituted as lost presence.

As postmodern tools computers promise mass-market subjectivity but in the context of replicability and ultimate anonymity. This dilemma lies at the heart of the presence *v.* absence debate. Hence the rhetoric of individual choice (choosing one's own pathway through a hypertext, making one's own edition) should not be imagined as identical with any authenticity of experience. The rhetoric is a fabric of modern consumer values with their own definable historical origins; it is in terms of a theory of consumption that we must understand the celebration of present and individual engagement and the abolition of consensual critical distance from the field of textual production and reception. It is here, too, that developments in electronic technology are forcing a belated consideration of some of the implications of Barthes's and Derrida's proposals for the 'death of the author'. Not only literary and social critics but intellectual property lawyers are concerned with the form of authors' rights which can be claimed for materials in the digital environment of data networks and information superhighways. Where mobility, instability, the permeability of text to text, and of authorial property to readerly reinterpretation and alteration are the dominant procedures of the electronic medium, what *is* an author and how do we constitute him/her in the interests of assigning rights?

The author is a relatively recent invention in the modern sense of an individual with whom a set of expressive statements (in verse or prose) can be said to originate and which can be properly credited to him/her as unique property. Authorship as recognition of the rights to reward of intellectual labour, and such labour as itself a species of property in the form in which ideas are presented, really dates in Europe and North America from the eighteenth century. As a concept it is decisively shaped by romantic theories of the solitary genius; what is copyrighted to the author is the interest in expression as original and organic form. For writers like Wordsworth and Coleridge in England, who helped shape the wide social reception of author as genius, the extension by the artist of a share in the production of meaning through the intensive labour of educated reading and reflection, virtually stamped the authorial imprint on the impressionable mind of the insightful reader. This is, of course, a metaphysical and metonymic extension of the understanding of copyright, but it helps us to see something of the conceptual shift which has taken place once ideas cease to be invested with bounded and fixed form and authors with the power of unique, and uniquely impressed (stamped with the author's copyright) utterance.

As Martha Woodmansee points out, electronic mail, on-line discussion lists, hypertext 'books', emphasize the 'collaborative nature of contemporary research and problem-solving' and are therefore 'hastening the demise of the illusion that writing is solitary and originary'.[21] She quotes from a review of Jay David Bolter's important book *Writing Space: The Computer, Hypertext, and the History of Writing* (1991) as it was issued in disk form. The reviewer writes:

I am now to some degree co-author of *my* particular version of the electronic book called *Writing Space*. And when I copy that version and pass it on to my friends (as Bolter specifically invites readers to do), they will no doubt make their own modifications and additions. It's conceivable that, after a sufficiently long period, only a small fraction of the material on the disk will have originated from Bolter's keyboard.[22]

Such participatory revision, comments Woodmansee, assumes 'an unending process of reading and writing which reverses the trajectory of print'; and she links this late twentieth-century reversion to those 'expressly collaborative' forms of writing that characterized the Middle Ages and the Renaissance and which found shape in 'commonplace books', themselves undifferentiated compilations of transcriptions, reworkings, and compositions which usually existed outside print culture.[23] In the longer perspective, Anglo-American copyright and Continental European authors' rights bear only a short-lived relation to the historical understanding of the identity of the author.

In different ways, the essays in this collection by Flanders and David Greetham point to the determinacy and fragility of the 'author-function' and to how the electronic environment is helping us to reposition authorship in a wider network of collaborative relations. Neither Flanders nor Greetham assumes the dependency of this reconception on postmodern practices but, like Woodmansee, they position it within a more extensive cultural survey—as part of the long and neglected history of women's authorship (where to be female and an author, or point of literary origin, imply a contradiction of terms), and as one aspect of the persistence of morphing from Ovid to the Mighty Morphin Power Rangers. As Greetham demonstrates, morphing or metamorphosis or mutability is 'a condition of nature' with implications for the coherence of the subject and for claims of ownership within the cultural sphere.

The problem of the subject, as it bears on issues of attributable labour, like the problem of the object (the real presence of the work or text), is not new to the world of electronic technology, but it is newly foregrounded and reshaped (or morphed) by the technologies which support Internet publication with its vast resources for the distribution, migration, repackaging, and redistribution of information. Peter Jaszi has argued that 'the conditions of the Internet environment today resemble those which prevailed at other moments of polymorphous collaboration, unrestrained plagiarism, and extraordinary cultural productivity—such as the Elizabethan stage or Holywood before 1915'.[24] How and even whether to police such a mobile environment, how and even whether to distinguish a subjective from a social appropriation of authority, whether and in what formal procedures we embody the disembodied practices of cyberspace, are hotly debated issues among interest groups as diverse as publishers and copyright lawyers on the one hand and techno-feminists on the other.

The essays in this volume represent a range of approaches to texts and text, though all assume a literary basis for their investigations. A dominant concern is the editing of literary texts, canonical and non-canonical, and the differences that the electronic medium might imply across a range of issues from interpreting the function and authority of annotation in a hypertextual model, to identifying what might form the permanent constituent features of text, and to distinguishing the impact that the double illegitimacy of female gender and electronic technology might make on traditional textual practices. Just as the essays adopt different positions in relation to text, so too they view the procedures of the electronic environment as more or less determining. Conner's thesis, with its linking of hypertext, ideology, and Twain's *Huckleberry Finn*, assumes the mutually supportive insights of postmodern critical theory and technology when it argues the case for defining hypertext as a fourth 'primary form of literary discourse' (after poetry, drama, and prose), with the cybernetic avatar as that which models a previous and independent phenomenon. In this case, the tendency towards hypertext is a feature of literary works regardless of the cybernetic possibilities of modelling, but in that modelling certain ideological positions are strengthened. We might compare this insight with McGann's point that electronic hypertext does not so much encourage the finding as the *making* of order.

Running through all the essays is a concern with change and with the possibilities of the electronic environment for assisting us in understanding change—change as newness and as the permanent state of things. For the most part, these essays are written by enthusiasts for and workers with electronic technologies. It is not always easy to move discussion of electronic technology beyond the narrowly technological because the details of that technology are themselves changing so quickly and demand incorporation in the critical assessment of its significance. The focus here, however, is as little as possible on 'information design' or the technicalities of producing electronic texts and as much as possible on those broader theoretical and cultural issues which seem to us to underly electronic practice as determinant and choice. The essays have been arranged so as to lead the reader who chooses to follow linear order from the speculative ground of McGann and Lamont's questionings ('what, if we shift from paper to electronic representation, may be the consequences?' 'how might our views with regard to certain textual issues change?') to the diversely theorized perspectives of Conner, Renear, and Flanders (positioning text in relation to a range of critical, philosophical, and gendered debates) and then to two pieces, by Robinson and Donaldson, in which general insights about text are informed by and grow from the particular, in their cases, from the practices involved in assembling large textbases. Framing the essays are an Introduction and Coda linking technological fashioning and change to the cultural developments that technology models and, in modelling, further validates as culturally significant.

NOTES

1. George P. Landow, *Hypertext: The Convergence of Contemporary Critical Theory and Technology* (Baltimore and London: Johns Hopkins University Press, 1992), p. 174; and Richard A. Lanham, *The Electronic Word: Democracy, Technology, and the Arts* (Chicago: University of Chicago Press, 1993), p. 23.
2. George Steiner, *Real Presences: Is There Anything in What We Say?* (London: Faber and Faber, 1989), p. 115; and Sven Birkerts, *The Gutenberg Elegies: The Fate of Reading in an Electronic Age* (New York: Ballantine Books, 1994), p. 138.
3. Gérard Genette, 'Structuralism and Literary Criticism', in *Figures of Literary Discourse*, trans. A. Sheridan (New York: Columbia University Press, 1982), p. 22.
4. Steiner, *Real Presences*, p. 10.
5. See the related argument in Richard Grusin, 'What Is an Electronic Author? Theory and the Technological Fallacy', in Robert Markley (ed.), *Virtual Realities and Their Discontents* (Baltimore and London: Johns Hopkins University Press, 1996), pp. 39–53.
6. Roland Barthes, 'From Work to Text', in *Image–Music–Text*, essays selected and translated by Stephen Heath (London: Fontana, 1977), pp. 155–64; and *Roland Barthes by Roland Barthes*, in *Barthes: Selected Writings*, ed. Susan Sontag (London: Fontana, 1982), pp. 418–19.
7. Barthes, 'From Work to Text', p. 161.
8. Michel Foucault, 'What Is an Author?' in Josué V. Harari (ed.), *Textual Strategies: Perspectives in Post-Structuralist Criticism* (Ithaca, NY: Cornell University Press, 1979), p. 159.
9. Julia Kristeva, 'Word, Dialogue, and Novel', in *The Kristeva Reader*, ed. Toril Moi, trans. Seán Hand, *et al.* (Oxford: Blackwell, 1986), pp. 36–7.
10. Barthes, 'From Work to Text', p. 161.

11. Julia Kristeva, *La Révolution du langage poétique* (Paris: Seuil, 1974), p. 339.
12. See, for example, two now classic studies, Jerome J. McGann, *A Critique of Modern Textual Criticism* (Chicago: University of Chicago Press, 1983); and D. F. McKenzie, *Bibliography and the Sociology of Texts* (London: British Library, 1986).
13. Landow, *Hypertext*, pp. 33–4.
14. J. Hillis Miller, *Illustration: Essays in Art and Culture* (Cambridge, Mass.: Harvard University Press, 1992), p. 34.
15. Raymond Williams, *Marxism and Literature* (Oxford: Oxford University Press, 1977), p. 54.
16. Jacques Derrida, *Positions*, trans. Alan Bass (Chicago: University of Chicago Press, 1981), p. 63.
17. Foucault, 'What Is an Author?', pp. 148 and 159.
18. See the description of what electronic text is in Patrick W. Conner, 'Hypertext in the Last Days of the Book', *Bulletin of the John Rylands University Library of Manchester*, 74 (1992), 17–20.
19. Miller, *Illustration*, pp. 11–12.
20. Alan Liu, 'Local Transcendence: Cultural Criticism, Postmodernism, and the Romanticism of Detail', *Representations*, 32 (1990), 77.
21. Martha Woodmansee, 'On the Author Effect: Recovering Collectivity', in Martha Woodmansee and Peter Jaszi (eds.), *The Construction of Authorship: Textual Appropriation in Law and Literature* (Durham, NC: Duke University Press, 1994), p. 25. On the modern conception of author as creator, see Mark Rose, *Authors and Owners: The Invention of Copyright* (Cambridge, Mass.: Harvard University Press, 1993).
22. Brian Eno, 'On Writing Space', *Artforum*, Nov. 1991, p. 14, cited in *Construction of Authorship*, p. 26.
23. Ibid., pp. 26–7.
24. Peter Jaszi, 'On the Author Effect: Contemporary Copyright and Collective Creativity', in *Construction of Authorship*, p. 55.

2

The Rationale of Hypertext

JEROME J. MCGANN

Lofty reflections on the cultural significance of information technology are commonplace now. Tedious as they can be, they serve an important social function. Some distribute general knowledge to society at large, some send it to particular groups whose professional history makes information about information an important and perhaps problematic issue.

Literary scholars comprise just this kind of group. If certain features of the new information technologies have overtaken us—for instance, the recent and massive turn to word processing—more advanced developments generate suspicion. When one speaks to colleagues about the emergence of the electronic library, information networks, or about the need and usefulness of making scholarly journals electronic, brows grow dark and troubled. And yet it is clear to anyone who has looked carefully at our postmodern condition that no real resistance to such developments is possible, even if it were desirable.

In this essay I will focus primarily on a particular feature of literary works—their physical character, whether audial or visible. I shall be pointing out why these features are important in a literary point of view and also sketching certain practical means for elucidating these textual features. This last matter—the central subject of the essay—is also the most difficult. The methodology I shall be discussing requires the scholar to learn to use a new set of scholarly tools.

One final introductory comment. My remarks here apply only to textual works that are instruments of scientific knowledge. The poet's view of text is necessarily very different. To the imagination, the materialities of text (oral, written, printed, electronic) are incarnational not vehicular forms. But for the scientist and scholar, the media of expression are primarily conceptual utilities, means rather than ends; to the degree that an expressive form hinders the conceptual goal (whether it be theoretical or practical), to that extent one will seek to evade or supersede it—perhaps even, in critical times, to develop new intellectual devices. But good poets do not really quarrel with their tools. As William Morris famously observed, 'You can't have art without resistance in the materials.'

THE BOOK AS A MACHINE OF KNOWLEDGE

This general context explains the need to give a clear answer to the question 'why': *why* take up these new editing methods, especially when the methods make (as shall be clear later) such demands upon us? At this point most scholars know about the increased speed and analytic power that computerization gives, and about the 'information highway' and its scholarly possibilities. Major changes in the forms of knowledge and information are taking place. From a literary person's point of view, however, the relevance of these changes can appear to be purely marginal: for whatever happens in the future, whatever new electronic poetry or fiction gets produced, the literature we inherit (to this date) is and will always be bookish.

Which is true—although that truth underscores what is crucial in all these events from the *scholar*'s point of view: we no longer have to use books to analyse and study other books or texts. That simple fact carries immense, even catastrophic, significance. Until now the book or codex form has been one of our most powerful tools for developing, storing, and disseminating information. In literary studies, the book has evolved (over many centuries) a set of scientific engines—specific kinds of books and discursive genres—of great power and complexity. Critical and other scholarly editions of our cultural inheritance are among the most distinguished achievements of our profession.

When we use books to study books, or hard-copy texts to analyse other hard-copy texts, the scale of the tools seriously limits the possible results. In studying the physical world, for example, it makes a great difference if the level of the analysis is experiential (direct) or mathematical (abstract). In a similar way, electronic tools in literary studies do not simply provide a new point of view on the materials, they lift one's general level of attention to a higher order. The difference between the codex and the electronic *Oxford English Dictionary* provides a simple but eloquent illustration of this. The electronic *OED* is a meta-book, i.e. it has consumed everything that the codex *OED* provides and reorganized it at a higher level. It is a research tool with greater powers of consciousness. As a result, the electronic *OED* can be read as a book or it can be used electronically. In the latter case it will generate readerly views of its information that cannot be had in the codex *OED* without unacceptable expenditures of time and labour.

Scholarly editions comprise the most fundamental tools in literary studies. Their development came in response to the complexity of literary works, especially those that had evolved through a long historical process (as one sees in the Bible, Homer, the plays of Shakespeare). To deal with these works, scholars invented an array of ingenious tools: facsimile editions, critical editions, editions with elaborate notes and contextual materials for clarifying a work's meaning. The limits of the book determined the development of the structural forms of these different mechanisms; those limits also necessitated the periodic re-creation of new editions as relevant materials appeared or disappeared, or as new interests arose.

So far as editing and textual studies are concerned, codex tools present serious difficulties. To make a new edition one has to duplicate the entire productive process, and then add to or modify the work as necessary. Furthermore, the historical process of documentary descent generates an increasingly complex textual network (the word 'text' derives from a word that means 'weaving'). Critical editions were developed to deal with exactly these situations. A magnificent array of textual machinery evolved over many centuries.

Brilliantly conceived, these works are nonetheless infamously difficult to read and use. Their problems arise because they deploy a book form to study another book form. This symmetry between the tool and its subject forces the scholar to invent analytic mechanisms that must be displayed and engaged at the primary reading level—e.g. apparatus structures, descriptive bibliographies, calculi of variants, shorthand reference forms, and so forth. The critical edition's apparatus, for example, exists only because no single book or manageable set of books can incorporate for analysis all of the relevant documents. In standard critical editions, the primary materials come before the reader in abbreviated and coded forms.

The problems grow more acute when readers want or need something beyond the semantic content of the primary textual materials—when one wants to hear the performance of a song or ballad, see a play, or look at the physical features of texts. Facsimile editions answer to some of these requirements, but once again the book form proves a stumbling-block in many cases. Because the facsimile edition stands in a one-to-one relation to its original, it has minimal analytic power—in sharp contrast to the critical edition. Facsimile editions are most useful not as analytic engines, but as tools for increasing access to rare works.

Editing in codex forms generates an archive of books and related materials. This archive then develops its own meta-structures—indexing and other study mechanisms—to facilitate navigation and analysis of the archive. Because the entire system develops through the codex form, however, duplicate, near-duplicate, or differential archives appear in different places. The crucial problem here is simple: the logical structures of the 'critical edition' function at the same level as the material being analysed. As a result, the full power of the logical structures is checked and constrained by being compelled to operate in a bookish format. If the coming of the book vastly increased the spread of knowledge and information, history has slowly revealed the formal limits of all hard copy's informational and critical powers. The archives are sinking in a white sea of paper.

Computerization allows us to read 'hard-copy' documents in a non-real, or as we now say a 'virtual', space-time environment. This consequence follows whether the hard copy is being marked up for electronic search and analysis, or whether it is being organized hypertextually. When a book is translated into electronic form, the book's (heretofore distributed) semantic and visual features can be made simultaneously present to each other. A book thus translated need not be read within the time-and-space frames established by the material characteristics of the book. If the hard copy to be translated comprises a large set of books and documents, the power of the translational work appears even more dramatically, since all those separate books and documents can also be made simultaneously present to each other, as well as all the parts of the documents.

Of course, the electronic text will be 'read' in normal space-time, even by its programmers: the mind that made (or that uses) both codex and computer is 'embodied'. This means that, from the user's point of view, computerization organizes (as it were) sequential engagements with non-sequential forms of knowledge and experience—immediate encounters with abstract or complexly mediated forms. If the limits of experience remain thus untranscended, through computerization's virtual enginery, however, the new tools offer a much clearer and more capacious view of one particular class or 'order of things'—in this case, the order of those things we call texts, books, documents.

HYPEREDITING AND HYPERMEDIA

The electronic environment of hyperediting frees one to a considerable extent from these codex-based limits. Indeed, computerization for the first time releases the logical categories of traditional critical editing to function at more optimal levels. But 'editing' text through word processors is not, in the view being taken here, 'hyperediting' because word-processing engines are structured only for expressive purposes. On the other hand, the deployment of 'hypertext' software should not be judged a necessity of hyperediting. The electronic *OED* does not use hypertext but it is certainly a hyperediting project. So too is the work initiated by Peter Robinson and the *Collate* program he has developed. To function in a 'hyper' mode, an editing project must use computerization as a means to secure freedom from the analytic limits of hard-copy text.[1]

Nonetheless, hypertext programs provide the clearest model for hyperediting. Hypertexts allow one to navigate through large masses of documents and to connect these documents, or parts of the documents, in complex ways. The relationships can be predefined (as in George Landow's various 'webs', like the Dickens Web) or they can be developed and pursued 'on the fly' (through the relationships created using a text encoding language, like SGML (Standard Generalized Markup Language) to markup a work). (For a discussion of SGML, see Renear's essay, pp. 107–26.) They are called hypermedia programs when they have the power to include audial and/or visual documents in the system. These documentary networks may or may not be interactively organized (for input by the reader/user). They can be distributed in self-contained forms (e.g. on CD-ROM disks, like the Harvard Perseus Project) or they can be structured for transmission through the Network. In this last case, the basic hypertext structure is raised to a higher power (but not to a higher level): a networked structure (say, WorldWideWeb) of local hypertexts opens out into a network of networks.

I rehearse these matters, which are familiar enough to increasing numbers of scholars, to remind us that the different purposes of different scholars determine the choice of an actual hyperediting procedure. The range of options also indicates that hyperediting should be seen as a nested series of operational possibilities (and problems). In my own view, for example, a fully networked hypermedia archive would be an optimal goal. Because such an archive of archives is not yet a practical achievement, however, one must make present design decisions in a future perfect tense. What that means in practice is the following: (1) that the hyperediting design for a specific project be imagined in terms of the largest and most ambitious goals of the project (rather than in terms of immediate hardware or software options); and (2) that the design be structured in the most modular and flexible way, so that inevitable and fast-breaking changes in hardware and software will have a minimal effect on the work as it is being built. In practice, then, one would not lock into a front-end hypertext system prematurely, or choose computer platforms or hardware because of current accessibility. Similarly, one wants to store data in the most complete forms possible (both as logically marked-up etext and as high-resolution digitized images). I have undertaken to develop *The Complete Writings and Pictures of Dante Gabriel Rossetti: A Hypermedia Research Archive* in order to test the adequacy and feasability of these principles and ideas (see Figure 1).

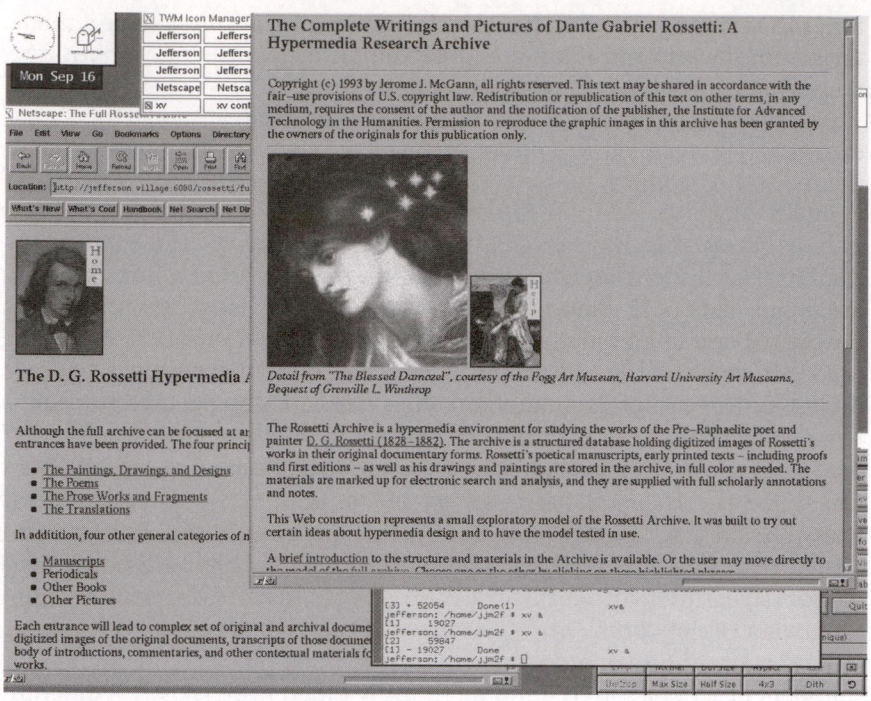

Fig. 1. This is a screen shot from two pages of the small demonstration model of the Rossetti Archive that was built for the WorldWideWeb: the introductory page and the top page of the Archive proper. This and seven other illustrations give screen shots of various moments within the demo model as they would occur in scholarly use. The sequence of illustrations means to give some idea of how the Rossetti Archive is structured. A more detailed introduction can be found within the electronic demo model itself; or see my essay 'The Rossetti Archive and Image-Based Electronic Editing', in Richard J. Finneran (ed.), *The Literary Text in the Digital Age* (Ann Arbor: University of Michigan Press, 1996), pp. 145–84. The first instalment of the Archive will be published in 1998 by the University of Michigan Press.

Obviously this essay cannot deal with all these matters in any extended way. One topic will be paramount: the importance, as I see it, of organizing a hyperediting project in hypermedia form. Hypereditions built of electronic text alone are easier to construct, of course, but they can only manipulate the semantic level of the original work. Hypermedia editions that incorporate audial and/or visual elements are preferable, since literary works are themselves always more or less elaborate multimedia forms. When Pound spoke of the three expressive functions of poetry— phanopoeia, melopoeia, and logopoeia—he defined the optimal expressive levels that all textual works possess by their nature as texts. Texts are language visible, auditional, and intellectual (gesture and (type)script; voice and instrumentation; syntax and usage).

THE NECESSITY OF HYPERMEDIA

The most direct way to show this need is through a set of examples. In these illustrations I shall move from a straightforward presentation of the elementary material demands raised by texts, to more complex interpretive issues that those demands create.

Example A

First, then, think about songs and ballads—think in particular about Robert Burns's ballad 'Tam Glen'. For a text we might turn to what is now widely regarded as the definitive (so-called) edition of Burns, the Kinsley/Clarendon Press edition, where it is printed from a manuscript text sent by Burns to James Johnson, who first published the ballad in his collection the *Scots Musical Museum* in 1790. Kinsley's (like Burns's and Johnson's) is a text for the eyes, and because the text of this essay is also typographical, I could easily reproduce it here.[2]

Yet the ballad interested Burns exactly because it was an auditional text. Under different circumstances I could give a reasonable reproduction of that ballad. I could play for you an audio version of, say, Jean Redpath singing the ballad to a score imitating the ballad as Burns might have heard it sung. Or I could play for you Andy Stewart's 'version' of the ballad, or others as well.

The words of 'Tam Glen' were in fact written by Burns, though the air for it is traditional. Many of the texts in Kinsley's edition of Burns, however, are hybrid works fashioned by Burns from Scots songs he collected and then modified, more or less drastically.[3] He did not hestitate to make his own changes in these works because in collecting his Scots songs he heard many versions. The ones he himself published, and the texts that come down to us through an edition like Kinsley's, do not represent the kinds of variety Burns would have known.

Besides, contemporary performances probably stand far removed from what Burns must have originally heard. In this sense, the Kinsley/Clarendon Press printed text is perhaps truer to its (printed) textual tradition than contemporary performances could be to their oral traditions. Nonetheless, if our primary care is towards preserving the original materials in a living way, could anyone prefer a paper text of such a work to an audial text?

'But that question compares apples and oranges', you will say. 'The tape is the equivalent of a popular, a modernized, an "uncritical" text. It is good for what it does, of course, but it cannot be imagined as a model for replacing what one gets in a complete critical edition like Kinsley/Clarendon.'

Then let us go further: would anyone who had it to choose prefer the Kinsley/Clarendon edition of Burns's complete works to an equivalent edition based primarily on audial texts?

Burns's work is grounded in an oral and song tradition. Paper editions are incompetent to render that most basic feature of his verse. (The same might be said, incidentally, of much of the work of Thomas Moore—a lesser writer than Burns altogether, of course, but a central romantic figure nonetheless, and one who has suffered badly from the inability of scholarship to preserve the memory of his work in living forms.)

The point is not to denigrate the Kinsley/Clarendon edition, which is in fact a model of scholarship. It gives us not only good reading texts, it supplies us with an apparatus, a glossary, excellent notes, and—a very nice feature—a few bars of sheet music for each text, so that we can hum up in our minds the memory of the original tunes. And all this in three volumes.

'Yes. And to have the equivalent in an oral form would take many tapes or disks. Besides, those musical documents wouldn't be able to organize and interrelate the audial materials the way the Kinsley/Clarendon edition has done with its textual materials—the way any good critical edition will do.'

But what if one could do that? What if one could have a critical edition of Burns's work in audial forms that allowed one to engage the songs in the same kind of scholarly environment that we know and value in works like the Kinsley/Clarendon edition? An environment allowing one to navigate between versions, to compare variants, an environment able to supply the central documents with a thick network of related critical and contextual information that helps to elucidate the works? What if one could do that? The point is, we can.

Example B

When I was asked to edit the *New Oxford Book of Romantic Period Verse* I wanted to print texts that stayed as close to the original ones as possible. I also wanted to print a good deal of the most characteristic and popular

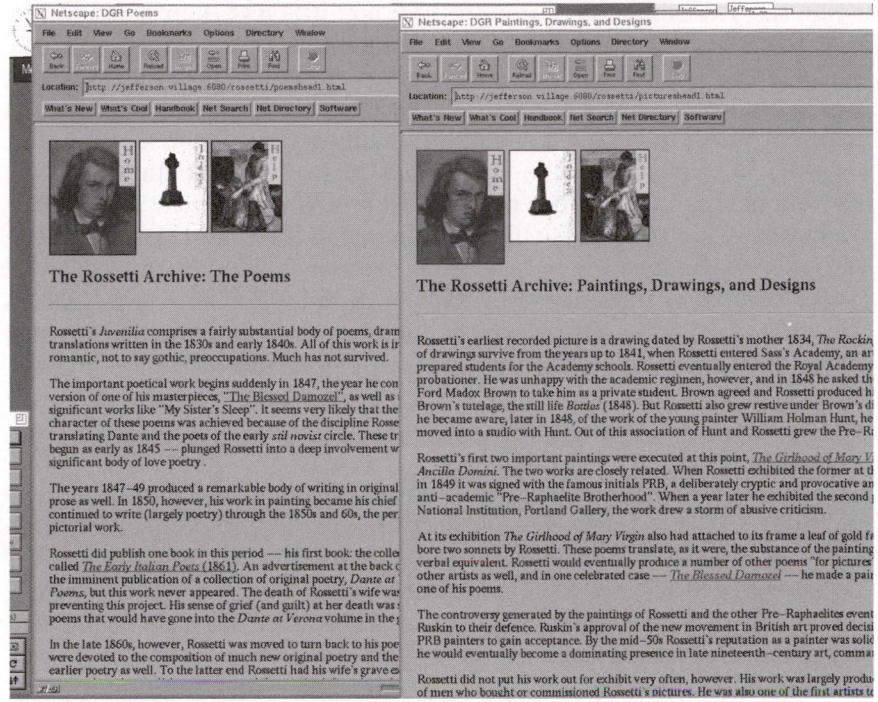

FIG. 2. This is a screen shot from the Introductory pages of the Poetry and the Pictures sections of the demo model of the Rossetti Archive. The texts that are highlighted indicate hypertext links to other Archive documents. The icons at the top of the pages are links to their named destinations. (In this example, as in all the others shown in these illustrations, the demo model gives only a small sample of the actual materials.)

work of the period, as well as work (for example, Blake's) that only came into prominence at a much later time.

So I wanted colour facsimiles of Blake, and colour facsimiles of a poem such as William Roscoe's 'The Butterfly's Ball and the Grasshopper's Feast'. And I wanted to print one of the most popular and important satires of the day, William Hone's 'The Political House that Jack Built', with the original (and closely integrated) Cruickshank illustrations. And I had other similar ideas. As it turned out, various commercial and institutional circumstances shot down most of these plans. All that remains of them is a facsimile of the wonderful Hone/Cruickshank satire.

The *New Oxford Book* is a reader's edition, not a critical edition. Nonetheless, it is a reader's edition sieved through a scholarly conscience. To give adequate reading texts of Blake, then, it ought to have given us colour facsimiles. The edition does not do that, and it is less than I had hoped as a result. Of course the edition does many other things, and does them (I hope) well. Its unusual organization is something not every press would have permitted, especially in such a well-established series. But in the matter of visual materials, the edition's limits are clear.

I give this example partly to foreground the technical, commercial, and institutional realities that determine what scholars can do in book forms. We have already glimpsed such determinants in the example from Burns. The present example reminds us how poetical texts frequently use the visual features of their media as part of their imaginative field. Just as Burns's poetry almost always exploits the language's auditional forms and materials, Blake's almost always exploits the print medium for expressive effects. A text of Blake's 'Songs', for example—whether critical or otherwise—that does not at a minimum give us a colour facsimile, is simply an inadequate text.

These two examples may stand as paradigms for a whole range of textual materials that scholarly editing to this point in time has not dealt with very well. We have had many fine editions of ballads and songs since the late eighteenth century, but none has been able to accommodate, except in minimal ways, the auditional features of the texts. Similarly, expressive typography and other visually significant features of book design have been handled to date in facsimile editions, which rarely—and never adequately—incorporate critical and scholarly apparatuses into their structure. The failure to meet the latter needs is especially apparent in the work produced during the periods I have been most involved with. The renaissance of printing that took place in the late nineteenth century utterly transformed the way poetry was conceived and written. In England, William Morris and D. G. Rossetti stand at the beginning of a poetical history that to this day shows no signs of abatement. The evolution of the modernist movement could (and at some point should) be written as a history of book production and text design.

These developments in England and America trace themselves back to William Blake, whose work was put into circulation and made historically significant largely through the efforts of the Pre-Raphaelites, especially Rossetti. Blake's work thus forecasts the massive opening of the textual field that took place in the nineteenth century, when image and word began to discover new and significant bibliographical relations. Technological breakthroughs such as lithography and steel engraving are more than causes accelerating these events. They are the signs of a culture-wide effort for the technical means to raise the expressive power of the book through visual design.

An adequate critical representation of such work has to this point been seriously hampered by the limits of the book as a critical tool. To date, for example, it has been impossible to produce a true critical edition of the works of Blake. Because Blake's texts operate simultaneously in two media, an adequate critical edition would have to marry a complete facsimile edition of all copies of Blake within the structure of a critical edition. One needs in such a case not a critical edition of Blake's work, but a critical archive. This archive, moreover, must be able to accommodate the collation of pictures and the parts of pictures with each other as well as with all kinds of purely textual materials. Hypermedia structures for the first time make this kind of archive possible; indeed, work towards the development of such a Blake archive is now underway.

The problem of editing Blake's work in a thoroughly critical way is not peculiar to Blake's idiosyncratic genius, however, it is symptomatic and widespread. To show how and why this is the case I offer three further examples, all from the nineteenth century. The first and third involve authors as famous as Blake, Emily Dickinson, and William Wordsworth. The second will also be brought forward under an authorial sign, the once celebrated but now forgotten poet Laetitia Elizabeth Landon. The examples of Dickinson and Landon will show the structure and extent of the editing problems already glimpsed through the example of Blake's work. We conclude with a discussion of the historical significance of the most recent critical editions of Wordsworth.

Example C

It has taken one hundred years for scholars to realize that a typographical edition of Dickinson's writings—whether of her poetry or even her letters—fundamentally misrepresents her literary work. A wholesale editorial revaluation of Dickinson is now well under way. A particularly telling example appeared recently in an article by Jeanne Holland on the Dickinson poem 'Alone and in a Circumstance' (J 1167). Holland's facsimile reprint of the poem shows a work structured in a close, even a dialectical, relation to its physical materials.[4]

Dickinson set up a kind of gravitational field for her writing when she fixed an uncancelled three-cent stamp (with a locomotive design) to a sheet of paper and then wrote her poem in the space she had thus imaginatively created. Whatever this poem 'means', the meaning has been visually designed—more in the manner of a painter or a graphic artist than in the manner of writers who are thinking of their language in semantic or—more generously—linguistic terms.

One could easily multiply instances of this kind of text construction in Dickinson's work. As we know, she refused what she called 'the auction' of print publication. All of her poetry—including those few things put

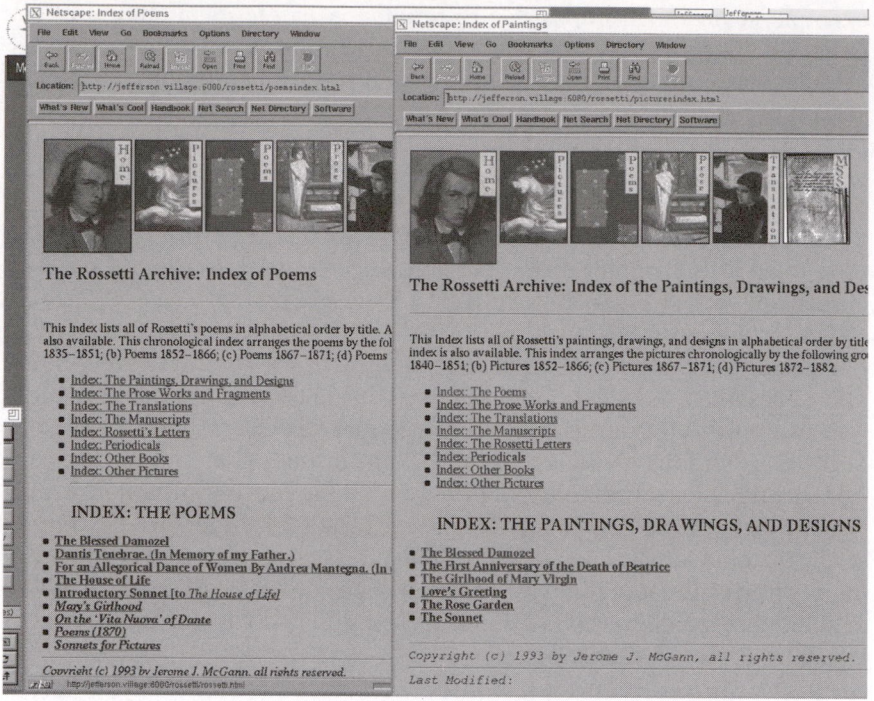

Fig. 3. This screen shot shows the demo Index pages for the Poetry and the Pictures sections of the Archive. All the icons are hyperlinked to their named destinations. The Index bullets are hyperlinks to those parts of the Archive, and each named work has a hyperlink to the top commentary page for that work.

into print during her lifetime without her permission—was produced as handicraft work. This means that her textual medium is treated in the writing process as an end in itself—ultimately, as part of the aesthetic field of the writing. Again and again in Dickinson's work we observe her using the physique of the page and her scripts as expressive vehicles of art. In an age of print publication, manuscripts of writers tend to stand *in medias res*, for they anticipate a final translation into that 'better world' conceived as the printed word. In Dickinson's case, however, the genres that determine the aspirations of her work are scriptural rather than bibliographical: commonplace book writing, on one hand, and letter writing on the other.

To edit her work adequately, then, one needs to integrate the mechanisms of critical editing into a facsimile edition—which is precisely the kind of thing that codex-based editing finds exceedingly difficult to do.

Example D

Here I shall turn to another kind of text—apparitionally very different, but finally closely related to Dickinson's work. Before we look at it, however, some preliminary comments may be useful.

The nineteenth century is famously the age of the novel. Quantities of verse continued to be written and read, of course, and the period has more than its share of poets who were either very important or very successful or both. Nonetheless, it is a commonplace that the period approximately defined by the deaths of Byron on one end, Tennyson on the other, was a great age of fictional prose.

This decline in the cultural fortunes of poetry, if in fact such occurred, has often been connected to the explosion of late romantic sentimental verse, a kind of writing typically associated with women or a feminized imagination. Dickinson, we know, became a great poet by exploiting and modifying the sentimental tradition that so evidently supports her work. In the version of this tale told by the ideologues of modernism, Dickinson did not simply exploit and modify the tradition, she exploded it altogether, and escaped thereby into greatness.

Like most such tales, this last inscribes a highly moralized fiction on a body of evident fact. For example, probably the most important venue for nineteenth-century poetry were the gift books and annuals that began to appear in the early 1820s and that dominated the market until late in the century. Scores of these works were produced, though now we remember them, if at all, in terms of a very few: *The Keepsake, Bijou, Forget-Me-Not*. Literary history pigeon-holed them years ago. They became a synonym for bad and sentimental writing, and to this day remain—properly too— an index to the feminization of culture.[5]

An equivalent textual condition develops in the world of nineteenth-century fiction. The genre of the novel underwent a great transformation as a consequence of new methods of producing and distributing these works. This story is now well known. Suffice it to say here that serialization (in its many forms) and the three-decker format had a decisive impact on the character of fiction writing. These and other new transmissional mechanisms not only gave authors fresh opportunities to change and revise their works, they complicated the fictional options in other ways as well. The illustrated novels of Dickens and Thackeray are simply the most outstanding examples of the generic changes being brought about through new methods of book production.

Out of this cultural context emerged one of the most distinctive minor genres of the period: the poem on the subject of a painting or picture. The form would be elaborated in remarkable ways by the Pre-Raphaelites, and

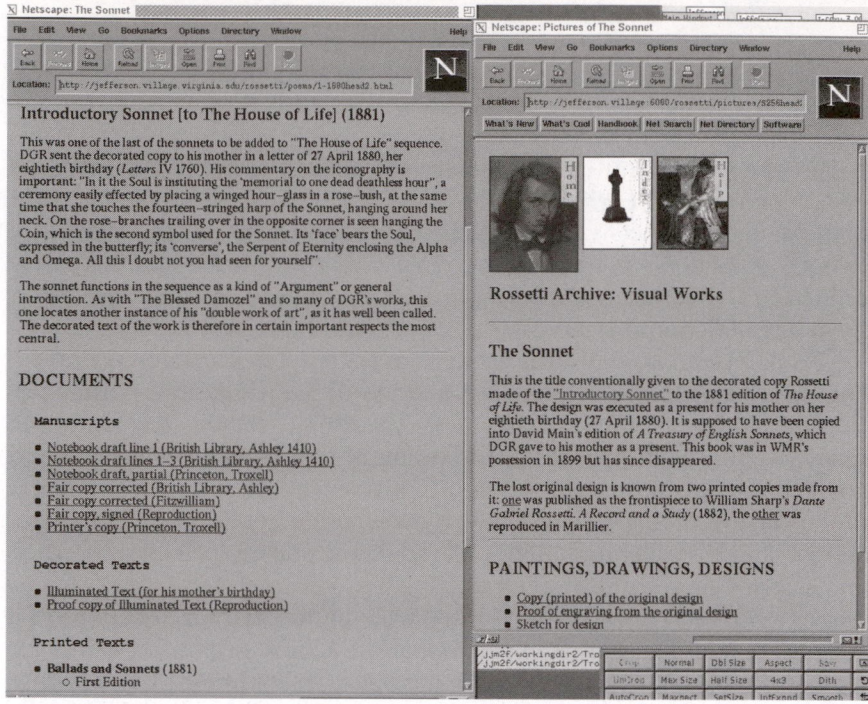

FIG. 4. This screen shot shows the demo of two related introductory commentary pages in the Archive. The pages supply critical introductions plus complete lists of all the known documentary states of the work in question (in this case, the introductory 'Sonnet' to *The House of Life*). If the work in question is a 'double work', i.e. if it involves both textual and pictorial elements, the commentary pages list all relevant textual and pictorial documents.

in particular by Rossetti, but it began much earlier. Good examples can be found throughout the early nineteenth century, but it was not extensively developed until the advent of the period of gift books and annuals. At that point the form undergoes a distinct mutation, as one can see by comparing (say) a poem like Wordsworth's 'Peele Castle' elegy with the picture-poems of Laetitia Elizabeth Landon. In Landon's work, Wordsworth's psychologically dynamic form passes beyond (perhaps also through) the Keatsian and Shelleyan process of aestheticization so brilliantly analysed in Hallam's essay on Tennyson's early poetry.[6] What is dynamic and psychological in Wordsworth becomes formal and literal in Landon and, after Landon, in Tennyson, whose early poetry is clearly written out of the same kind of sensibility.

The queen of the annuals, Landon was obliged to write a great many poems for pictures, and her work nicely illustrates the two dominant stylistic procedures encouraged by the genre. First is the poem that tries to render, more or less faithfully, the details of the picture's imagery. To this is added, or interwoven with it, an interpretive element. Some of Landon's best known works are of this kind: for example, 'A Child Screening a Dove from a Hawk', after Stewardson, and 'The Enchanted Island', after Danby.

Both of these poems are from Landon's 1825 series 'Poetical Sketches for Modern Pictures' (published in the volume *The Troubador, and Other Poems*). Because the texts were originally printed without accompanying engravings, we might think that a scholarly edition now could suitably forgo reproducing their related pictures. The opposite, it seems to me, is true. Wordsworth's Peele Castle poem, for instance, does not absolutely need its picture, is not integrated into its visual materials the way Landon's poems are. For her part, Landon has not just written poems after pictures that have moved her, she has written picture-poems for an audience whom she expects to be familiar with the pictures. In each case we are dealing with a very different 'picture of the mind' ('Tintern Abbey', 61). Wordsworth takes his picture from an imagination of the individual person—ultimately, from the figure Wordsworth made of himself in his verse. By contrast, Landon's individual—her figure of herself—is everywhere represented in her work as a function of social codes and attitudes. In this respect her work recalls Burns's: though many of his songs were printed without (sheet) music, they nonetheless bear their music in their heart, like the original solitary reaper, and they expect their audience to be familiar with it. (On the other hand, Burns stands closer to Wordsworth to the extent that his audience has forgotten or lost touch with those songs.)

Many—perhaps even most—of Landon's picture-poems were printed with engravings of the pictures. This happens because of the generic character of the gift book, which was primarily organized around its visual materials. Texts, both prose and verse, were written in relation to pictures rather than (as in illustrated editions of Scott or Dickens) the other way round. A typical example comes in *The Keepsake* for 1829: Landon's untitled piece written after Landseer's portrait of *Georgiana, the Duchess of Bedford* ('Lady, thy face is very beautiful'). (See Figure 5 for the text and the engraving.)

121

Lady, thy face is very beautiful,
A calm and stately beauty: thy dark hair
Hangs as the passing winds paid homage there;
And gems, such gems as only princes cull
From earth's rich veins, are round thy neck and arm;
Ivory, with just one touch of colour warm;
And thy white robe floats queen-like, suiting well
A shape such as in ancient pictures dwell!
 If thou hadst lived in that old haunted time,
When sovereign Beauty was a thing sublime,
For which knights went to battle, and her glove
Had even more of glory than of love;—
Hadst thou lived in those days, how chivalrie,
With brand and banner, would have honour'd thee!
Then had this picture been a chronicle,
Of whose contents might only poets tell
What king had worn thy chains, what heroes sigh'd,
What thousands nameless, hopeless, for thee died.
But thou art of the Present—there is nought
About thee for the dreaming minstrel's thought,
Save vague imagination, which still lives
Upon the charmed light all beauty gives.
What hath romancing lute, or fancied line,
Or colour'd words to do with thee or thine?
No, the chords sleep in silence at thy feet,
They have no measures for thy music meet;
The poet hath no part in it, his dream
Would too much idleness of flattery seem;
And to that lovely picture only pays
The wordless homage of a lingering gaze.

L. E. L.

GEORGIANA.
DUCHESS OF BEDFORD.

Printed by Mrs Queen.

Published for the Proprietor, by T. Hurst & Cⁿ, St Pauls Churchyard and R. Jennings, 2, Poultry.

FIG. 5. This is the illustration of *Georgiana, the Duchess of Bedford* as it appears in the 1829 *Keepsake*, facing the text of Landon's poem.

As with much of Landon's best work, these lines evolve a kind of anti-poem that self-consciously exploits its own factitiousness. Much could be said about its mannered poeticality, the work's false elegancies that startle and disturb the reader from the outset—as the word 'very' in the first line emphasizes. But I leave such readings for another more appropriate time. Here it is sufficient to see, and to say, that the poem properly exists in the closest kind of relation with the actual picture, as Landon's socio-economic treatment of her subject emphasizes. Furthermore, in this case art's relation to the economics of class, so central to Landseer's original painting, receives a full bourgeois reinscription.

The textual situation here is subtle and complex. Proceeding from the semantic wordplay in line 19 ('But thou art of the Present'), we begin to observe the relationship that this work is fashioning, in every sense, between text and picture. For instance, at the semantic level the poem simultaneously reflects upon its nominal subject, the Duchess, and addresses its real subject, the 'art of the Present'. For Landon's poem is not written on the Duchess or painting so much as on the relation of the two. As such, the most important subject of all is neither Duchess nor painting, it is *The Keepsake* itself and its (reproduced) engraving.

Here one wants to recall the fact that Landseer's fame as an artist was largely secured through the engravings that broadcast his work rather than through the original oils. The 'Georgiana, the Duchess of Bedford' is 'of the Present' in several senses, all of which are important to Landon. But most important are the contemporary artistic representations of the Duchess—the painting, the engraving, and now Landon's poem, the last two being framed and represented in *The Keepsake for MDCCCXXIX*, which is how the title-page reads. Signifiers of Beauty, each comes forward here in a self-conscious, perhaps even a shameless, state of artistic exhaustion. Completely integrated, the engraving, the poem, and the book correspond precisely to what Marx would shortly call 'the soul of the commodity'.

The picture-poem was a characteristic form in gift books and annuals, which often constructed themselves around sets or groups of pictures rather than collections of texts. Contributors were asked to write poems *to* specific pictures, just as novelists of the period were asked to write novels in three volumes, or in a sequence of episodes of a certain number and size. Under such circumstances, the poets all but completely abandoned the usual romantic conventions of sincerity. If the conventions appear at all, as they often do in Landon, they tend to come like ghosts, conscious of their afterlife. *In Memoriam* is the epic of all such writing.

In this example from Landon I have allowed myself to range beyond bibliographical issues into interpretive commentary. I have done this because literary history has long invisibilized Landon and the gift-book traditions she used. And yet it is a historical fact that for fifty years and more that tradition was a dominating influence on imaginative writing that exploited relatively brief forms (like lyric and short story). Indeed, it could easily be argued that Landon wrote in and through the single most important (and institutionally based) poetic genre of the period. Even more interesting, this genre was not a conceptual form (like epic, sonnet, or the novel) but a material one: the gift book and literary annual. As we know, 'serious' people long ago stopped reading writers like Landon and Felicia Hemans. But their work will perforce become difficult to understand if we

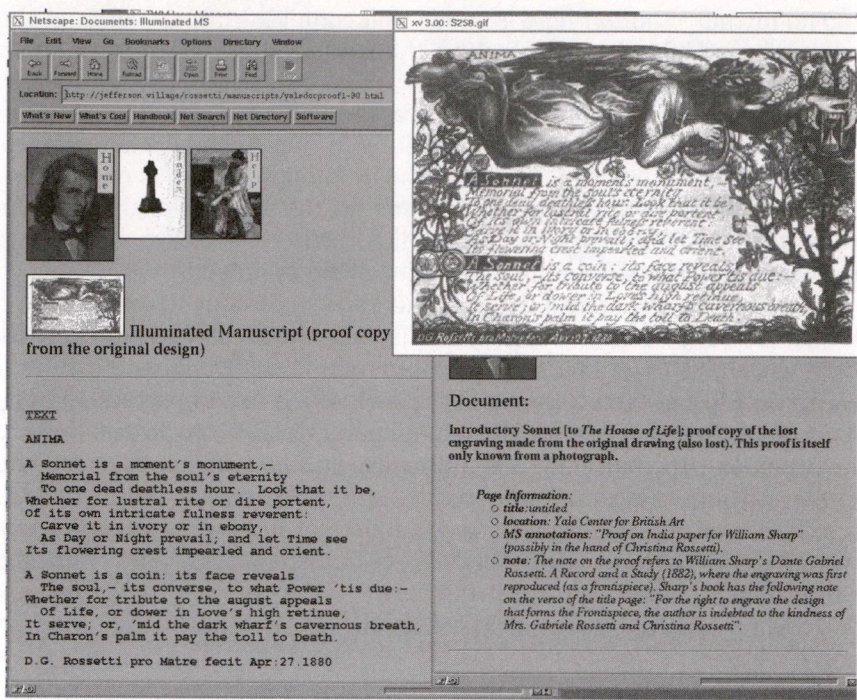

FIG. 6. This screen shot depicts three electronic documents simultaneously: a facsimile of the illuminated version of the 'Sonnet'; an alphanumeric representation of that document (in modified diplomatic transcription); and the commentary page that comes with these documents. The Rossetti Archive is designed so that the scholar can open and study an indefinite number of the Archive's files at the same time.

do not receive it in forms that at least approximate its original imaginative condition. In Landon's case, the pictorial and ornamental context of gift-book production can be torn away from her work only at the cost of its destruction.

The example of Landon therefore culminates my answer to the question of 'why' one would want to exploit hypermedia environments in scholarly work. I submit that no edition aspiring to represent the kinds of textual situation we have been examining would be happy with the removal of any of the materials, or—what often happens—with the translation of concrete textual features into those thin, abstract presences: a bibliographical notation or a scholar's narrativized description. I submit further that every critical and scholarly edition will be—has been—forced into such abstractions when it aspires, *within the physical constraints of a tradititional book format*, to a comprehensive treatment of its materials. The more complex the materials, the more abstract and/or cumbersome the edition becomes.

Example E

In this case I ask you to recall the Cornell Wordsworth, in particular the three volumes devoted to *The Prelude*: Stephen Parrish's edition of the 'Two Book' *Prelude* (1977), W. J. B. Owen's edition of the 'Fourteen Book' *Prelude* (1985), and Mark Reed's edition of the 'Thirteen Book' *Prelude* (1993). All three are models of their kind, meticulous and thorough. Nonetheless, in their heroic efforts to represent that original complex and unstable scene of writing, these editions—*coming at just the historical moment that they do*—have put a period to codex-based scholarly editing.

Here is a true story that may help to explain my meaning. Several years ago I wrote to Mark Reed to ask who was going to edit the 'Five Book' *Prelude*. He wrote back and said there would be no such edition since (1) that particular form of the work only attained a fleeting existence, and (2) the *Prelude* project was already dauntingly large and, from the publisher's point of view, textually repetitive. Instead, his edition would provide a narrative description and textual history of the 'Five Book' *Prelude*. He sent me a copy of this narrative, which eventually appeared as part of his edition.

Mark Reed narrativized the 'Five Book' *Prelude* for one reason only: the book format (including the commercial factors governing that format) did not lend itself to printing yet another *Prelude* volume in the Cornell series. Too much of the material was viewable in the other volumes. Indeed, the limits of the codex imposed all kinds of constraints on the editors of Wordsworth's great uncompleted work, so that one will find it difficult to use: on one hand full of scholar's codes, on the other cumbersome when one wishes to compare different documents and texts.

As I have already pointed out, these problems inhere in the codex form itself, which constrains the user of the critical edition to manipulate difficult systems of abbreviation, and to read texts that have (typically) transformed the original documents in radical ways. In an electronic edition, however, both of these hindrances can be removed. Precisely because an electronic edition is not itself a book, it is able to establish itself in a theoretical position that supervenes the (textual and bookish) materials it wishes to study. The operations carried out by the traditional book-based abbreviation systems continue to be performed in the electronic edition, of course, for they are central to the whole idea of the scholar's critical edition. In the computerized edition, however, the reader does not have to learn or even encounter the codes in order to execute critical operations (e.g. moving back and forth across different parts of books or separate volumes, carrying out analytic searches and comparisons). These operations are performed on command but out of sight. In addition, of course, the computerized structure allows the reader to undertake searches and analyses of the material that would have been impossible, even unimaginable, in a codex environment.

CONCLUSION: THE ROSSETTI HYPERMEDIA ARCHIVE

Hyperediting is what scholars will be doing for a long time. Many difficult problems will have to be dealt with, of course, including major problems hardly touched on here: questions of copyright, for instance, or the whole array of problems posed by the emergence of the vast electronic information network that is even now coming into being. In the immediate context, multimedia hyperediting poses its own special difficulties.

For instance, hypermedia projects (like Perseus, for instance) are notably constrained by a structural feature of the digitized images they employ. When these images are introduced into a hypermedia structure, they have had to serve as simple illustrations; for the (bitmapped) information in the digitized image cannot be searched and analysed as electronic texts can be.

How to incorporate digitized images into the computational field is not simply a problem that hyperediting must *solve*, it is a problem created by the very arrival of the possibilities of hyperediting. In my own case, the Rossetti Hypermedia Archive was begun exactly because the project forced an engagement with this problem. Those of us who were involved with the Rossetti Archive from the beginning spent virtually the entire first year working at this problem. In the end we arrived at a double approach: first, to design a structure of SGML markup tags for the physical features of all the types of documents contained in the Rossetti Archive (textual as well as pictorial); and second, to develop an image tool that permits one to attach anchors to specific features of digitized images. Both of these tools effectively open visual (and potentially audial) materials to the full computational power of the hyperediting environment. At this writing the DTDs (Document Type Definitions) for all textual materials, including digitized materials, are fully operational. The image tool is currently in its first release.

It is important to realize that the Rossetti project is an archive rather than an edition. When a book is produced it literally closes its covers on itself. If its work is continued, a new edition, or other related books, have to be (similarly) produced. A work like the Rossetti Hypermedia Archive has escaped that bibliographical limitation. It has been built so that its

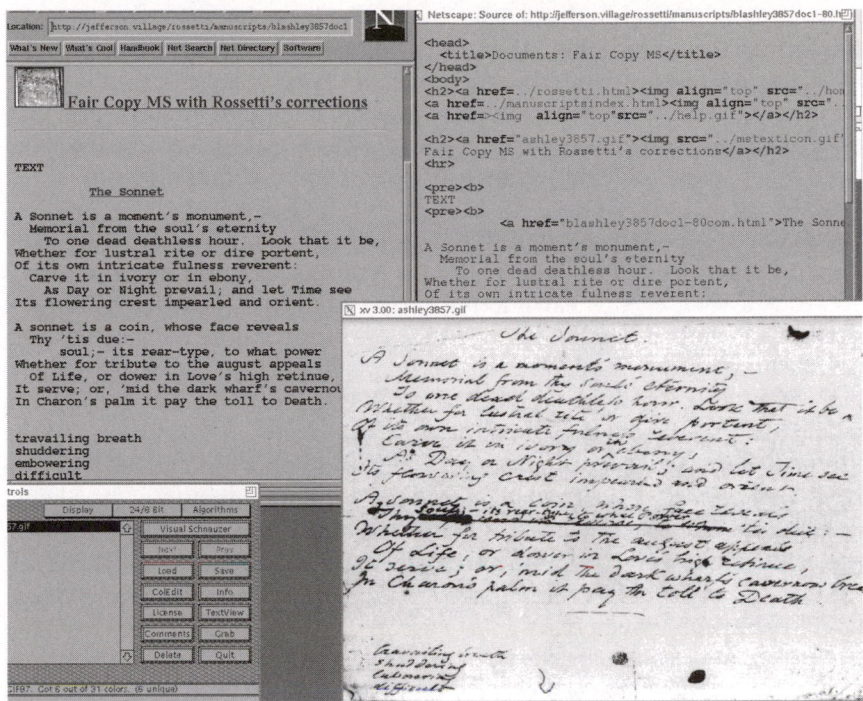

Fig. 7. This is a screen shot of three other documents related to the introductory 'Sonnet': a facsimile of one of the manuscripts in the British Library; the diplomatic transcription of that manuscript; and the HTML-marked text that stands behind the latter. In the Rossetti Archive as it is actually being built, all these electronic files are marked in SGML for full structured search and analysis. (The image at the lower left is the panel for manipulating visual images in a UNIX environment and has nothing as such to do with the Archive. It appears here only because it was needed to construct these screen shots for paper publication.)

contents and its webwork of relations (both internal and external) can be indefinitely expanded and developed.

The 'hyper' organization has also permitted the Archive to escape another bookish horizon which has profoundly affected editorial theory and textual scholarship. A major aspect of this scholarship has been the investigation of ancient texts—in particular, the scholarly reconstruction of such works from textual remains that have been seriously broken over time. Such work encouraged scholars to focus on a single text, the ideal goal of their reconstructive operations.

In more modern periods, however, the textual remains are often very numerous. The history of the texts of Wordsworth and Blake and Dickinson is not seriously fractured. Indeed, the scholarly problem in such cases is how to sort out the relations of the documents and put all those relationships on display. However, the goals of classical scholarship and the material formalities of the book encouraged scholars to imagine and produce single-focus works—editions that organized themselves around what used to be called a 'definitive' text, the source and end and test of all the others.

Whatever the virtues of this kind of focus—there are many—one would like to be free to choose it or not, as one needs. In most cases scholars confront a vast, even a bewildering, array of documents. Determining a single focus can be analytically useful, even imperative for certain purposes. On the other hand, one can easily imagine situations where a single determining focus hinders critical study. Besides, in many other cases one would like the possibility to make *ad hoc* or provisional choices among the full array of textual alternatives—to shift the point of focus at will and need. One cannot perform such operations within the horizon of the book. A hypermedia project like the Rossetti Archive offers just these kinds of possibilities, for the data in the Archive is not organized hierarchically. It resembles more that fabulous circle whose centre is everywhere and whose circumference is nowhere.

The change from paper-based text to electronic text is one of those elementary shifts—like the change from manuscript to print—that is so revolutionary we can only glimpse at this point what it entails. Nonetheless, certain essential things are clear even now. The computerized edition can store vastly greater quantities of documentary materials, and it can be built to organize, access, and analyse those materials not only more quickly and easily, but at depths no paper-based edition could hope to achieve. At the moment these works cannot be made as cheaply or as easily as books. But very soon, I am talking about a few years, these electronic tools will not only be far cheaper, they will also be commonplace. Already scholars are creating electronic editions in many fields and languages, and are thereby establishing the conventions for the practice of Hyperediting. The Rossetti Archive is one project of this kind.

CODA: A NOTE ON THE DECENTRED TEXT

Editors and textual theorists interested in computerized texts appear to differ on a significant point: whether or not hyperediting requires (even if it be at some deep and invisible level) a central 'text' for organizing the hypertext of documents. My judgement is that it doesn't.

The question here can and often does get quite muddled. Enthusiasts for hypertext sometimes make extravagant philosophical claims, and sceptics are then drawn towards sardonic reactions. Hypertext is no more a sign of the Last Days than was moveable type five centuries ago.

To say that a hypertext is not centrally organized does not mean—at least does not mean to me—that the hypertext structure has no governing order(s), even at a theoretical level. Clearly such a structure has many ordered parts and sections, and the entirety of the structure is organized for directed searches and analytic operations. In these respects the hypertext is always structured according to some initial set of design plans that are keyed to the specific materials in the hypertext, and the imagined needs of the users of those materials.

Two matters are crucial to remember here, however. First, the specific material design of a hypertext is theoretically open to alterations of its contents and its organizational elements at all points and at any time. Unlike a traditional book or set of books, the hypertext need never be 'complete'—though of course one could choose to shut the structure down if one wanted, close its covers as it were. But the hypertextual order contains an inertia that moves against such a shutdown. So, for example, if one were to create a hypertext of (say) *King Lear*, the 'edition' *as it is a hypertext* can pass forward in time indefinitely. Someone will have to manage it, but if it remains hypertextual it will incorporate and then go beyond its initial design and management. It will evolve and change over time, it will gather new bodies of material, its organizational substructures will get modified, perhaps quite drastically.

The second point goes to the matter of the conceptual form of hypertext as such (as opposed to the specific implementation of that form for certain materials and purposes). Unlike a traditional edition, a hypertext is not organized to focus attention on one particular text or set of texts. It is ordered to disperse attention as broadly as possible. Of course it is true that every *particular* hypertext at any particular point in time will have established preferred sets of arrangements and orderings, and these could be less, or more, decentralized. The point is that the hypertext, unlike the book, encourages greater decentralization of design. Hypertext provides the means for establishing an indefinite number of 'centres', and for expanding their number as well as altering their relationships. One is encouraged not so much to find as to make order—and then to make it again and again, as established orderings expose their limits.

An important historical fact might be usefully recalled: that the Internet, which is an archive of archives, was originally designed precisely as a decentred, non-hierarchical structure. The point was to have an information network that could be destroyed or cut at any point, at any number of points, and still remain intact as a structured informational network. The theory of hypertext flows directly from this way of imagining a non-centralized structure of complex relationships. With hypertext, as with the

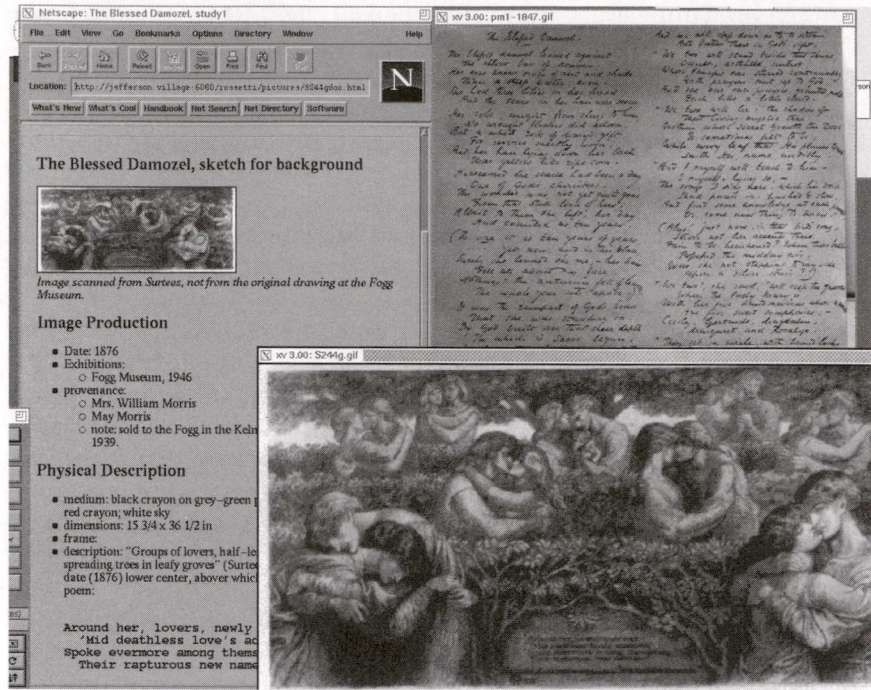

F<small>IG</small>. 8. This screen shot depicts three files relevant to the study of 'The Blessed Damozel': a facsimile of the Pierpont Morgan manuscript; a facsimile (from the Fogg Museum) of the finished sketch for the background of the finished oil painting; and part of the commentary page for the latter. The icon of the sketch shown on the commentary page is hyperlinked to the sketch.

Net, the separate parts of the ensemble (nodes on the Net, files in a hypertext) are independently structured units. That kind of organization ensures that relationships and connections can be established and developed in arbitrary and stochastic patterns.

This kind of organizational form resembles our oldest extant hypertextual structure, the library, which is also an archive (or in many cases an archive of archives). As with the Internet and hypertext, a library is organized for indefinite expansion. Its logical organization (e.g. the Library of Congress (LC) system) can be accommodated to any kind of physical environment, and it is neutral with respect to user demands and navigation. Moreover, the library is logically 'complete' no matter how many volumes it contains—no matter how many are lost or added.

The non-centralized character of such an ordering scheme is very clear if one reflects even briefly on the experience of library browsing. You are interested in, say, Dante Gabriel Rossetti's writings. So you move to that

LC location in the library (any library). You stand before a set of books and other documents, which may be more or less extensive. *Nothing in that body of materials tells you where to begin or what volume to pull down. It is up to you to make such a decision.*

You can only find your way to that point in the library if you can negotiate its logical structure; and further browsing (or directed research) requires an even greater self-conscious understanding of the organization. Neophite library users are often intimidated by a library precisely because they cannot immediately tell how to use it. Guides to a library will explain its logical structure as well as the physical implementation of that structure. Even so, they are conceived in the same spirit as the Internet and hypertext.

Subnets (or substructures) of these kinds of organization may be more or less hierarchically organized than other substructures. In a library, for example, historical orderings of various kinds appear everywhere. Nevertheless, these local basins of order are arbitrary with respect to the total archive. This result obtains because each unit of the organization (each document and also each set of documents), like each node on the Internet, is logically defined as an independent item.

In a hypertext, each document (or part of a document) can therefore be connected to every other document (or document part) in any way one chooses to define a connection. Relationships do not have to be organized in terms of a measure or standard (though subgroups of organization can be arbitrarily defined as non-arbitrary forms). From a scholarly editor's point of view, this structure means that every text or even every portion of a text (i.e. every logical unit in the hypertext) has an absolute value within the structure as a whole unless its absolute character is specifically modified.

The Rossetti Archive organizes its texts, pictures, and other documents in this kind of noncentralized form. So when one goes to read a poetical work, no documentary state of the work is privileged over the others. All options are presented for the reader's choice. Among those options are arbitrary constraints that can be placed on the choices available. These constraints, which can be defined at any level of the organization, can be invoked or revoked at will. The point is that the structure preserves the independence of every document because the organization, like the Net, is 'divided into packets, [with] each packet separately addressed'. Since each of these packets has 'its own authority to originate, pass, and receive messages', each is free to 'wind its way through the [archive] on an individual basis'.[7] Of course that is a metaphoric way of putting the matter: files in a hypertext, like documents in a library, are not active agents. It is the user who moves through the hypertext. Nevertheless, the ordering of the hypertext materials is, by default, arbitrary and discrete. If the archive

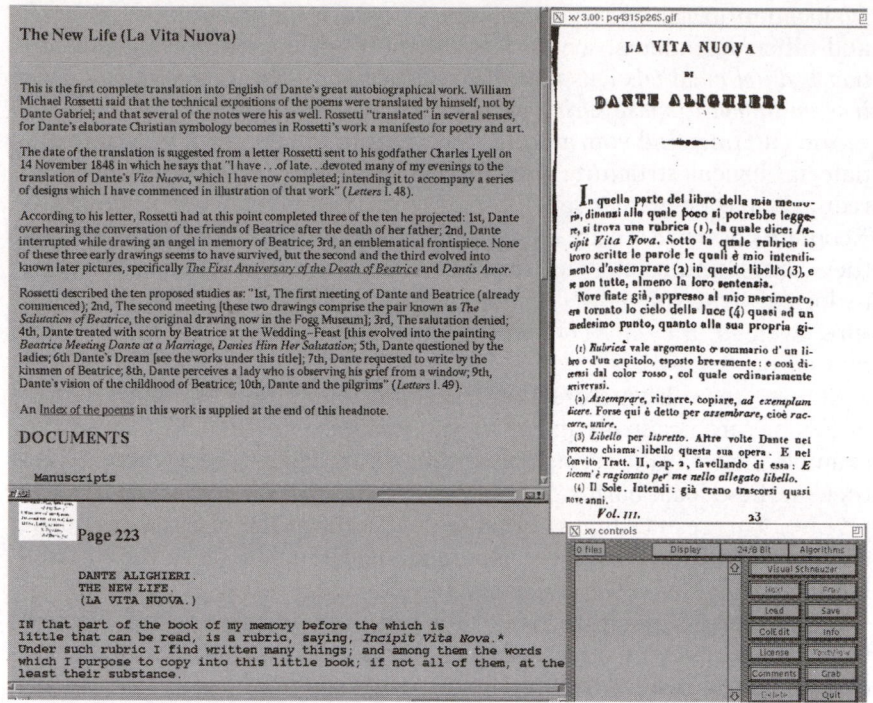

The New Life (La Vita Nuova)

This is the first complete translation into English of Dante's great autobiographical work. William Michael Rossetti said that the technical expositions of the poems were translated by himself, not by Dante Gabriel; and that several of the notes were his as well. Rossetti "translated" in several senses, for Dante's elaborate Christian symbology becomes in Rossetti's work a manifesto for poetry and art.

The date of the translation is suggested from a letter Rossetti sent to his godfather Charles Lyell on 14 November 1848 in which he says that "I have ...of late. ..devoted many of my evenings to the translation of Dante's *Vita Nuova*, which I have now completed; intending it to accompany a series of designs which I have commenced in illustration of that work" (*Letters* I. 48).

According to his letter, Rossetti had at this point completed three of the ten he projected: 1st, Dante overhearing the conversation of the friends of Beatrice after the death of her father; 2nd, Dante interrupted while drawing an angel in memory of Beatrice; 3rd, an emblematical frontispiece. None of these three early drawings seems to have survived, but the second and the third evolved into known later pictures, specifically *The First Anniversary of the Death of Beatrice* and *Dantis Amor*.

Rossetti described the ten proposed studies as: "1st, The first meeting of Dante and Beatrice (already commenced); 2nd, The second meeting [these two drawings comprise the pair known as *The Salutation of Beatrice*, the original drawing now in the Fogg Museum]; 3rd, The salutation denied; 4th, Dante treated with scorn by Beatrice at the Wedding–Feast [this evolved into the painting *Beatrice Meeting Dante at a Marriage, Denies Him Her Salutation*; 5th, Dante questioned by the ladies; 6th Dante's Dream [see the works under this title]; 7th, Dante requested to write by the kinsmen of Beatrice; 8th, Dante perceives a lady who is observing his grief from a window; 9th, Dante's vision of the childhood of Beatrice; 10th, Dante and the pilgrims" (*Letters* I. 49).

An Index of the poems in this work is supplied at the end of this headnote.

DOCUMENTS

Manuscripts

Page 223

DANTE ALIGHIERI.
THE NEW LIFE.
(LA VITA NUOVA.)

IN that part of the book of my memory before the which is little that can be read, is a rubric, saying, *Incipit Vita Nova.** Under such rubric I find written many things; and among them the words which I purpose to copy into this little book; if not all of them, at the least their substance.

LA VITA NUOVA
DI
DANTE ALIGHIERI

In quella parte del libro della mia memoria, dinanzi alla quale poco si potrebbe leggere, si trova una rubrica (1), la quale dice: *Incipit Vita Nova*. Sotto la quale rubrica io trovo scritte le parole le quali è mio intendimento d'assemprare (2) in questo libello (3), e se non tutte, almeno la loro sentenzia.

Nove fiate già, appresso al mio nascimento, era tornato lo cielo della luce (4) quasi ad un medesimo punto, quanto alla sua propria gi-

(1) *Rubrica* vale argomento o sommario d'un libro o d'un capitolo, esposto brevemente: e così dicesi dal color rosso, col quale ordinariamente scriverasi.

(2) *Assemprare*, ritrarre, copiare, *ad exemplum licere*. Forse qui è detto per assemprare, cioè raccorre, unire.

(3) *Libello* per *libretto*. Altre volte Dante nel processo chiama. libello questa sua opera. E nel Convito Tratt. II., cap. 2, favellando di essa: *E siccom' è ragionato per me nello allegato libello.*

(4) Il Sole. Intendi: già erano trascorsi quasi nove anni.

Vol. III.   23

Fig. 9. This is a screen shot from a moment in the Translations section of the Archive. It shows a portion of the critical introduction to Rossetti's translation of the *Vita Nuova*; the original Italian text from the edition that Rossetti actually used; and a diplomatic rendering of the page from Rossetti's *The Early Italian Poets* that corresponds to Dante's text. The icon partly visible in the diplomatic text, if clicked, would take the user to a facsimile of that page. All the diplomatic texts in the archive have such icons.

contains any more centralized or hierarchical structures, these have to be (arbitrarily) introduced. Furthermore, if they are introduced, the extent of their authority over the user has to be (arbitrarily) defined as well.

The problem here returns us once again to the fundamental issue of the relation of (hard copy) text to (electronic) hypertext. The decentralized forms of hypertextual archives clearly possess logical structure. That structure is designed to facilitate navigation through the archived materials irrespective of the purposes of the navigation.[8] When the hypertext is used to manage study of and navigation through complex bodies of (hard copy) documentary materials—the kinds that traditional scholarly editors deal with—a special type of 'decentralism' appears. The exigencies of the book form forced editorial scholars to develop fixed points of relation—the 'definitive text', 'copy text', 'ideal text', 'Ur text', 'standard text', and so forth—in order to conduct a book-bound navigation (by coded forms) through large bodies of documentary materials. Such fixed points no longer have to govern the ordering of the documents. As with the nodes on the Internet, every documentary moment in the hypertext is absolute with respect to the archive as a whole, or with respect to any subarchive that may have been (arbitrarily) defined within the archive. In this sense, computerized environments have established the new 'Rationale of hypertext'.[9]

NOTES

1. The simplest definition of hypertext is Theodore Nelson's, 'nonsequential writing', *Literary Machines* (Sausalito, Calif.: Mindful, 1990, 5.2). Nelson's book is a classic introduction to hypertext. For other introductory information about hypertext and hypermedia, and about the projects mentioned in this and the next paragraphs, see Emily Berk and Joseph Devlin (eds.), *Hypertext / Hypermedia Handbook* (Internet Publications, New York: McGraw Hill, 1991); Paul Delany and George P. Landow (eds.), *The Digital Word: Text-Based Computing in the Humanities* (Cambridge, Mass.: MIT Press, 1993); George P. Landow, *Hypertext: The Convergence of Contemporary Critical Theory and Technology* (Baltimore: Johns Hopkins University Press, 1992); Paul Delany and George P. Landow (eds.), *Hypermedia and Literary Studies* (Cambridge Mass.: MIT Press, 1991); Jay David Bolter, *Writing Space: The Computer, Hypertext, and the History of Writing* (Hillsdale, NJ: Lawrence Erlbaum, 1991).
2. See *The Poems and Songs of Robert Burns*, ed. James Kinsley (Oxford: Clarendon Press, 1968), i. 435–6.
3. See, for example, the ballad 'Tam Lin' (ibid., Kinsley no. 558, ii. 836–41).
4. This revaluation of Dickinson studies was sparked by the great facsimile edition of the poet's original fascicles, *The Manuscript Books of Emily Dickinson*, ed. R. W. Franklin (2 vols.; Cambridge, Mass.: Belknap Press, Harvard University Press, 1981). Since then the work of Susan Howe and her students has been only slightly less significant, especially the recently published edition of Dickinson's fragments, *Emily Dickinson's Open Folios: Scenes of Reading, Surfaces of Writing*, ed. Marta L. Werner (Ann Arbor: University of Michigan Press, 1995); and the essay by Jeanne Holland, 'Scraps, Stamps, and Cutouts: Emily Dickinson's Domestic Technologies of Publication', in Katherine O'Brien O'Keeffe and Margaret J. M. Ezell (eds.), *Cultural Artifacts and the Production of Meaning* (Ann Arbor: University of Michigan Press, 1994), pp. 139–82. Howe's seminal essay is indispensable: 'These Flames and Generosities of the Heart: Emily Dickinson and the Illogic of Sumptuary Values', *Sulfur*, 28 (Spring 1991), 134–55. See also Paula Bennett, 'By a Mouth that Cannot Speak: Spectral Presence in Emily Dickinson's Letters', *Emily Dickinson Journal*, 1 (1992), 76–99; and my own 'Emily Dickinson's Visible Language', ibid., 2 (1993), 40–57. Martha Nell Smith is currently the head of the Emily Dickinson Editorial Collective, a group of scholars committed to seeing Dickinson's work re-edited so

as to expose its 'sumptuary values', i.e. the scripts and visible designs that are such an important feature of the writing.

5. See Andrew Boyle, *An Index to the Annuals*, vol. i (vol. ii never printed) (London: privately printed by Andrew Boyle, 1967); F. W. Faxon, *Literary Annuals and Gift Books: A Bibliography 1823–1903* (originally printed 1912, reprinted Boston: Pinner, Private Libraries Assoc., 1973); Anne Renier, *Friendship's Offering: An Essay on the Annuals and Gift Books of the 19th Century* (London: Private Libraries Assoc., 1964); Alison Adburgham, *Silver Fork Society: Fashionable Life and Literature from 1814 to 1840* (London: Constable, 1983).

6. Arthur Henry Hallam, 'On Some of the Characteristics of Modern Poetry, and on the Lyrical Poems of Alfred Tennyson', reprinted from the *Englishman's Magazine* (Aug. 1931) in *The Writings of Arthur Hallam*, ed. T. H. Vail Motter (New York and London: Modern Language Assoc. of America, 1943), pp. 182–97.

7. Quoted from Bruce Sterling, 'Internet', *Magazine of Fantasy and Science Fiction*, Science Column no. 5 (Feb. 1993). I quote here from the text of the column that was made available through a Network mailing list.

8. For discussion of the structure of hypertext (and a critique of rather loose representations of its decentralized form), see Ross Atkinson, 'Networks, Hypertext, and Academic Information Services: Some Longer Range Implications', *College and Research Libraries*, 54: 3 (May 1993), 199–215.

9. Textual scholars will understand that this essay has been written in a conscious revisionary relation to W. W. Greg's great essay 'The Rationale of Copy-Text', which had such a profound influence on twentieth-century textual scholarship. For Greg's essay, see *Studies in Bibliography*, 3 (1950–1), 19–36.

3

Annotating a Text: Literary Theory and Electronic Hypertext

CLAIRE LAMONT

Textual editions of English literary authors do not always carry annotations. Indeed some of the most ambitious do not, like the Clarendon Dickens. But many do, as do many more modest editions. By annotations I mean those notes which in the conventions of modern editing appear not with the textual notes but in a separate list. They may be printed at the foot of the page, or in a list at the end of the volume. They will be called simply 'Notes' or perhaps 'Explanatory Notes', to differentiate them from 'Textual Notes', and that heading will cover different kinds of information. Typically annotations can be marshalled into two rough categories, those which remove obscurities and those which manifest sources. The very fact that a list of annotations usually contains different kinds of information might lead us to expect theoretical problems. Much annotation is produced with apparently little questioning of the rationale of the activity.[1] There have been, however, two major developments in recent years which bring the problems of annotation to the forefront of critical attention. The first is a growing awareness of the theoretical problems of annotation in the light of modern literary theory; and the second is the development of the electronic hypertext which has promised easier access to a larger quantity of annotation than has been possible in the traditionally printed book.[2] The aim of this essay is to consider annotation as it has traditionally been practised in the light of these two challenges, modern literary theory and the electronic hypertext.[3]

Annotation has a long history. Texts of value have always attracted annotation and the Middle Ages saw extensive commentaries to biblical, legal, and medical texts. The annotation of secular works of English literature was not common until the eighteenth century when the skills of the textual editor were extended first to Shakespeare and then to other poets. The annotation of novels, although anticipated by Walter Scott's annotation of his own novels, was not common until the twentieth century and was still being justified quite recently.[4] Annotations deliver a text into another world, the world of scholarship. They draw attention to the fact that there have been previous readers. They invite the new reader to join the party of those who have already read the work and left their traces in the annotation.

This is achieved by the activity of the annotator, who may be doing much more than annotating the text. The annotator, who may be acting alone or collaboratively, may be also the textual editor, may write a critical introduction, may make a selection of recent criticism for suggested 'Further Reading'. Amid all these activities it is possible that the theoretical basis for annotation is not seriously questioned. After all annotation supplies what many readers want. Textual editing may be seen as a tribute to the text, as much as for the satisfaction of the reader. Annotations, however, satisfy the demand of the market-place, especially now that so many literary works have been appropriated by institutional education at all its levels. In the case of some literary works one wonders how many readers there are who are not planning to write an essay in the near future? Readers not only want to enjoy the act of reading, but many of them are aware that they will have to give an account of it very shortly. That context is bound to leave its marks on the book, among which are the annotations. The increased quantity of annotation appearing in modern editions and reprints seems to testify to *demand*.[5] With such an impetus behind the activity, the annotator might suppose that the difficulties are only practical, that of finding the relevant information. Practical problems soon, however, merge into theoretical problems.

The first question to confront the annotator is what to annotate? Words and allusions that the modern reader might not understand? Fine, but which reader? We have all read annotations which carefully tell us the years of Queen Elizabeth's reign and then pass silently over a really recondite allusion. We are used to editions like *The Twickenham Edition of the Poems of Alexander Pope* which does not translate references to Latin poets. Editors of Scottish literature frequently face the problem of James VI of Scotland who in 1603 became James I of England. Some readers will not know that, but those who do may be touchy about being told. The annotator will therefore have to form a view—inevitably inadequate—of who the reader is. So a practical problem becomes a theoretical one pretty quickly. Reader-response criticism has given us the concept of the 'implied reader'. Annotations will also have an implied reader, who may not be the same reader as the implied reader of the text. There is scarcely a note, or lack of one, that does not imply the reader. This example comes from the Arden edition of *Macbeth*. In the first act a Captain describing the military heroism of Macbeth and Banquo says:

> Except they meant to bathe in reeking wounds,
> Or memorize another Golgotha,
> I cannot tell—

> (I. ii. 40–2)

The Arden edition, dating from 1951, has no note on Golgotha, imply-ing a reader who does not need to be told.[6] There are a lot of cultural assumptions behind that omission.

I have suggested that one of the aims of annotation is to remove obscur-ity. The annotator will recognize different sorts of obscurity: some obscur-ities seem to inhere in the text; others are the result of the reader's experience. Those obscurities which seem to be within the text will prob-ably be the subject of a textual note as well as an annotation. The assump-tion behind both sorts of note is that the text should communicate with clarity, and that it is only by some accident that it does not. Even with this assumption annotation is not straightforward. Take, for example, the last two lines of Keats's 'Ode on a Grecian Urn'. The textual notes of an edition will explain the crux in terms of the placing of inverted commas, and the authority of the texts containing the variant readings. Where there is a textual crux should the annotator offer simply a reading of the text that the textual editor has chosen, or should he or she attempt a brief survey of all the readings that have gained credit? Two distinguished Keats editors, John Barnard for Penguin and Miriam Allott for Longman, have chosen the latter. In annotating the last two lines of the 'Ode on a Grecian Urn', Barnard lists five possible answers to the question who is speaking and to whom? Allott offers a choice of six opinions on the meaning of the lines and their relevance to the rest of the poem.[7] There is presumably a difference between offering one reading and five or six.

Other sorts of obscurity have their source in the reader. Some texts do not communicate with clarity because of the passage of time, or change in social circumstances, between its original production and the reader. Annotation in these cases involves historical or social reconstruction to recover meaning. Traditionally annotators who have reflected on this activ-ity have explained it as attempting to give the modern reader the know-ledge which could have been assumed among the text's original readers. In Ian Jack's words, 'The principal duty of an annotator is to attempt to enable his contemporaries to read a book as its original audience read it.'[8] Ian Small, however, has pointed out the impossibility of knowing who the original readers were, whether we are looking for (in his terms) *actual*, *potential*, or *possible* readers,[9] an impossibility mirroring that of knowing who are the modern readers. A number of presuppositions have to be made about the reader when it comes to marrying the daily knowledge of the past with the partial ignorance of the present.

Annotations of the types I have outlined may justify themselves to the traditional annotator by the fact that the reader can be supposed to want them. Passages in some texts are likely to cause uneasiness in the reader which might be to some extent assuaged by a note. At the least the attempt to provide a note communicates the fact that someone else has thought there was a difficulty. But many annotations cannot be justified in that way. Many annotations do not simply respond to the reader's anticipated need for a note, but appear to be based on the recognition that the modern reader will *not* feel the need for a note but *should*. Annotators working on late eighteenth-century texts have found it necessary to tell readers that Dr Johnson's definition of the word 'candid' was 'Without malice; without deceit; fair; open; ingenuous'. The reader may have been perfectly happy making sense of the passage assuming the word to mean 'directly truthful, even when telling the truth is uncomfortable or unwelcome'.[10] The reader of nineteenth-century novels may be happy enough with the knowledge of, say, ecclesiastical organization or social etiquette which he or she already has. The annotator may think, however, that the reading would be enriched by giving sharper detail. This involves telling the reader first that there is the possibility of obscurity and then attempting to remove it. This is not exactly response to perceived need.

The convention of the annotated text may also create the appetite it feeds. It is likely that some texts contain material that was never in a simple sense *understood* by the majority of its original readers. Take for example the novels of Walter Scott. They contain scenes of dialogue by speakers of non-standard English. The Scottish novels have dialogue in Scots; several of the novels contain passages in low-life English and thieves' cant. It can hardly be supposed that as the Waverley novels came to command large audiences in the whole of Britain and North America all readers would understand these language varieties. There were some complaints at the time, but most contemporary readers seem to have been satisfied. Presumably they understood enough; unintelligibility itself communicates something. Perhaps readers had faith that the details could be explained and did not ask for a demonstration. A modern annotator can deliver the demonstration, but in making all the language varieties in the text equally accessible the annotations are probably making for a kind of reading that was scarcely ever possible for the original readers.

The sorts of annotation that I have mentioned so far traditionally justify themselves by reference to either the obscurity of the text or the ignorance of the reader. This is understandable in a commonsense way. But it does not take much reflection to see that there are theoretical pitfalls at every stage. Such annotations all suppose the sovereignty of the text, and in modern literary theory that assumption is in dispute. Even in the context of a theory of literature that maintains the sovereignty of the text, annotation poses difficulties. It is often pointed out that annotations tend to diminish a text, by limiting the interpretative potential in favour of one reading, or at any rate a lesser range of possibilities than the plurality of the text might command.[11] That is no doubt true of even the most valiant annotator of Keats. New Critics would attribute the unsatisfactoriness of annotation to the mysterious unattainability of literature. If the text is sovereign, annotation will always tend to fail because despite its supposed aim of opening avenues of interpretation it will have a tendency to close many more. That is summed up in Jacques Derrida's epigram, 'the fate . . . of an annotation is to be always bad; and the better it is, the worse it is.'[12]

Modern literary theorists approach the problem from a different basic assumption. Modern theory has challenged the view that meaning is located in the text. Here are theoretical quicksands for annotators. If there is any dominant emphasis in modern literary theory, it is that meaning is not inherent in a text, but is created by the reader or by the act of reading. The very ambition, therefore, to annotate a text pre-empts the whole hermeneutic enquiry. What happens to the act of reading if an annotator slips in between reader and text with a note? Readers read in the light of their own experience of previous texts; do we acknowledge that one of these might be a carefully placed note, read more or less concurrently with the reading of the text? Do such notes get subsumed into the text in the act of reading, so challenging our idea of what the text is anyway?

Stanley Fish has commented on this impasse in his 'Interpreting the Variorum'. He mentions annotators' difficulties with the last two lines of Milton's sonnet starting 'Lawrence of virtuous father virtuous son'. The last two lines are:

> He who of those delights can judge, and spare
> To interpose them oft, is not unwise.

The debate is over the word 'spare'. Fish, in allusion to the activities of the traditional annotator, writes, 'to consult dictionaries, grammars, and histories is to assume that meanings can be specified independently of the activity of reading'.[13] Fish's view is that to specify the possible meanings of 'spare' is positivist; reader-oriented analysis, on the other hand, will give 'experiential' readings. And experiential readings are famously fraught with indeterminacy and deferral of meaning. A note could be added to the text, but for the reader it would only add another layer of indeterminacy.

Has the shift to the sovereignty of the reader in literary theory made annotation in the traditional sense impossible? All annotators by now must be aware of the danger of claiming that meaning is lodged in the text. But the theory of the interaction between reader and text which constitutes the act of reading is still in debate. Annotators should realize that they are operating in a war zone.

To remove obscurities, verbal or referential, is the commonest reason for a note, and modern annotators will pause before literary theories concerned with interpretation, the construction of meaning, the reader and the act of reading. Another type of annotation is that which attributes sources, either a source for an allusion in the text, or a source for the text itself. Closely associated with that is the citation of parallels, either in other works by the author or in the work of others. Those are a different sort of annotation. If notes directed at obscurity are concerned with the text and the reader, source notes usually point to the author. Why should one want them if one is not interested in the author, or at least in the genesis of the text? In 1968 Roland Barthes famously declared the author to be dead,[14] and although creditable attempts at resuscitation have been made, the health of the patient cannot be taken for granted. A consequence of putting source material into annotations is that the information may be read as making a point about authorial intention. Such annotations lead to source-based readings of the text, along the lines of 'this is obscure, but the source reveals what the submerged line of thought is.' Authorial intention has been another theoretical battleground since W. K. Wimsatt and Monroe C. Beardsley's famous essay entitled 'The Intentional Fallacy'.[15]

Modern literary theorists take differing views over the author. The more phenomenological theorists may regard the author as dead; but that is not the case for the more sociological theorists. It is obvious that feminist critics do not want the author to die before being found to be a woman. And psychoanalytic critics want the author on the couch rather than dead. I will say no more except that the author, should you wish him or her dead in your edition, is likely to come back to life through the manifestation of sources and parallels.

Source study is of course an old-fashioned term. It has been overtaken by the concept of intertextuality, first propounded by Julia Kristeva in 1966. Kristeva is keen to separate intertextuality from simple source study.[16] Laurent Jenny offers a useful definition when he says that he proposes 'to speak of intertextuality only where there can be found in a text elements exhibiting a structure created previous to the text'.[17] Annotators often find that there is another structure present in their text: it may be another written text; it may be a different kind of structure, like for instance a card game. The game of ombre in *The Rape of the Lock* has long been an annotator's playground. Annotators of Jane Austen's novels know that when her characters sit down to cards the reader will see more in the episode if the rules and social nuances of the specific game being played are known. There is a social text operating intertextually in the novel. It is a challenge to the annotator not only to pin-point the source, but to indicate following from it the structures intertextually present in the text.

I have tried to suggest some of the commonest types of information found in annotations. In fact the activity is so little policed that many other sorts of note may be found, or not found. One sort of note that is only sporadically found concerns the relation between fact and fiction, or between different levels of fictionality. Early in *Macbeth* Banquo asks 'How far is't call'd to Forres?' (I. iii. 39) That is a real place-name; the Arden edition does not tell us where Forres is. Perhaps that is justified; why should today's reader have some specific geographical information which Jacobean audiences did not, and which perhaps Shakespeare himself did not have? But take a Scott novel. It is Scott's procedure as a historical novelist to insert fictitious place-names into a setting established by real ones. Should an annotator point out which are fictitious and which not? That is in old-fashioned terms the question of fact and fiction. To use more modern terminology it is the question as to whether texts can refer to something outside themselves existing on a different level of reality. Is there a 'real world' outside the text?[18] Does Edinburgh mean our Edinburgh when it occurs in a Scott novel, or is it a fictionalized city with the same name?

Theories of reading, theories of the author, and the question of the text's reference to a world outside itself—these are all theoretical problems besetting traditional annotation. One can also find in annotated editions notes which do not seem to account for themselves at all except as examples of something the annotator found interesting, outrageous, or piquant. Among these are brief quotations from earlier reviewers and critics. Some of these may assist the reading of the text; others are perhaps the attempt to squeeze into the edition material for which the editorial apparatus makes no other provision; one may regret that others are there for the relief of the annotator, settling scores with the past.

The reader of an annotated text may know less than other readers— because the annotation has created a dependent reader and has closed off possibilities—or more—because told more than any individual reader has ever known before. Either way, something has been done to the reader by the annotator. It is this realization which has made the most recent commentators on annotation regard it as a question of *power*.

The debate about annotation may start by considering the claims of the text and the claims of the reader, and it might be agreed that annotation involves a mediation between the two. But what about the third party, the annotator? It might be supposed that the annotator is the servant of the two former, anxiously seeking to form a bond between text and reader. Modern commentators are more likely to stress, however, the power of the annotator. Annotation is only required when there is already an alienation between text and reader. It can be claimed that the annotator enters as mediator only when the other two are weakened—when the text is failing to communicate and the reader failing to read—a suitable opportunity for an insidious take-over. The critical view of the annotator is that he or she, in the guise of offering help, is knowingly or otherwise controlling the situation by both enabling and limiting interpretation of the text and both serving and creating its reader. It might be claimed that all forms of criticism are an exercise of power over a text, but traditional annotation exerts its power more invisibly than most. Ralph Hanna in a stimulating article on this subject points out that the diffused form in which annotations appear prevents the power of the annotator as interpreter from being perceived. Twentieth-century annotators 'are required to fragment their activities into tasks presented as rhetorically discrete, so that they can never appear whole consciousnesses in touch with the text'.[19] In Hanna's view the disparate presentation of annotation is a tacit acknowledgement of the guilt of the annotator, guilty of 'an aggression directed at both the community that sanctions annotation and the text that inspires it'.[20]

To turn from contemporary theoretical considerations of annotation to the electronic hypertext is to turn from a theology of guilt to a theology of liberation. It has been usual to speak of hypertext in terms of liberation, liberation from the constraints of the traditional book form. Although this rhetoric has sometimes been tempered by the recognition that designing a literary hypertext so as to fulfil its proponents' ideals is not an easy task, the enterprise is buoyed up with the optimism of the freed prisoner. What are the freedoms to which the electronic medium invites us? They are usually proposed as freedom from the print medium, freedom from the organizational conventions and the space and time limitations of the book, and, particularly claimed for literary hypertext, freedom from 'linearity' and freedom to 'decentre' a text.[21] Most of these are spatial concepts, drawing on the fact that the electronic environment is not subject to the dimensional limitations of the book. What is the effect of these freedoms on the idea of annotating a text?

Electronic hypertext is a network of *nodes* of information connected by *links*. The user *navigates* the system by utilizing its links, and as the system expands and as one hypertext is connected to others the potential scope for navigation becomes ever larger and the interlocking systems ever more complex. In addition to links supplied by the creators of the systems, links can often be added by their users. The determined navigator who may start by following links deliberately built into the system may thereafter find him- or herself navigating beyond any previously envisaged route in a voyage of exploration. Hypertext can also use *multimedia*, meaning that it stores not only words but also graphics, sound, and video. (Where I refer to this enriched form of hypertext, I shall use the term *hypermedia*.) Hypertext may also be *interactive*, meaning that the user can control many features of the system, add, delete, or converse with it. In what follows I shall bear in mind the larger picture of hypertext speaking unto hypertext, but shall start from the more limited version of literary hypertext as an electronic package designed round a literary text. I should like to ask what happens to the concept of annotation in hypertext, and I shall do so with reference to the freedoms suggested above, which are all one way or another freedoms from the constraints of the book. I have marshalled these under three headings, space, linearity, and the centre.

To move from book to hypertext or hypermedia involves a change of medium; it adds to print and fixed illustration the possibility of moving pictures and sound. It also involves a change in form, from the physical form of the codex to the 'electronic environment'. Books are bound; hypertext is fluid and unbounded. A consequence for annotation is that you can have more of it.

Annotation has always been limited by the physical form of the book and by conventions of suitability which the book fostered. If annotations are placed at the foot of the page it is usually thought unacceptable if they usurp most of the page. If they are at the end of the book quantity is less important, but conventions of appropriateness apply there too. Because in a book you can to some extent see the whole quantity of annotation at once you can see whether it is disproportionate to the text. The tendency of annotations to overwhelm the text visibly has been the target of satire, for instance in Pope's edition of *The Dunciad* of 1729. Despite the fact that excessive annotation has long been presented as a manifestation of the dangerous stupidity of misguided scholarship, there has been a desire for more and more of it. There has been a demand not simply for annotation to help the first-time reader but annotation that attempts to record every interpretation or comment that has ever been made. This used to be satisfied, to the extent that it was, by the variorum edition. Hypertext fulfils the ambitions of the variorum. It certainly removes the constraints under which the editors of Keats's 'Ode on a Grecian Urn' drew up their succinct lists of interpretations.

One can allow the mind to fantasize on the endless amount of annotation that could be stored in hypertext, as an example of opportunity or as a species of modern nightmare. Suppose one were annotating a text which contained an allusion to *As You Like It*. The traditional annotator would identify the allusion, giving the reference and a few lines of the play. Hypertext could give more, the whole scene of the play, indeed the whole play. It could give an account of Shakespeare and his achievements in dramatic comedy. It could give access to allusions to *As You Like It* in other works by the same author; it could (supposing anyone had the information to hand) give a list of all other literary works which had ever alluded to *As You Like It*. Practicality might cause this process to stop somewhere, but in theory why should it?

The consequences of losing the codex form do not concern only quantity. The book form has conventions for the presentation of a text and its editorial apparatus, what Gérard Genette calls its paratextual material.[22]

A common format is for a critical introduction to be placed before the text in an edition, and for textual emendations to go immediately after the text followed by annotations and a glossary. Hypertext will remove this visual representation of material, and because of the freedom from space constraints may make it unnecessary to differentiate between annotations and a glossary, and may require that the difference between criticism and annotation be thought out anew. It might be asked, therefore, whether the whole concept of annotation might disappear? Curiously in the electronic world where so many other distinctions disappear the concept of annotation is still viable. If annotation in the sense in which I have been using it is information which is linked to a specific passage in the text then, so long as hypertext information is accessed by links from the text, the sense of an annotation is retained even if the destination of the links is expanded almost out of recognition.

Whatever the theoretical possibilities, in practice the concept of annotation is preserved in hypertext programmes currently in use. To take Hypercard, one of the most popular hypermedia systems, for example: the 'note button' leads the reader to what could be like a traditional annotation, giving brief information designed to be useful at that point in reading the text. After reading the note the reader would be expected to backtrack to the text. It would be the *scholar* rather than the *reader* who would follow further links leading from the note, thus getting further and further from the text.

The fluid nature of hypertext has another consequence for annotation in that it frees it from the temporal fixedness of the printed edition. New information cannot be taken into a book, or errors corrected, until the publication of another edition. Hypertext makes possible constant updating and correction. If the hypertext operates interactively it could become a forum for debate over controversial annotations. Hypertext allows for the unsettling modern virtue of being provisional.

Hypertext has obvious advantages for annotation. It would be delightful if reading the Monument scene in *Antony and Cleopatra* (v. ii) one could have easy access to a depiction of the Jacobean stage with some hints as to the use of the balcony in that scene, to say nothing of accounts, photographs, and video of how it had been staged in later generations. It would be similarly delightful if coming across an allusion to a folk-song while reading one could hear it sung. And the quantity of annotation so generated might escape the criticism of the author of *The Dunciad* because it is only *potential* quantity and would be invisible until summoned. It would not usurp the page or add weight to the book.

Among so many advantages it is worth asking whether there are any disadvantages to losing the form of the book? There may be practical disadvantages for the reader but I shall confine myself to the consideration of annotation. Freeing oneself from the format of the codex requires one to ask about that form which has become so familiar. The book form has a different relationship to different literary genres. It does not have a primary relationship to drama, whose medium is primarily the theatre. It does have a primary relationship with the novel, as appeals to the 'gentle reader' and confidences like 'Reader, I married him' bear witness.[23] The consequence of moving out of the book into another form will therefore have a greater consequence for literary texts which in themselves presuppose the book. Hypertext editions and annotations of such texts will need to have a type of annotation not required while the text and its modern editions are using the same form. It will be necessary to explain, for instance, three-volume publication, or the fact that in a codex you can tell visually when you are nearing the end.[24] The rhetoric of liberation is in this respect more appropriate for hypertexts concerned with drama and orally transmitted poetry than with the novel. Dramatic and some poetic texts have perhaps always been diminished by the medium of the book; the novel, which has a traditional affinity with the book, may be diminished by the electronic medium.

The question of linearity is frequently raised as part of the rhetoric of liberation associated with hypertext. Hypertext will free us from the linearity of the print medium, or of the book. It is part of the revenge being taken by the late twentieth century, offered for the first time since the adoption of the codex[25] an alternative as the prime medium of communication, on what is now seen as an inflexible mentor. Linearity in such discussions is usually reckoned to be a bad thing. It may be as well to withhold judgement, however, until certain distinctions have been made. The question of linearity can be asked about a text itself, about different versions of a text and about the paratextual situation. Kathryn Sutherland has pointed out aspects of narrative which have always tended to subvert linearity.[26] In another essay in this book Jerome McGann explores the question of linearity among variant texts. Annotation obviously raises the question of linearity. There will be no linear reading of a text, in either book or electronic form, if the reader is breaking off repeatedly to read annotations.

I have mentioned that it is conventional in editions of literary authors for annotations to be placed either at the foot of the page or at the end of the book. They are likely also to be in a smaller type size than the text. It is more likely that annotation to poetry and drama will be at the foot of the page; it is rare to see annotations to novels at the foot of the page. Although the placing of annotations may be influenced by printing costs, there are probably other reasons for the conventions that hold in the printed book. Annotations to novels are usually at the end of the book because convention likes to present novel readers with a 'clean page'. Why should readers of plays and poems not have an equal need of a clean page? Presumably because those genres do not have the same affinity with the book as the novel. The concept of the clean page influences another decision, whether the presence of annotations should be signalled in the text by such means as superscript numerals. One reason why some editors prefer to have their annotations at the end of the book is that if there are no superscript numerals in the text the reader need not know they are there.

The problem with superscript numerals, or any other signal indicating an annotation, is that they are an invitation to break the 'linear' experience of reading the text. They are arrows out of the text, functioning like links in the hypertext environment. If annotations are not signalled it is possible for the reader to use them, but without disturbing the linear integrity of the reading. There are after all readers who read all the annotations at the end of the book together after finishing the text, and the editor who places them there may be hoping they would be read in that way. The question as to whether annotations are to be signalled in the text has to be addressed in hypertext as in a book. The chief disadvantage to not signalling their presence is the constant arousal of the reader's curiosity ('Is there a note?') and frustration if there is no note after one has searched the back of the book or clicked a command. The habit of reading all the annotations at once after reading the text (or even before) is not particularly easy to achieve in hypertext because of the quantity of potential information and because it is accessed by links activated by choice and demand. There is not in hypertext an equivalent to letting your eye run down a page of annotations.

Annotations have raised the question of linearity probably from the first annotations to be made. In medieval and early printed books it was common to put annotations on the same page as the text, not only at the foot, but also in the margins. It is uncommon now for annotations to English literary texts to be in a margin. That privileged position is retained for an author's self-annotation, like the marginal glosses to the 1817 edition of *The Ancient Mariner*. There is, however, a particular danger of placing annotations very close to a text: the danger that they will be taken to be part of the text. Confusion between text and gloss has been noticed several times in medieval commentaries. There is a paradox here: hypertext offers freedom from linearity, but it is in an electronic medium rather than in the book that the unintended absorption of annotation into a text is more likely to occur. As Derrida has pointed out, 'The computer today makes possible the fluid integration of the digression or supplement into the course of linear writing, whereas the rigidity and heaviness of other instruments and props (including the typewriter and tape recorder) limit such an integration.'[27]

Unintended confusion between text and annotation in modern editions of English literary works is always possible, but not particularly likely in view of the printing and editorial conventions designed to prevent it. Deliberate removal of signifiers distinguishing the two might be a feature of works manifesting a postmodern view of textual relationships. In all that I have written above, however, it has been assumed that we know what is text and what is annotation. That is because the text is the *centre* of the activity. But another part of the liberation rhetoric of hypertext is that it decentres. What are the problems for a literary text and its annotations if the text is dethroned, is not the centre from which the annotations gain their *raison d'être?* One can imagine an instance of decentring brought about by annotation that one might welcome: if annotation was concerned to reveal an intertextual relationship it might be useful to have the two texts share, or take turns in the centre. In most instances where annotation tended to decentre the text, however, it would probably be an unintended consequence of the quantity of annotation that hypertext can deploy. I have stuck to the value-charged word *centre*. Why not use a more neutral term, like *axis* which has been proposed by George Landow and Paul Delany in an attempt to find a value-free term to describe the organizational principle in hypertext?[28] The reason for using a word like centre is that whatever terms are used for a text and its annotations—centre and peripheries, primary and secondary—they should maintain the basic distinction between them. This distinction has been explained sociologically and philosophically. It is because the text has value that society empowers the annotator to annotate it.[29] Derrida explains the necessary secondariness of annotation with reference to linguistic philosophy. The text is a performative act:

a text whose very structure precludes its ever being second, secondary, explanatory, a text that is never pedagogical, descriptive, constative, theoretical, interpretive—in other words, it never comes after another text upon which it would depend, however little—if one considers that a text so absolutely performative, self-sufficient, self-interpretive, initial, and inaugural, and poetic in the strong sense of the word, is a divine speech act or divine writing, then the hierarchical relationship between the main text and the annotations . . . reproduces a theologico-political model.[30]

More than one argument in this chapter has ended with uncertainty about the text itself. It will be apparent that any literary theory which is sceptical about the possibility of putting boundaries to a text will have difficulty in formulating a theory of annotation. Such sceptics will live in a world of postmodern proliferation which hypertext will not cause but might model. Traditional annotation privileges its text above the annotations. Literary hypertext programs currently in use do so too, if not intentionally then actually because since in hypertext you cannot *see the whole* the ordering of access to information is more important than it is in a book. In fact it is likely to be intentional. Lynette Hunter uses the phrase 'central text hypermedia' to differentiate it from other kinds like, for instance, 'topic-driven hypermedia'.[31] Any hypertext aiming to annotate a literary text will be likely to be an example of 'central text hypermedia'.

With uncertainty about the text goes uncertainty about the author and the editor. Traditionally it could be assumed that the text was the work of the author and the annotations the work of the editor. This is the question of power again. Who has authority over the different elements in a paratextual situation? This is another area where hypertext has been said to promise liberation. Because agency in hypertext may be dispersed among many it is possible to pretend it is not there. Because it can present so much information it is possible to pretend that there has been no selection. Hypertext appears to be free of control because it offers *everything* and we the consumers can *choose*. But it does not contain everything, only a lot.[32] And somebody made the selection, even if simply by stopping, by failing to program a link. Who? The difficulty in admitting the answer to this is witnessed by the current uses of the title *author* in discussions of hypertext. Hypertexts are sometimes referred to as having an editor, but more frequently as having an author. Hypertexts in modern usage are *authored*.[33] There is another use of the term 'author' in the literature of hypertext to mean a reader whose voyage of navigation takes routes individual to that voyager although potentially available to any.[34] As I remarked above traditional annotators have been accused of usurping power; in the world of hypertext the accusation is defused by calling everyone involved, whether author, annotator, or reader, an author. It is the ultimate liberation that everyone involved should be an author. But in a hypertext which is based on a central text it is important not to lose the distinction between an author and an editor: an author is *sui generis*; an editor should be working within some editorial policy. In such a hypertext the annotator is selecting, even if the selection is over what the reader reads first rather than after a long navigational voyage, and will face the same theoretical questions as the book-bound annotator.

The question remains does hypertext simply let you do *more* of what the book tried to do, and using multimedia do it more successfully? If that is the case one may have old theoretical worries but one would not have new ones, unless one can envisage the concept of having *too much*. As I have indicated there is enough to worry about in the whole undertaking of annotation. In hypertext the capacity to supply annotations is greatly increased, but the dimensions of the text and the capacity of the reader remain unaltered. The amount of material which can be amassed for potential access is formidable if the annotating intention is dispersed into an electronic network. There is a danger that the reader will lose first the text, and then him- or herself in the mazes of hyperspace. This sort of thing has happened before, in the book format. It is a feature of reformations to ditch the commentaries and go back to the text.

Although these dangers are present there are some features of hypertext which mitigate them. The problem of quantity is lessened in practice by graded access. In a literary hypertext the central text is always a lodestar for the navigator. The danger of quantity is lessened also by the fact that hypertext annotation, like annotation in a book, has its implied reader. This is apparent in the descriptions of available hypertexts in terms of the level of student they are designed for. Of course as the navigator gets further and further from home, and especially if one hypertext is connected to another, he or she may sail out of protected waters and feel the full buffet of unmediated knowledge, but this should not happen by accident. The freedom from the space limitations of the book allows the opportunity to draw clearer distinctions in a literary hypertext between the different sorts of material traditionally included in annotations, and to distinguish between information useful to the reader, which should be accessible one step away from the text, and the much wider variety of material wanted by that person when turned into a scholar.

I said at the outset that annotators do not always appear to have considered the theoretical aspects of their task. Are hypertext 'authors' likely to do better on this score? After all, it does not appear that the change of medium to hypertext removes any of the worries about annotation arising from literary theory. It may obscure them, however, because of the rhetoric of freedom associated with hypertext. Hypertext may free us from the limitations of the book, but not from the sorts of question about the nature of reading which theorists ask. Literary theorists are critical of the power of the annotator over the text and over the reader; hypertext exerts the same power, either through an individual annotator or through the power dispersed in the system. Writers on hypertext have bypassed these questions by their stress on choice, and the uncontrolled market-place. It is strange how the exponents of hypertext have echoed the vocabulary of the politics of the last fifteen years in suggesting that debate about value can be pre-empted by increasing choice, and that freedom consists in its not being obvious who is controlling the system. It is not encouraging to know that if one is lost in hyperspace one is probably theoretically as well as practically lost.

I have tried to show that annotating a literary text raises theoretical problems, which are not removed in hypertext. So should we still do it? As the momentum towards more annotation seems unstoppable in both book and electronic form that seems at least an impractical question. It would help things along if one could adduce some arguments in justification of annotation. I shall offer two, one relating to annotation as an aspect of scholarship, and one drawing on the ideas of Derrida in relation to texts and their annotation.

I started this chapter by describing annotation in the context of textual editions of English literary works. There is always an argument in favour of annotation where a text is edited because of the close relation between the two activities. In dealing with an obscurity in a text the textual editor and annotator will work together. (In practice these two may be the same person, but it clarifies the issue to see them as separate.) The textual editor faced with an apparent obscurity would ask the annotator whether a meaning could in fact be arrived at from the text as it stood. If the annotator pointed out that the passage contained language now obsolete, or a suppressed quotation, the textual editor could relax. But what happens to the information that removed the uncertainty about the text? If it is suppressed it is likely that the reader will stumble over the same obscurity. An annotation will explain the textual decision to do nothing. The same happens the other way round: it is not uncommon for an annotator to be the first person to suspect the text. Good annotating confirms good textual editing and makes it manifest.

I mentioned also at the outset that some textual editions do not contain annotations. Fewer still contain critical introductions. There may be local reasons for these decisions; but if one had to offer a general explanation for the absence of critical and annotatory material from textual editions one would point to the traditional wariness between literary critics and textual critics. Literary critics, and following them literary theorists, tend to have no role for textual editors, except as people who do the donkey work before the real geniuses move in. Textual editors in return have tended to regard critics as practitioners of imprecise and self-indulgent disciplines compared with their own. They have not countenanced anything critical because 'it will go out of date'. We might agree that it will; but do we agree with the submerged comparison, 'it will go out of date, while the work of the textual editor will not'? The refusal to include interpretative paratextual material went with a certain phase of textual theory, in which textual editing was seen as a rigorous, quasi-scientific activity which if not done for all time was at least done for a very long time. While the textual editor was held above the vicissitudes of this mortal condition no wonder we had editions which gave only the text and some stark textual notes. Now that the whole editorial process is recognized to be within a time and culture the need to banish interpretation is gone.

That is fortunate, given the paratextual expansion promised by hypertext. The danger may be, in the current situation, that we see ourselves as so immersed in our culture that we have no rationale for behaving otherwise than as if totally determined by it. We could just let hypertexts happen, and regard them as a manifestation of the postmodern condition. But literary hypertexts should not just happen by accretion. Nothing need be banished from a hypertext network, but some things should always be closer to home. If one annotates because one values the text there is no point in attempting to put it in a value-free environment. So far as annotation is concerned such an attempt would in any case fail because, in Derrida's words, 'no annotation is neutral'.[35] If you do anything to a text you are interpreting, whether you are annotating or adding networks of paratextual material. If this arouses anxiety it might be assuaged by recalling that the society that has hypertext also has the xerox machine and a plain copy of a text is easily obtained.

The second justification for annotation that I wish to adduce derives from Derrida's view of the 'double bind' which makes annotation necessary. As I have mentioned above Derrida draws a distinction between 'an originary text or speech act' and annotations which are secondary to it. In the passage that follows, he points out the 'double bind' whereby texts which are in one sense 'independent and self-sufficient' cry out for annotation. Such a text:

says to the reader or auditor, 'Be quiet, all has been said, you have nothing to say, obey in silence,' while at the same time it implores, it cries out, it says, 'Read me and respond: if you want to read me and hear me, you must understand me, know me, interpret me, translate me, and hence, in responding to me and speaking to me, you must begin to speak in my place, to enter into a rivalry with me.' The more a text is 'unannotatable,' the more it generates and cries out for annotation: this is the paradox and the double bind.[36]

English literary texts have joined sacred texts in crying out for annotation. We are the heirs of ancient traditions of annotation; we have also internalized a pattern, perhaps mythical as much as historical, whereby if texts attract too much annotation they provoke reformation. We want the generous pluralism of extensive annotation; but we do not want to lose the purity of the text. We have been debating this for centuries; hypertext has produced another arena in which the debate may continue.

NOTES

1. Most of the discussion of the rationale of annotation that there has been has come from the major editorial series. Examples include Martin C. Battestin, 'A Rationale of Literary Annotation: The Example of Fielding's Novels', *Studies in Bibliography*, 34 (1981), 1–22; Ian Jack, 'Novels and those "Necessary Evils": Annotating the Brontës', *Essays in Criticism*, 32 (1982), 321–37; David Hewitt *et al.* (eds.), *The Edinburgh Edition of the Waverley Novels: A Guide for Editors* (Aberdeen: Edinburgh Edition of the Waverley Novels, 1996), pp. 100–8.

2. Stephen A. Barney (ed.), *Annotation and Its Texts* (New York and Oxford: Oxford University Press, 1991), the papers of a conference on annotation held at the University of California Research Institute in 1988; Paul Delany and George P. Landow (eds.), *Hypermedia and Literary Studies* (Cambridge, Mass. and London: MIT Press, 1991); George P. Landow, *Hypertext: The Convergence of Contemporary Critical Theory and Technology* (Baltimore and London: Johns Hopkins University Press, 1992).

3. I should note here that in this chapter I am concerned with annotation of English literary texts from recent centuries, and I am not addressing the question of self-annotation.

4. Stephen Wall, 'Annotated English Novels?', *Essays in Criticism*, 32 (1982), 1–8.

5. An example of expanding annotation may be found in the Penguin editions of Jane Austen's *Pride and Prejudice*. The edition by Tony Tanner (1972) contains four explanatory notes; the new edition by Vivien Jones (1996) contains nineteen pages of annotations. It should be added that there are dissentient voices concerning the purpose of annotation. Laurent Mayali asserts that 'the multiplication of critical apparatus does not enhance the authority of the text itself but achieves the recognition of the annotator within the academic discipline' ('For a Political Economy of Annotation', in Barney (ed.), *Annotation and Its Texts*, pp. 187–8). The present writer, being an annotator herself, eschews such scepticism.

6. *Macbeth*, ed. Kenneth Muir, The Arden Shakespeare (London: Methuen, 1951 and frequently reprinted), p. 8.

7. *John Keats: The Complete Poems*, ed. John Barnard (Harmondsworth: Penguin, 1973), p. 652; *The Poems of John Keats*, ed. Miriam Allott (London: Longman, 1970), p. 538.

8. Jack, 'Novels and those "Necessary Evils" ', p. 323.

9. Ian Small, 'The Editor as Annotator as Ideal Reader', in Ian Small and Marcus Walsh (eds.), *The Theory and Practice of Text-Editing* (Cambridge: Cambridge University Press, 1991), pp. 197–206.

10. Samuel Johnson, *A Dictionary of the English Language*, 1755 (London: Times Books, 1979); *Longman Dictionary of Contemporary English* (Harlow, Essex: Longman, 1978).

11. John H. Middendorf, reviewing Martin C. Battestin's edition of *Tom Jones* for the Wesleyan Edition of the Works of Henry Fielding (1974), made this comment on annotation: 'Obviously the editor's interests and previous knowledge come into play, and though these may be, as here, of the most responsible and wide-ranging sort, may they not also, especially in an imposing edition like this, forestall fresh responses and invite an end to debate?' (*Johnsonian News Letter*, 35 (Mar. 1975), 2).

12. Jacques Derrida, 'This Is Not an Oral Footnote', in Barney (ed.), *Annotation and Its Texts*, p. 193.

13. Stanley Fish, 'Interpreting the Variorum', in *Is There a Text in This Class? The Authority of Interpretive Communities* (Cambridge Mass. and London: Harvard University Press, 1980), pp. 149–52.

14. Roland Barthes, 'The Death of the Author', in *Image–Music–Text*, trans. Stephen Heath (London: Fontana, 1977), pp. 142–8.

15. This article, which first appeared in 1946, was revised and collected in W. K. Wimsatt, *The Verbal Icon: Studies in the Meaning of Poetry* (Lexington: University of Kentucky Press, 1954).

16. Julia Kristeva first elaborated her concept of intertextuality, in 'Word, Dialogue and Novel', published in *Séméiotiké* (Paris: Seuil, 1969); she stressed its difference from source study in 'Revolution in Poetic Language' (1974), trans. Margaret Waller, in *The Kristeva Reader*, ed. Toril Moi (Oxford: Basil Blackwell, 1986), p. 111.

17. Laurent Jenny, 'The Strategy of Form', trans. R. Carter, in Tzvetan Todorov (ed.), *French Literary Theory Today* (Cambridge: Cambridge University Press, 1982), p. 40.

18. If there is not, it is hard to justify annotation. As Stephen Wall has pointed out, 'Annotation, after all, is only a means (although an essential one) to better contextual understanding. The modern reader who thinks of texts simply as sign-clusters running wild in the desert will not worry about its absence' (Wall, 'Annotated English Novels?', p. 8).

19. Ralph Hanna III, 'Annotation as Social Practice', in Barney (ed.), *Annotation and Its Texts*, pp. 180–1.

20. Ibid., p. 179.

21. See, for instance, George P. Landow and Paul Delany, 'Hypertext, Hypermedia and Literary Studies: The State of the Art', in their *Hypermedia and Literary Studies* (1991): 'We can define *Hypertext* as the use of the computer to transcend the linear, bounded and fixed qualities of the traditional written text' (p. 3).

22. Gérard Genette, *Palimpsestes: La Littérature au second degré* (Paris: Seuil, 1982), p. 9.

23. The first sentence of the last chapter of Charlotte Brontë's *Jane Eyre* (1847).

24. Jane Austen draws humorous attention to this fact in the last chapter of *Northanger Abbey*: 'The anxiety, which in this state of their attachment must be the portion of Henry and Catherine . . . can hardly extend, I fear, to the bosom of my readers, who will see in the tell-tale compression of the pages before them, that we are all hastening together to perfect felicity' (ed. Marilyn Butler (Harmondsworth: Penguin, 1995), p. 217).

25. The codex form was adopted in Europe in the early centuries AD. (Colin H. Roberts and T. C. Skeat, *The Birth of the Codex* (London: published for The British Academy by Oxford University Press, 1983).)

26. Kathryn Sutherland, 'A Guide through the Labyrinth: Dickens's *Little Dorrit* as Hypertext', *Literary and Linguistic Computing*, 5 (1990), 305–9.

27. Derrida, 'This Is Not an Oral Footnote', in Barney (ed.), *Annotation and Its Texts*, p. 199.

28. Landow and Delany, 'Hypertext, Hypermedia and Literary Studies', in id., *Hypermedia and Literary Studies*, p. 18.

29. Mayali, 'For a Political Economy of Annotation', in Barney (ed.), *Annotation and Its Texts*, pp. 185–91.

30. Derrida, 'This Is Not an Oral Footnote', in ibid., p. 193.
31. L. Hunter, 'Hypermedia Narration: Providing Social Contexts for Methodo-logy', *Conference Abstracts* (Association for Literary and Linguistic Computing-Association for Computers and the Humanities Conference, Apr. 1992), p. 144.
32. On this, see Ian Small, 'Text-editing and the Computer: Facts and Values', in Warren Chernaik, Caroline Davis, and Marilyn Deegan (eds.), *The Politics of the Electronic Text* (Oxford: Office for Humanities Communication, Oxford University Computing Services, 1993), pp. 25–30.
33. See, for instance, Marilyn Deegan, Stuart Lee, and Nicola Timbrell, *An Intro-duction to Multimedia for Academic Use* (Oxford: Oxford University Computing Services, 1996), ch. 2, 'Authoring', pp. 13–25.
34. For instance Jay David Bolter, *Writing Space: The Computer, Hypertext, and the History of Writing* (Hillsdale, NJ: Lawrence Erlbaum Associates, 1991), p. 3.
35. Derrida, 'This Is Not an Oral Footnote', in Barney (ed.), *Annotation and Its Texts*, p. 195.
36. Ibid., p. 202.

4

Lighting out for the Territory: Hypertext, Ideology, and *Huckleberry Finn*

PATRICK W. CONNER

Tom's most well, now, and got his bullet around his neck on a watch-guard for a watch, and is always seeing what time it is, and so there ain't nothing more to write about, and I am rotten glad of it, because if I'd a knowed what a trouble it was to make a book I wouldn't a tackled it and ain't agoing to no more. But I reckon I got to light out for the territory ahead of the rest, because aunt Sally she's going to adopt me and sivilize me and I can't stand it. I been there before.

THE END, YOURS TRULY HUCK FINN.[1]

I

Hypertext is an interesting term, because it has to bridge an unusual semiotic gap: it is used to name a cybernetic phenomenon in which a text appearing on a computer monitor can be used to access another text stored elsewhere, either online or in memory; or it may be used as a new term in the realm of critical theory to refer to a decentred, infinitely referential kind of discourse. In this essay, I intend to argue that any critical use of the term 'hypertext' must take into account how the object so termed may be modelled in the cybernetic context, because—at least, in the case of hyper-text—the connection between literary criticism and technology is mutu-ally supportive of both domains, and each serves the ideologies of the other.

To provide a case study in support of this position, I shall examine cer-tain conjunctions of ideology and structure in Mark Twain's *Adventures of Huckleberry Finn*. Samuel Clemens (for whom 'Mark Twain' was a pseud-onym) did not have access to the term 'hypertext', yet he endowed a cer-tain open structure within *Huckleberry Finn* with an ideology which reflects the fundamental assumptions of a recognizable American myth; this myth, which focuses on the relative positions of the individual and society, and an ambiguous attitude towards boundaries and difference, is relevant to the underlying assumptions of those critics and software designers who are currently championing cybernetic hypertext.

Contrary to an undefined, non-technical approach to hypertext in which any notion of linked texts and non-centred discourse may be held to be hypertextual with all the virtues that is assumed to convey, I intend to insist on a more narrow, technical definition of the phenomenon in this study. It will be my contention that the critical test of a tendency towards hypertext in a work of literature should be the ability to model the work as a hypertext in a context which makes explicit the relationships between the nodes and links. Such a model requires the critic to specify where links should be located and what happens to the reader who follows them; such a model further requires the critic to consider the relationship of the reader to a text which has been traditionally taken as a unified whole, and which in its modelled form, must be accessible in parts. One brief example of the sort of problem which a 'modelled' reading brings out might be a consideration of Huckleberry Finn's concluding statement that he will 'light out for the territory', rather than let Aunt Sallie 'adopt . . . and sivilize' him. The open-ended hypertext version of *The Adventures of Huckleberry Finn* would, of necessity, have to include a link to 'the territory'. Movement appears to characterize the web of *Huckleberry Finn* (indeed, the Mississippi comprises the structural principle of the web), and each place Huck stops must be linked to the tale along the River. But if we read the book as a hypertext, we cannot easily specify the order in which the events along the river may be encountered by the reader; if we model the hypertext version to follow the sequence in the printed text, we will have created a narrative with none of the choices we expect to be provided in a hypertext. In order to know how to link the territory, we have to consider the ramifications of those places to which it might be linked, and indeed we might choose to model the work with the territory linked to several places. Is there not always the possibility of 'lighting out for the territory', or is that only a possibility after a given event on the river? Or is it not possible except as the only path for Huck away from the Phelps' farm?

Of course, we are not obliged actually to make real hypertexts out of Twain's work, but in considering that possibility, we ground our critical insights in our efforts to deconstruct the text at a level of larger units than Derrida dealt with; indeed, we are—as Foucault would have us do—looking at the structure of the archive from which our text was first assembled.

II

Emblazoning 'The end' and his name at this point of the part of his narrative which is known to readers as Mark Twain's *Adventures of Huckleberry Finn* did not, in fact, bring Huck's narrative of Huckleberry Finn and Tom

Sawyer to an end. In 1884, a year before *Huckleberry Finn* was published, Samuel Clemens began to write the next part, 'Huck Finn and Tom Sawyer among the Indians'. He apparently did not complete this text and never published it during his lifetime.[2] Nevertheless, he clearly responded to the impulse to continue the story by building upon Tom Sawyer's suggestion on the penultimate page of *Adventures of Huckleberry Finn* that he, Jim, and Huck go into the areas west of Arkansas known in the 1850s as the 'Indian Territories' to pursue 'howling adventures amongst the Injuns' (p. 361), a scheme which Huck concludes he will have to undertake ahead of the other two or risk being 'sivilized' again.

That last paragraph of the published *Adventures of Huckleberry Finn* is a crystallization of Mark Twain's technique throughout the book. The paragraph leaps from Tom's bravado and boyish pride in having been shot like a noble soldier in a romantic novel, to an observation on the difficulty of 'making' a book, to the final declaration that the character's sense of self-worth—if not his salvation—is incompatible with the demands of the 'sivilized' culture. The whole work is clearly concerned with personal ethics exercised in the face of community standards, and the last paragraph in fact identifies three American icons which are often used to represent ways the individual may be figured in the dialectic between the individual and the community: Tom as brash Yank or 'cowboy' whose links with similar types ranging from the performances of Errol Flynn to Lyndon Johnson are easy to establish; Huck as the ideologue and loner who is reflected, albeit in different ways, in popular myths about James Dean and Henry Thoreau is also a clear part of the American cultural landscape; and Huck as inventer, both in the rhetorical and technological senses of one who makes or 'invents' his story at the same time as he creates or 'invents' the medium in which the story exists—in this case, the kind of book he has laboured to make—takes a position we can find in the autobiographical writings of Benjamin Franklin and Frederick Douglas, although Huck is probably not an autobiographical alter-ego of the author. Unlike the cowboy and the loner, however, the American character as maker of his own book in both senses does not appear to have been captured in recent popular culture; nevertheless, it is very much a part of American literary tradition, mirrored in the character of Ishmael in Herman Melville's *Moby Dick*, the narrating persona of Washington Irving's *The Sketch Book*, Thoreau's *Walden*, Whitman's *Leaves of Grass*, and the modern poets who discovered how a typewriter is linked to poetic composition—Eliot, Pound, and e. e. cummings, for example. All are writers who, like Huck Finn, laboured with the technologies of writing as a primary condition of their writing and therefore as a part of themselves as subject.[3]

'You don't know about me, without you have read a book by the name of "The Adventures of Tom Sawyer," but that ain't no matter,' Huck declares at the very beginning of his narrative.[4] For the purpose of this essay, the significant part of that statement is that Huck's origin, by his own admission, lies in a book over which he himself had no control, and that his own narration will take the form of a subsequent book.[5] What books do and how they do it are mentioned fifty-one times in the work, with possibly the most salient observation made by Tom Sawyer when he tries to organize his pirate gang by the book in Chapter 2. At that point, Ben Rogers demurs on holding prisoners for ransom, although none of the boys understands the meaning of the word 'ransom'.[6] Tom explains why they cannot ransom their prisoners with a club:

Because it ain't in the books so—that's why. Now Ben Rogers, do you want to do things regular, or don't you?—that's the idea. Don't you reckon that the people that made the books knows what's the correct thing to do? Do you reckon you can learn 'em anything? Not by a good deal. No, sir, we'll just go on and ransom them in the regular way. (p. 11)

It is indeed this very attitude towards the authority of books in the context of setting up a band of renegades which allows the reader to construct innocence and naïvety where the text in fact advocates the most violent and repugnant behaviour. Children as young as these deal in such heinous acts regularly in American cities—or so it is reported—but we still read Tom Sawyer's plans for his pirate gang without concern for juvenile crime because of the paradoxical stance we take towards books, a stance which Mark Twain satirizes in his making of a new kind of book, as written by Huckleberry Finn. On the one hand, Tom's bookishness (or 'nerdish' behaviour, we might say today) obviates his threat as a delinquent; on the other hand, we are comforted that he does not understand the books he has read.

When we miss how book culture is both subverted and reinscribed in this work, then we naturally miss the importance of the escape sequence at the end of the book which has led so many good readers into despair. What must be realized is that Mark Twain returns at the end of Huck's book to the final subversion of the authority of Tom's sort of reading and of the book's place in culture generally by replacing Tom's pirate fantasy with a real opportunity to use his romantic brand of book learning to set Jim free. In point of fact, the boys have the means and motivations to allow Jim to escape at any time, and Tom even knows that Jim has been legally manumitted from slavery. The only thing which in fact keeps Jim prisoner is Tom's allegiance to his books. When Huck sees no need to have Jim work at sawing off his own leg or even the leg of his bed when he can simply lift the bed and slip the chain off, Tom expostulates:

Well, if that ain't just like you, Huck Finn. You can get up the infant-schooliest ways of going at a thing. Why, hain't you ever read any books at all?—Baron

Trenck, nor Casanova, nor Benvenuto Chelleeny, nor Henri IV., nor none of them heroes? Who ever heard of getting a prisoner loose in such an old-maidy way as that? No; the way all the best authorities does is to saw the bed-leg in two. (p. 299)

Of course, Tom is not citing texts, but using books as cultural authority. In a way, his position argues Mark Twain's 'Notice' following the title-page, 'Persons attempting to find a motive in this narrative will be prosecuted; persons attempting to find a moral in it will be banished; persons attempting to find a plot in it will be shot. By order of the author per G.G., Chief of Ordnance' (p. xxv). Whoever G.G. may have been,[7] he is the authority to enforce the author's desire that this book have no authority—or at least no authority in the sense that Tom, Miss Watson, and the Shepherdson clan have reified literary authority in their own lives with desperate, or even disastrous, consequences.

   Although it seems to me that Tom Sawyer provides Mark Twain's best example of the most pernicious reader and exploiter of books, he does not provide the work's only strategy for resisting a misappropriated bookish culture; indeed, almost every event and every character in the work can be read in this context. From Chapter I, Huck evinces impatience with this use of texts as cultural authorities, but he has no control over it.

Pretty soon I wanted to smoke, and asked the widow to let me. But she wouldn't. She said it was a mean practice and wasn't clean, and I must try to not do it any more. That is just the way with some people. They get down on a thing when they don't know nothing about it. Here she was a bothering about Moses, which was no kin to her, and no use to anybody, being gone, you see, yet finding a power of fault with me for doing a thing that had some good in it. And she took snuff, too; of course that was all right, because she done it herself. (p. 3)

He contrasts books and smoking again when he describes his days locked in Pap Finn's cabin: 'It was kind of lazy and jolly, laying off comfortable all day, smoking and fishing, and no books nor study' (p. 30). Huck takes a decidedly materialist view of the position of books in his environment: there must be more than abstract value, there must be some purpose in what they represent. To paraphrase him, they must be of some *use* to somebody. The table with books arranged on it in the Grangerford household is a good example of this society's approach to literature and texts as iconic parts of its culture in contrast to Huck's materialist valuation of these things.

This table had a cover made out of beautiful oil-cloth, with a red and blue spread-eagle painted on it, and a painted border all around. It come all the way from Philadelphia, they said. There was some books, too, piled up perfectly exact, on each corner of the table. One was a big family Bible, full of pictures. One was 'Pilgrim's Progress,' about a man that left his family it didn't say why. I read considerable in it now and then. The statements was interesting, but tough. Another was 'Friendship's Offering,' full of beautiful stuff and poetry; but I didn't read the poetry. Another was Henry Clay's Speeches, and another was Dr. Gunn's Family Medicine, which told you all about what to do if a body was sick or dead. There was a hymn book, and a lot of other books. And there was nice split-bottom chairs, and perfectly sound, too—not bagged down in the middle and busted, like an old basket. (p. 137)

The chairs are the only thing which occasion genuine admiration. But Huck's attitude towards books notwithstanding, the influence of romantic texts on the culture at large is clearly overwhelming. It is, in fact, enmeshed with the material culture of the fictional work as a means of identifying with it. The steamboat which Huck and Jim find wrecked and sinking was named the *Walter Scott*, after the great romantic novelist (p. 89),[8] and in Chapter 32 when Huck arrives at the Phelps' farm masquerading as Tom, Aunt Sally recalls another injured steamboat, the *Lally Rook* (p. 279). In fact, a sidewheeler named *Lallah Rookh* after the title of Thomas Moore's romantic epic poem (1817) actually operated on the Mississippi River between 1838 and 1847.[9] Because *Huckleberry Finn* is set in the 1840s, we should not be surprised that he mentions these particular works, but it is not Mark Twain's purpose to burlesque a single literary period, but rather an ill-defined corpus of adventures or romances, both sentimental and swashbuckling, which were never set in America, and seldom touched on problems relevant to an American's experience, except as they might address universal issues. The lies the self-proclaimed Duke of Bridgewater and unanointed King of France create about their royal origins are other extensions of the romantic narrative being trotted out in frontier garb. Indeed, the whole farce played out at the Peter Wilks' home where the old frauds pretend to be English nobility assumes that the community will be enchanted by—but nevertheless completely unfamiliar with—anything identified as a matter of English culture. The Duke and King's attempt to play Shakespeare through the river towns makes up a further dimension of the cultural pretensions of these communities. Shakespeare was, in fact, quite popular in the small-town opera houses of nineteenth-century America, as much out of a desire to enhance cultural associations as to enjoy the plays. The final farce of Jim's unnecessary imprisonment at the Phelps' farm can be read as Tom's attempt similarly to materialize the swashbuckling novels and memoirs he has been reading. The implicit absurdity and cruelty of this part of the book are clear indictments of the whole textualizing process Mark Twain continuously battles in *Huck Finn*.

In this context, then, a central question for the reader would seem to be the inconsistency of the content of the work in its response to the literary, the bookish, and to text-making in general when contrasted to the display of effort Huck undertakes to make his book. But such inconsistency is resolved when we realize that *The Adventures of Huckleberry Finn* is a proto-hypertext, and as such, it strives to realign ideology and textuality.[10]

A hypertext is a series of nodes, which may be episodic or otherwise definable, which are connected through a variety of short texts we call links. As a hypertext, Huck's book strives to be exactly what the works Americans appropriated from Europe are, for the most part, not. Huck's book represents a series of interpretative sites which act almost like miniature battlefields. This concept is important, because such sites allow the same ideology to be tested over and over, each time under different circumstances. Each site provides another reason for American culture to rethink its alliance with its European begetters, and the sum of these sites linked together is particularly persuasive. This conflict between an inherited settler-colonialism which manifests itself in continual references to European textuality and the author's implied necessity for a cultural revolution as its only antidote creates the parameters within which Mark Twain's ideology is expressed. 'I am said to be a revolutionist in my sympathies, by birth, by breeding and by principle', he wrote in an essay in defence of Maxim Gorki; 'I am always on the side of the revolutionists, because there never was a revolution unless there were some oppressive and intolerable conditions against which to revolute.'[11]

These intolerable conditions described in the narrative of *Adventures of Huckleberry Finn* are those we usually identify with post-colonial conditions in a society newly freed of an imperialist governance; but post-revolutionary America anticipated the pattern of association with Great Britain which the later Commonwealth nations took up. That is, it maintained commercial, diplomatic, and ideological ties with the power it had rebelled against, and—although British reviewers tended to laugh frequently at American efforts at literature and art—many Americans maintained their sense of an English identity for a number of years after the American Revolution.[12] By the 1880s, when Mark Twain was writing *Huck Finn*, however, yet another war—the Civil War—had been endured; non-English emigrants had entered the young country by the hundreds of thousands, thus diluting the 'Englishness' of the American lineage; and immense new fortunes were being made in oil, steel, coal, shipping, journalism, and banking. These fortunes created their own imperial dynasties no less rapacious than their pre-revolutionary war counterparts, but these raptors were at least home-grown. By the time of the publication of the book in 1885, there was a clear will to nationhood and national culture, in part because the aftermath of the American Civil War made that a necessary desire, but also in part because Americans were obliged to forget whatever was contrary to their collective nationness. It is as true today as it was a century ago: when Americans are obligated to remember a US colonial *mentalité*, they do not find there the alterity of what was anterior; they are obliged to find instead some source or trigger of the collective construction of nationness. Homi Bhabha explains the phenomenon thus:

> To be obliged to forget—in the construction of the national present—is not a question of historical memory; it is the construction of a discourse on society that *performs* the problematic totalization of the national will. That strange time—forgetting to remember—is a place of 'partial identification' inscribed in the daily plebiscite which represents the performative discourse of the people.[13]

Mark Twain, perhaps implicitly identifying himself again with the revolutionary, attempted to expose that totalizing performative discourse of the national present in *Adventures of Huckleberry Finn* by representing the textuality anterior to (but still very much embedded in) the present as a residual menace. He is only able to achieve his goals because he resists the form of another nineteenth-century totalizing discourse, the novel. *Huckleberry Finn* was not meant by Mark Twain to be identified as a novel. Certainly, this is the point made in the Author's 'Notice' prepended to the work wherein he declares his prose fiction work to be free of motive, moral, and plot, and thereby declares it to be no novel. He adopts, instead, the form of hypertext whose nodes and links serve as wedges to break apart what Bhabha calls 'the totalization of the national will'.

Nodes and links are the structures which comprise a hypertext, but they are more than formalist abstractions, for both are forms which only exist where there is content; that is, they are discursive forms. As Julia Kristeva, among others, points out, 'a discourse bears and imposes an ideology'.[14] The semiotic potential of a node, however, is different from the same potential of a link, and the ideology expressed in one cannot be similarly expressed in the other. In fact, it may be fair to say that the ideological coherence of a hypertext is found in the complementarity of its links with its nodes.

This should not be surprising, since we have long known that genre affects content. In the broadest sense of the word, textual adjustment is motivated by ideological concerns, whether those concerns have to do with establishing the text, defining chronology and temporal boundaries in a narrative, or defining texture and space in a descriptive exercise; and the evolution of genres has depended upon matching ideological content within its 'ideologically correct' frame.[15]

If links and nodes operate like separate genres, then we need to view the phenomenon of hypertext in a way which will permit us to understand how two genres may be complementary in a single work. One way to do this is to say that hypertext is a literary genre itself, and links and nodes are the sub-genres which comprise it. I do not think that is true, however. Rather, hypertext is a primary form of literary discourse, like prose, poetry, and drama. It is, however, a form constructed so as to accommodate multiple genres.[16] This is so not only because hypertext cannot be subsumed beneath any of the other three primary forms named,[17] but also because, like each of the other primary forms of literary discourse, hypertext presents a new form concurrent with a new technology of textualization.[18] Moreover, like the three established forms, this one is inclusive of those which preceded it. If we think of poetry as the primary form of oral literature; of prose as the primary form established with writing; and of drama as the form accompanying not only the development of print technology, but of an early modern/modern technology of representing a fuller semiotic range of the text in the successive technologies of the stage, of film, and of television, then hypertext is the primary form literary discourse must take to exploit the post-modern technologies offered by network computing.[19] Of course, a hypertext is not restricted to cybernetic dissemination, even when the high-status version of a hypertext is its networked form. As each form has developed, it has embraced the other forms available to it. Prose texts can incorporate a certain amount of poetry without losing their status as prose—Boethius *De Consolatio Philosophiae* is an example—but poetry has no place for prose. Dramatic texts may include either poetry or prose—indeed, the fledgeling drama of the late Middle Ages and the Renaissance often employed both—but drama clearly embraces, and is not embraced by, the first two forms. Hypertext allows the inclusion of all of the earlier forms to define nodes in their own rights, but—like the drama—it clearly embraces and is not embraced by the other primary forms.

I am not, of course, suggesting that the technology which allowed a form to achieve a measure of cultural dominance was in fact the progenitor of that form. There have always been poetry, prose, drama, and hypertext, but material culture has responded to them differently at different times. I have shown elsewhere that manuscript technologies could and did support the development of proto-hypertext one thousand years ago, and of course the drama achieved a period of expression during classical antiquity when it fell in with the technology of public spectacle.[20] It is noteworthy that the classical drama embraced only poetry, albeit in a great variety of subforms. Once Christianity saw to the dismissal of the drama in the West, we had to wait until the attitude which dismissed it was changed, and for the means of production to develop again for its representation. On a smaller scale, the same thing happened when English theatres were reopened at the restoration of King Charles II, having been closed for twenty years during the Cromwellian protectorate. The technology of dramatic production (including the production of play-texts) had been suspended for two decades, and had to catch up, as it were, with the socio-technological context of the 1660s. The use of elaborate new rigging for the presentation of Charles II's masques was a part of this, as was the use of female actors for female roles. The technology of print did not, throughout the age of movable type, much favour the development of hypertext, so that the modern age in its broadest sense, from—say— 1500 to 1918, corresponds almost wholly to the development of a print culture, and has little place for this form of discourse as a literary form; nevertheless, the end of the modern age is presaged, like the end of every era, in its own developments, and Joyce and Faulkner's modernism clearly sought to explore varieties of hypertext before an efficient technology for its production had been devised.[21] Certainly, one of the feats of the Early Modern period is the 'discovery' and exploitation of the Americas, and in those cultures which sprang from this colonizing impulse, new subjects and purposes—indeed, new ideologies—sprang up (and are springing up) in the respective post-colonial periods of cultures once determined by Western Europe. Such cultural upheavals are bound to lead writers and readers to adjust the available forms of discourse anew, and in doing so, to re-establish a form which had been overshadowed.

When the United States was trying to carve its own post-colonial foundation, the primary literary discourse which it most successfully employed and passed along in what became the canon of American literature was, I argue, a form of hypertext.[22] Mark Twain's *Adventures of Huckleberry Finn* was first published in 1885, twenty years after the American Civil War, an event which for all intents and purposes must be seen as the predictable confrontation of colonial and anti-colonial forces. In a way that has not become a part of popular culture nor received history about that war in the United States, the Confederacy represented the colonial forces and the Union side the anti-colonial; the issues around which the war swirled, including slavery, economic issues, and political issues, can be analysed as resting on distinctions which would either maintain the *status quo* which evolved during the period of English settler-colonialism, or would dismantle it.[23]

The American Civil War took place in 1861–5; *Adventures of Huckleberry Finn* was set in the Mississippi River valley twenty years before the war, and published twenty years after it in 1885. Looking back two decades after the Civil War, then, Mark Twain constructed a culture in *Huck Finn* which we must imagine the losers of that war were fighting to preserve, a culture derived from England during the colonial period, and transformed, like most colonial representations of the imperial culture, into something quite grotesque. 'The most serious blow suffered by the colonized is to be removed from history and from the community,' Albert Memmi wrote; '[c]olonization usurps any free role in either war or peace, every decision contributing to his destiny and that of the world, and all cultural and social responsibility.'[24] *Adventures of Huckleberry Finn* is filled with clans and families and people who quite clearly have been removed from the history of the time and place which people ostensibly like them did, in fact, inhabit. These people were living in the Mississippi River valley at a time when westward expansion was defining the development of the new nation, farming technology was rapidly allowing the great farming states west of the Mississippi to develop impressive economies, and numerous debates raged not only on abolitionist issues, but on women's concerns, and on Indian affairs. Except for a few epithets aimed by various characters against abolitionists, none of this is a part of the work. These characters are not primarily portraits of people from the period and place of the book's setting as many critics have wanted to claim, but rather they figure the texts of the European—mostly English—colonizers.

Only Jim and Pap Finn cannot read which is why, in different ways, neither of them is complicit in the cultural imperialism the work labours to subvert. It is probably important for Huck's own role in the book that he be *sui generis*, that he face the world which has been defined by the colonizer's books without any predisposition towards those books or the ideas they promulgate. Pap thus proclaims Huck's immaculate conception:

'. . . And looky here—you drop that school, you hear? I'll learn people to bring up a boy to put on airs over his own father and let on to be better'n what *he* is. You lemme catch you fooling around that school again, you hear? Your mother couldn't read, and she couldn't write, nuther, before she died. None of the family couldn't before *they* died. I can't; and here you're a-swelling yourself up like this. I ain't the man to stand it—you hear? Say, lemme hear you read.'

I took up a book and begun something about General Washington and the wars. When I'd read about a half a minute, he fetched the book a whack with his hand and knocked it across the house. (p. 24)

It is, of course, appropriate that George Washington should be the subject of Huck's reading, for Mark Twain continued to use Washington, the paradigmatic anti-colonialist, as an image of the anti-imperialist force throughout his life.[25]

III

I have, I admit, taken the long way around to demonstrate that the work Mark Twain's *Adventures of Huckleberry Finn* does is ideological in the most political sense, and that the means of addressing the ideological is clearly through the subversion of established literary conventions. Everyone in the book, except Huck, Jim, and Pap, is manipulated by a romanticized, sentimentalized image of an ideal world which eschews the ethical and political realities facing the United States on the eve of the Civil War; all of the characters, except Pap who lives outside any community and Jim and Huck who traverse them all, inhabit 'imagined communities'.[26] It is these communities which represent the nodes in any hypertextual analysis of *Adventures of Huckleberry Finn*, and it is precisely their 'imagined' dimension which allows them to represent what, at some level, we suspect to be representative of a sort of national consciousness.

If the nodes in this hypertext are 'imagined communities', what goes into the production of such communities? We are tipped off to this in Mark Twain's note labelled 'Explanatory':

IN this book a number of dialects are used, to wit: the Missouri negro dialect; the extremest form of the backwoods Southwestern dialect; the ordinary 'Pike Country' dialect; and four modified varieties of this last. The shadings have not been done in a haphazard fashion, or by guesswork; but painstakingly, and with the trustworthy guidance and support of personal familiarity with these several forms of speech.

I make this explanation for the reason that without it many readers would suppose that all these characters were trying to talk alike and not succeeding.

THE AUTHOR.

Only specialists in the history of American English are likely to spend much time sorting through the dialects preserved and/or created in *Huckleberry Finn*, but—as Benedict Anderson has observed in discussing the communalization of nations—the signal point at which a community becomes 'emotionally plausible and politically viable' is when it is united under the banner of a vernacular language promulgated by provincial printers:

What I am proposing is that neither economic interest, Liberalism, nor Enlightenment could, or did, create *in themselves* the *kind*, or shape, of imagined community to be defended from these regimes' depredations; to put it another way, none provided the framework of a new consciousness—the scarcely-seen periphery of its vision—as opposed to centre-field objects of its admiration or disgust.[27] In accomplishing *this* specific task, pilgrim creole functionaries and provincial creole printmen played the decisive historic role.[28]

Anderson makes this observation on the basis of his earlier conclusion that 'the convergence of capitalism and print technology on the fatal diversity of human language created the possibility of a new form of imagined community, which in its basic morphology set the stage for the modern nation'.[29] The thirteen colonies of North America expanded westward by growing communities at the margins of 'sivilization' (as Huck Finn would have it), ultimately making a vast archipelago of little communities each solidified within its own elastic boundaries by capitalist economies dedicated to identifiable commodities[30] and by the technologies of printing which both defined an official language for them and promulgated information in it.[31] We have statistics for the period between 1691 and 1820 which indicate that there were more than 2,120 newspapers published in thirty colonies and states, and 22 per cent or 461 of these operated for more than ten years. The newspaper was a remarkably stable force for a common culture in most communities, and it has been observed that we should not be surprised that it was Benjamin Franklin, a printer and a journalist, who founded the postal system in the United States, whose role in the development of communities is apparent.[32] Nor is it surprising that a man with such interests became, at that time, a definer of the nation, nor that a person like Samuel Clemens was to redefine it later.

Language and culture are, of course, closely related—synonymous, many would say. Edward Said's extension of Anderson's point, then, is particularly important:

The concept of the national language is central, but without the practice of a national culture—from slogans to pamphlets and newspapers, from folktales and heroes to epic poetry, novels and drama—the language is inert; national culture organizes and sustains communal memory, as when early defeats in African resistance stories are resumed ('they took our weapons in 1903; now we are taking them back'); it reinhabits the landscape using restored ways of life, heroes, heroines, and exploits; it formulates expressions and emotions of pride as well as defiance, which in turn form the backbone of the principal national independence parties.[33]

The configurations which I see as hypertextual nodes in Mark Twain's book are defined in these ways and by these things. Of course, the communities of people Huck visits are not nations, Anderson, Bhabha, and Said's valuable comments notwithstanding, but neither are they, in truth, river communities; they are iconic constructions, as literary creations always are, and they figure nineteenth-century antebellum American communities because we are told that is what they are and because we recognize enough of their contents as belonging to a certain time in history and to people of a certain class in that time. That does not mean, however, that they are not—either ontogenetically or metaphorically—nations.

If we were to try to set *Adventures of Huckleberry Finn* up on the World Wide Web as a hypertext, we would find it easy enough to do; the problem which would arise, however, is the same problem we encounter when we see a film or play based on a novel. Olivier's *Wuthering Heights* is not Emily Brontë's *Wuthering Heights*, yet both works are somehow related. But even though a film may display many excellencies, it cannot reproduce the experience of the novel; the novel is a different discourse. It may be, however, that Laurence Olivier and Emily Brontë's two versions of *Wuthering Heights* do indeed belong to a grander hypertext, in which the visual scenes of the film are linked to the texts on which they are founded.

It is very important to understand that *Adventures of Huckleberry Finn* may be presented and conceived as a hypertext, because that will allow us to evaluate and interpret it in new ways and differently from the way we do when we regard it as an obvious kind of nineteenth-century novel. On the other hand, if we can only think of hypertext in its cybernetic avatar, then we shall find a very different *Huckleberry Finn* on the Web than we have in the printed form, because—if for no other reason—we shall have to create more links than the written form offers, links which are never explicitly specified in the book, and these would make very different readings possible. I have, in fact, avoided using the word 'novel' to designate *Huck Finn* in this study, not because a hypertext can never inhabit the fictional form we call a novel, but because the hypertext which is contained in the nexus of narrative and character which we think of as a novel is not the same hypertext which exists free of any novelistic constraints, as I think this one does.

As a node in the hypertext, each imagined community figures as a space for the discussion of a topic, and, if Huck's book is indeed a hypertext, the nodes should be more or less independent of one another. While there may be a first node, there is no last node—that is, any node which must be final in the narrative. A hypertext narrative is comprised of a series of narremes whose connections are always contingent. That means that there can be no planned development of a character, setting, or a plot beyond the boundaries of the node which contains it, except insofar as the particular logic of linking is complementary to the nodes being linked. That is to say, a link can promote the literary development of character or plot only if it links a node which is subordinate to or necessarily dependent upon the previous node in some fashion. For example, in the sort of hypertext used as online documentation for many computing applications, a node which explains a concept in a previous node is linked to the concept (usually by means of a content word) and it clearly develops the previous node; equally clearly, it constitutes material subordinate to and thus controlled by the previous node. We do not, however, have that kind of linkage in *Huckleberry Finn* and the fact that we do not is mainly responsible for what has been regarded as a problematic ending to the story.

In his own self-made book on hunting for big game and identifying great literature, *Green Hills of Africa*, Ernest Hemingway wrote the thing about *Adventures of Huckleberry Finn* to which everyone alludes, but which no one quotes nowadays:

All modern American literature comes from one book by Mark Twain called *Huckleberry Finn*. If you read it you must stop where the Nigger Jim is stolen from the boys. That is the real end. The rest is just cheating. But it's the best book we've had. All American writing comes from that. There was nothing before. There has been nothing as good since.[34]

When this was published in 1935, Hemingway was a decade closer to the publication of Mark Twain's book than we are to the publication of Hemingway's book. Whether the twelve chapters dealing with Jim's captivity at the Phelps' farm is 'cheating' or not is, nevertheless, beside the point. Hemingway wanted the novel to end elsewhere, as have many readers, and that—as much as any other reason—may be an excellent indication that the novel works as a hypertext should, allowing the reader to assert his or her own arrangement of its nodes. In a recent passionate, smart, but negative review of the book, Jane Smiley articulates the great problem with the whole novel (she would have it be a novel) once we mistake the captivity episode for a novelistic resolution:

As with all bad endings, the problem really lies at the beginning, and at the beginning of *The Adventures of Huckleberry Finn* neither Huck nor Twain takes Jim's desire for freedom at all seriously; that is, they do not accord it the respect that a man's passion deserves. The sign of this is that not only do the two never cross the Mississippi to Illinois, a free state, but they hardly even consider it. In both *Tom Sawyer* and *Huckleberry Finn*, the Jackson's Island scenes show that such a crossing, even in secret, is both possible and routine, and even though it would present legal difficulties for an escaped slave, these would certainly pose no more hardship than locating the mouth of the Ohio and then finding passage up it. It is true that there could have been slave catchers in pursuit (though the novel ostensibly takes place in the 1840s and the Fugitive Slave Act was not passed until 1850), but Twain's moral failure, once Huck and Jim link up, is never even to account for their choice to go down the river rather than across it. What this reveals is that for all his lip service to real attachment between white boy and black man, Twain really saw Jim as no more than Huck's sidekick, homoerotic or otherwise.[35]

On the one hand, Smiley would clearly like to create her own episode for the book, again demonstrating the power of its hypertextual structure. The episode she would create would not work, however, for she imagines a sustained tale of the underground railroad which could not be generated by the imagined communities which make up Mark Twain's nodes in this hypertext, but which would require a series of subordinated linkings quite unlike the work already produced and which the author has stipulated to be plotless in his prepended 'Notice'. Nor, as we shall see, will the texts of the links themselves support the reading she would prefer, even though they focus on Huck and Jim's relationship. On the other hand, Smiley is mostly correct when she claims that Jim never rises above being Huck's sidekick. While I, too, wish that a book so popular as this one had a major contribution to make towards transforming America's inability to resolve its racist attitudes one hundred and thirty-some years after President Lincoln's proclamation of emancipation, this book does not do that.

While Mark Twain was no racist, at least in such terms as racial issues could be represented during the days of Reconstruction, neither is this book concerned, as Harriet Beecher Stowe's *Uncle Tom's Cabin* was concerned when it was published in 1851–2, with significant issues of racism, perhaps because when *Huckleberry Finn* was written, slavery had been outlawed throughout the country for two decades, but the fundamental issues of resolving racial strife separate from abolishing slavery had not yet been articulated for most white Americans.[36] As we shall see in the discussion below on implicit links, Mark Twain does make a contribution towards articulating those issues. The work is clearly and realistically *racialist*; that is, it accepts the premiss that race creates significant distinctions among people, although it equally attempts to repudiate a *racist* agenda within that context. Every node is primarily concerned with a society which has misconceived itself through its textuality, and the point is made in each community's public perception of Jim that their colonialized textualities refuse to recognize the complexity of America's racial makeup. That is the point in the Silas Phelps node in which white texts do not merely contextualize Jim as a prisoner, but enslave him in a form of absurdity which many readers can no longer read as satiric. In Mark Twain's book, cultural imperialism—primarily, the romantic sentimentalism of Western Europe—had invaded the United States, and was the root of cultural stagnation, perversity, and violence, all under the guise of civilization. With such a broad satiric target, racism is but a part of what animates his attack. As I have already argued, the ideological content is a function of the hypertextual dimension of the work. Because in each node a community may be imagined which is characterized by romanticized, sentimentalized, or melodramatic themes, often alluding directly to identifiable romances and novels ranging from the works of Sir Walter Scott to Thomas Carlyle, then the book's theme—that we are beset by a kind of untailored, off-the-rack civilization which fits neither our problems, our people, nor our times—is intensified by repetition as we move from node to node.

A critical analysis of a hypertext requires of course an attentiveness to both structure and ideology, because the integrity of a hypertext is clearly dependent on both the dyadic configuration of nodes and links which comprise its unique structure on the one hand and the production of complex meaning on the other.[37] Nevertheless, it is the cultural work which the book does—hypertext or not—which ultimately must be of interest. It may well be that the definition of a hypertext should be derived from the Marxian notion of production itself. I should like to define a hypertext as a textual process which consists of a base and a superstructure: the base is comprised of the various operations of linking and conditions under which linking takes place; from it the material text with all of its divergencies, digressions, and differences is continuously generated.

The base is, of course, larger than merely a categorization of hypertextual operations, for these constitute but one realization of the possible material transformations of the conditions of production—within the larger category of language in this instance.[38] Such an assumption deposits any individual hypertext, e.g. *Adventures of Huckleberry Finn*, as a function of the superstructure, the realm of the ideological. Louis Althusser has already suggested that an intimate relationship exists between ideology and reading practices, which is why he included literature among the ideological apparatuses which contribute to the process of reproducing the relations of production, the social relationships which are the necessary condition for the existence and perpetuation of the capitalist mode of production.[39] But unlike the other primary forms—poetry, prose, and drama—which Althusser means to include within his adjustment to the Marxist paradigm, hypertext is necessarily more protean with regard at any instant to reading practices (and therefore the ideologies) they invite. Reading practices can vary with different readers, or with the same readers over time or even in the course of the same hypertext. Focusing on the reader as a key to textual production explains why I feel justified in claiming that hypertext is a textual *process* of *continuous* generation which requires us to view this textual form as primarily a constituent of social operations.

I am also concerned to make clear that this definition is not designed merely to accommodate cybernetic hypertexts. The reading of printed texts as hypertexts is just as protean as the reading of cybernetic hypertexts. This is because the dyadic base of links and nodes in our description of hypertextuality works against over-determined readings. For this reason, George Landow connects hypertext with Jacques Derrida and deconstruction in the first sentence of his pioneering critique of cybernetic hypertext and literary theory.[40] Links, by the process of linking and not by the means of delivery (whether electronic or through print), resist closure at all levels. The primary difference between cybernetic and printed hypertexts is a difference directly derived from the material conditions of the production of the text.

Raymond Williams anticipated this observation a decade before the effect of computers on textuality was foreseen in the popular media. 'For they [electronic means of transmission] are always more than new technologies, in the limited sense,' he wrote. 'They are *means* of production, developed in direct if complex relations with profoundly changing and extending social and cultural relationships: changes elsewhere recognizable as deep political and economic transformations.'[41] We have hardly begun to deal with a number of issues which the ubiquity and immanence of electronic texts will require us to tackle. As I drafted a first version of this essay, the Communications Decency Act, which would censor material made available in the USA through the Internet, was being heard in

Federal Court in Philadelphia.[42] The court found the Act unconstitutional, but most citizens and lawmakers, including President Clinton, remain confused by what appears to be a form of textuality which is clearly unmanageable by the usual means available to individual societies;[43] therefore, we can expect significant changes in a social order obliged to seek the means both to control socially and to accommodate economically this new form of textual production, although we cannot predict how these changes will emerge. Those in favour of censoring the Internet argued that it harbours inappropriate material for children. The proto-hypertext, *Adventures of Huckleberry Finn*, occasioned a similar public outcry, also based on what some people viewed as inappropriate material for children.[44] But while only a handful of newspapers fought over the decision to ban *Huck Finn* made by the public library of Concord, Massachusetts, no less than an Act of Congress was thought an appropriate response to the perception of a threatening textuality on the Internet, so overwhelming are the implications of the power of this new agent of distribution.[45]

While cybernetic hypertexts may have a marked influence on society, it is the means of their production which will cause a textual revolution, and not the fact of their hypertextuality. Cybernetic hypertexts are more clearly non-linear than printed hypertexts, because the electronic medium makes possible a variety of ways to allow the reader to navigate a text, and readers, whose desires are of course conditioned by their own cultural and social relationships, choose among such paths to satisfy those desires as the writer(s), similarly conditioned, may have supplied. Where the means of textual production is defined by print, as with *Adventures of Huckleberry Finn*, the reader normally reads in a linear fashion from beginning to end, at least when reading the work for the first time. But both cybernetic hypertexts and print hypertexts are generated from a base which contains all of the paradigmatic possibilities of interaction between nodes and links. Whether the reader acquires the text via a linear reading or an electronic 'surfing' is hardly germane to the way in which the work will be mediated through the other entities and apparatuses which make up the superstructure wherein the psyche of the social being is formed.[46] Rather, it is the arrangement, as it were, of the text within the reader's consciousness, regardless of how it was 'input', which makes it a vehicle of an ideology. A hypertext, subsequently presenting itself to the reader as a series of nodes and links, similarly creates the possibility for multiple ideological perspectives.

We have explored the way the nodes in *Huckleberry Finn* are constructed around imagined communities whose textuality reveals a settler-colonialism that attempted to appropriate the culture of the colonizer (England, for the most part) through grotesque readings and pre-determined applications of its texts. Mark Twain undermines this means of creating a national subject through his humour and satire on the one hand, and on the other, with the portrayal of the inevitable violence visited upon a society which has authorized a textuality of no special relevance to its own social base. In that respect, *Adventures of Huckleberry Finn* is a very serious social text. The eight nodes I have identified in the Appendix to this study all share Mark Twain's apparent distaste for the fundamental principles of the communities they seek to display; the Jackson Island sequence, as idyllic as the descriptions of the river and sky help make it, is nevertheless—with only Huck and Jim to people it—clearly a community *manqué*. Each of these nodes examines a different aspect of the so-called 'national character'. A single ideology apparently underlies, however, all eight of these nodes, and that ideology speaks to the need for the texts on which a society depends to reflect the material circumstances of that society.[47]

IV

If the ideology of the nodes is central to a hypertextual interpretation of the book, then the links between the nodes must participate in that interpretation; this is only possible if hypertextual links can also be regarded as capable of carrying ideological content as well as nodes. This is a point we shall have to examine in some detail, because the cybernetic model of hypertext—from which we tend to draw our understanding of the form—would superficially suggest that links are merely structural. Although a word or phrase may be made to serve a linking function by tagging it to render it 'hot' (that is, electronically capable of providing access to another node), a linking text is necessarily a more complex 'utterance' than unlinked text, whether or not it is tagged for cybernetic display; such complexity will either reorganize the ideological content of an utterance to serve both as ordinary discourse and as linking discourse, or it will, in the act of defining the link, create a new content for it which must operate parallel to its original content and thus create a nexus of ideologies. Linking generates *amplificatio* which is always a reorganization or enhancement of an explicit or implicit assertion.[48] The choice of a link's content is therefore always an ideological choice. So while the ideology of linking may appear to be of a more abstract kind than is read in the nodes, it nevertheless is extremely significant in the development of a work's totalizing theme.

It would seem, however, that matters of linking are so different in cybernetic hypertexts and print hypertexts like *Adventures of Huckleberry Finn* that we might argue that the two forms of hypertext are quite unrelated, and should, perhaps, be called by different names. I do not, however, subscribe to this view, because—in fact—the disparity between linking processes is, at least for the purposes of literary analysis, merely illusional. Here are some sample cybernetic hypertext links:

<A href = 'http://web.syr.edu/~fjzwick/twainwww.html'>**Mark Twain** </A>

<A href = 'http://web.syr.edu/~fjzwick/twainwww.html'> **materials concerning Mark Twain on the World Wide Web**</A>

<A href = 'http://web.syr.edu/~fjzwick/twainwww.html'> **the greatest satirist America has produced**</A>

<A href = 'http://web.syr.edu/~fjzwick/twainwww.html'> **Jim Zwick's series of web pages dedicated to Mark Twain's writing and politics**</A>

These links are encoded in HTML, the hypertext markup language, each embedded within a longer text on an internet site, where the tagging enclosed within the angle brackets will render the text, here in bold type, as linked to the same electronic address in each instance given, <http://web.syr.edu/~fjzwick/twainwww.html>. The user of the hypertext will not see this address encoded in the main text, but only the emboldened words, which usually will be a different colour from unlinked parts of the text. The linked text will govern the perspective of the reader, so that, although each link above will lead to the same homepage with its attendant texts, the reader will come to those texts predisposed to the aspect of their content supplied in the linking text. A link is not merely a point of access to another node; a link establishes an ideology pertinent to gaining a node. I have written elsewhere that even a footnote reference number is a link to a second node, either as a comment or a citation or both.[49] Obviously, an ideology is expressed in whose work is cited and what is said about it, but that inheres in the node accessed, and not properly in the numeral or asterisk which references it. The ideology of the numeral, however, is also present in both printed and cybernetic hypertext. The desire to amplify is expressed even in the mere existence of the footnote reference. What is expressed here, however, is more than mere desire to amplify; in a footnote, it is often a matter of one's *duty*, *privilege*, or *adulation* to cite, and that something of that order is referenced clearly is triggered by the mere reference itself, no matter how uninvolved the numeral- or asterisk-signifier itself may be.[50]

I shall distinguish between two sorts of links in *Adventures of Huckleberry Finn*, 'associative links' and 'implicit links'. By the former, I mean those links in the book which help demarcate the major nodes while creating a bit of narrative to move the reader along Mark Twain's planned path, as required by his print technology.[51] As the appendix to this paper will make clear (see pp. 103–5), the chapter—a type of 'structure-representing link'—is not structurally co-terminus with the major nodes in *Huckleberry Finn*.[52] Therefore, Mark Twain is obliged to separate the nodes in definite ways through a series of associative links which represent the end of one node and supply a point from which the reader can gain entrance to the next.

[At the end of the First node] When I lit my candle and went up to my room that night, there set Pap, his own self! (p. 22)

[At the end of the Pap node] There was a little gray in the sky, now; so I stepped into the woods and laid down for a nap before breakfast. (p. 44)

[At the end of the Jackson Island node] We slept most all day, and started out at night, a little ways behind a monstrous long raft that was as long going by as a procession. (p. 106)

[At the end of the Rafters node] It was one of these long, slanting, two-mile crossings, so I was a good long time in getting over. I made a safe landing, and clum up the bank. (p. 131)

[At the end of the Feud node] Then we hung up our signal lantern and judged that we was free and safe once more. I hadn't had a bit to eat since yesterday; so Jim he got out some corn-dodgers and buttermilk, and pork and cabbage, and greens—there ain't nothing in the world so good, when it's cooked rights—and whilst I eat my supper we talked, and had a good time. (pp. 154–5)

[At the end of the Frauds node] Next day, towards night, we laid up under a little willow towhead out in the middle, where there was a village on each side of the river, and the duke and the king begun to lay out a plan for working them towns. (p. 203)

[At the end of the Peter Wilks node] We dasn't stop again at any town, for days and days, kept right along down the river. We was down south in the warm weather, now, and a mighty long ways from home. (p. 265)

[At the end of the Silas Phelps node] But I reckon I got to light out for the territory ahead of the rest, because aunt Sally she's going to adopt me and sivilize me and I can't stand it. I been there before. (p. 362)

Other readers may prefer to cite slightly different parts of the same passages these were drawn from; that is not a barrier to the argument being advanced here, because Mark Twain was not writing cybernetic hypertext in which links must be formally embraced by conventions of the markup language; his links test the boundaries of the genre simply by providing the means of associating one node with another. Print technology permits full passages to link long stretches of discourse, because amplification of an expression in print is only achieved by the production of further discourse, whereas cybernetic hypertext permits a reduction of signifiers, although —as has been observed—without a reduction of ideological content.

The links which terminate the first and last nodes could easily serve as cybernetic links, with 'Pap' designated as the hot word in the first, and 'territory' as the hot word in the last. But we are not restricted to single-word signifiers in hypertext of any kind, and it will be useful to think of the longer links—of which I may have captured but fragments—in terms of what V. N. Voloshinov says about the word as a concept of expression:

In point of fact, *word is a two-sided act*. It is determined equally by *whose* word it is and *for whom* it is meant. As word, it is precisely *the product of the reciprocal relationship between speaker and listener, addresser and addressee*. Each and every word expresses the 'one' in relation to the 'other'. I give myself verbal shape from another's point of view, ultimately, from the point of view of the community to which I belong. A word is a bridge thrown between myself and another. If one end of the bridge depends on me, then the other depends on my addressee. A word is territory shared by both addresser and addressee, by the speaker and his interlocutor.[53]

Although the link is syntactically more complex than Voloshinov's 'word', his remarks serve as a foundation for comprehending what is basic to the link, because it is the fundamental part of a hypertext (nodes are but discourses of a known order) and clearly serves the hypertext as 'a two-sided act', equally determined by where it links from and where it links to. A link is 'precisely the product of the reciprocal relationship between addresser and addressee' or writer and reader, because a link 'expresses the "one" in relation to the "other"'. The reader is given interpretative direction from the writer's intelligence concerning where the text may go, which is ultimately derived from the ideological community to which he or she belongs. A link is 'a bridge thrown between' the hypertext writer and the hypertext reader. If one end of the bridge depends on the writer, then the other depends on the reader. A link is 'territory shared by both addresser and addressee', by the writer and the reader. Links are, to expand Voloshinov's conception of 'word', hyper-words.

A link connects nodes, but it bridges the hypertext writer and hypertext reader because it must be specifically created by the writer for the reader's orientation, and thus must derive from the writer's sense of a 'stabilized *social audience* that comprises the environment in which reasons, motives, values, and so on are fashioned', an audience to which the reader naturally contributes.[54]

In view of this, it should not be remarkable that the associative links at the ends of the nodes should be so consistently *domestic*. Huck is about to go to bed for the night when he discovers Pap waiting for him; after counterfeiting his own murder, the link tells us he took a nap before breakfast; at the end of the Jackson Island node, readers are told that Jim and

Huck slept during the day and travelled at night; at the end of the Rafters node when the pair is separated in the water's rush, the language betrays no anxiety, but the measured safety we equate with domesticity; at the end of the Feud node, Huck and Jim are safe again as they settle down to eat; in the next node, they lay up together under a clump of willows; at the end of the Peter Wilks node, they drift for days into the dreaded south, where the link describes not fear but only the warm weather. With such comfort on the river, it is no wonder that Huck opts for the 'territory' rather than the alternative domesticity offered by Aunt Sally.

Many critics of this work have noted the idyllic river scenes in contrast to the brutal life ashore, but that is not the contrast these links in fact offer. Indeed, many dangers are met on the river, and—as we learn in the Silas Phelps node (pp. 361–2)—Pap Finn was found murdered in a brothel drifting on the flood.[55] Rather, these links describing the elemental pleasures of sleeping, eating, resting safely, talking, and affection serve to reinforce the notion that it is 'sivilization' or the extended elaboration of pleasures civilization affords which is perverse. The imagined communities constructed in each node are linked by the constant reminder of what both Mark Twain and his stabilized social audience wanted to believe about the inherent nature of humans, a point he made more explicitly in the essay entitled, 'A Defense of General Funston'.

We are *made*, brick by brick, of *influences*, patiently built up around the framework of our born dispositions. It is the sole process of construction; there is no other. Every man and woman and child is an influence; a daily and hourly influence which never ceases from work and never ceases from affecting for good or evil the characters about it—some contributing gold-dust, some contributing trash-dust, but in either case helping on the building, and never stopping to rest. The shoemaker helps to build his two-dozen associates; the pickpocket helps to build his four dozen associates; the village clergyman helps to build his five hundred associates; the renowned bank-robber's name and fame help to build his hundred associates and three thousand persons whom he has never seen; the renowned philanthropist's labors and the benevolent millionaire's gifts move to kindly works and generous outlays of money a hundred thousand persons whom they have never met and never will meet; and to the building of the character of every individual thus moved these movers have added a brick; the unprincipled newspaper adds a baseness to a million decaying character-fabrics every day; the high-principled newspaper adds a daily betterment to the character-fabric of another million. The swiftly-enriched wrecker and robber of railway systems lowers the commercial morals of a whole nation for three generations. A [George] Washington, standing upon the world's utmost summit, eternally visible, eternally clothed in light, a serene, inspiring, heartening example and admonition, is an influence which raises the level of character in all receptive men and peoples, alien and domestic; and the term of its gracious work is not measurable by fleeting generations, but only by the lingering march of the centuries.[56]

The associative links, then, are the moments unreached by those contrasting influences which Mark Twain records in the staccato style of bustling gilded-age towns and cities. The links at the ends of the nodes in *Huck Finn* are the territory the writer and reader can share.

There is a second kind of link in *Huckleberry Finn* which can be identified as an 'implicit link'. According to DeRose, implicit links are links which 'can be inferred algorithmically from elements comprising the source document'. Every word in a text is linked in this sense to a lexicon of the language in which the text is written. We can systematically and mechanically generate the lemmatized form in the lexicon from the words in the text, and therefore link each word to its dictionary entry.[57] And while 'algorithmical' may seem to refer to a situation which can only be duplicated in cybernetic hypertext, the identification of interpretative sites in a text by means of the systematic application of an authoritative matrix of concepts is as old as literature itself. St Augustine and St Jerome's commentaries on the Psalms demonstrate this repeatedly, wherein the matter of the New Testament and the interpretations accruing to it are used to interpret references in the Psalms, thus implicitly linking Hebrew songs to different Christian purposes.[58] Psychoanalytical approaches to reading are similarly algorithmic, using Sigmund Freud or Jacques Lacan's works, among others, to define the matrix from which an interpretation may be generated.

Certainly, a desideratum for the future will be a poetics of hypertextual linking, in which the fundamental principles of examining such texts can be thought through more rigorously than in the present study. To say, however, that the implicit link is generated from an interpretative matrix is only to say that it participates in the transformative and symbolic dimensions of textuality. In order to distinguish its role in a hypertext, we will need to return to Voloshinov's linguistic considerations, wherein we shall find the implicit link analogous to his sense of 'expression': '[The] simplest, rough definition [of 'expression'] is: something which, having in some way taken shape and definition in the psyche of an individual, is outwardly objectified for others with the help of external signs of some kind.'[59] As an associative link shares the qualities of Voloshinov's 'word', so an implicit link shares a similar space with 'expression'. Just as an expression is usually constituted of words, so we shall find that implicit links are constituted of associative links. At the basis of any linking operation is the sharing of territory between writer and reader, which is the same as saying that all links are essentially associative. We should not be surprised, then, that the text's major nodes—the 'imagined communities' in *Huck Finn*—are linked associatively. The implicit link, however, allows the writer and reader to step beyond the confines of the series of nodes we have examined so far, and to discover relationships between the text at hand

and other, larger dimensions of the cultures and ideologies which produced the text and which read it.

When Voloshinov describes an expression as taking 'shape and definition in the psyche of an individual', he is arguing that language does not merely constitute itself, but that behind the expression in that ill-defined place called the 'psyche' there is a connection between the actor and the language he or she enacts wherein the expressible is formulated; there is first of all, we may assert, desire. But expression is dependent upon two elements: not only must we have the inner something which is expressible, but an expression equally requires an outward objectification. 'In any case, all the creative and organizing forces of expression are within', Voloshinov argues. 'Everything outer is merely passive material for manipulation by the inner element. Expression is formed basically within and then merely shifts to the outside.'[60]

Because we are used to thinking of consciousness as interior and individual, we have to be careful in how we apply Voloshinov's distinction to the implicit link, because the inner/outer binary does not quite work for hypertextual analysis. Hypertext is socially constructed, if only because it is open-ended, and authors must be thought to 'contribute' to it rather than simply to impose a text. The 'creative and organizing' forces of an implicit link are embedded within the interpretative matrix of the culture following those links. For example, the privileged selection of New Testament, liturgical, and patristic materials which constituted Jerome and Augustine's matrices for reading the Hebrew texts we call the Psalms is a case is point. There is moreover an equally large body of rabbinical literature on interpreting the Psalms in the Hebrew tradition, and this, too, is dependent upon a matrix of images, signs, principles, and equivalencies from Hebrew culture.[61] These matrices are the creative and organizing forces of the implicit link, and it is because of their existence that we can infer where these links occur in the hypertext, without having to preprocess or 'tag' each link. Just as we can have a computer process a text using a predetermined lexicon in order to link untagged items to their appropriate lexical nodes, so we may generate implicit links in a text by processing it against a relevant matrix of cultural materials, and thus generate a web of connections between the hypertext and the culture in which it is being read. Each implicit link can then be said to express the content of the matrix within the text to which it is linked; that is, it is the material of the matrix which is shifted to the external or 'realized' form it takes within the hypertext.

I hasten to point out that an implicit link is not merely an allusion to another text or to a cultural commonplace. An implicit link brings to bear on a text the whole weight of the matrix to which it is linked. Whereas an associative link connects nodes more or less of equal weight, an implicit link connects one node in the hypertext to the whole cultural process which informs it through the interface of what I have called an interpretational 'matrix'. The matrix is not just a convenient construct for analysis, but is made up of those forms of which writers and readers of hypertext are sensible within the boundaries of the matrix. An interpretational matrix is multi-dimensioned, and it may be viewed synchronically, diachronically, socially, politically, or in other ways; ideologies espoused through implicit links are given form via this matrix.[62]

It will be useful here to examine the way such a matrix might work to elucidate the complexity of *Adventures of Huckleberry Finn*. As I have already suggested, Mark Twain's work is not in this book concerned primarily with issues of race; it is instead concerned with combating the tendency of post-colonial cultures to fall into the trap of adopting a textuality (and therefore a culture) which is unresponsive to their needs and unrelated to their conditions. The book, written twenty years after the US Civil War, is set in the 1840s, about twenty years before the emancipation of US slaves, and the period of its setting as well as that of its writing virtually guarantees that attitudes towards race and slavery will nevertheless have to have a place in the book, the author's focus on other things notwithstanding. The relationship between Jim and Huck of course requires that, as well. The advantage of the hypertextual concept of implicit linking is that it allows a text to subtend with additional materials the structure created through associative links. I should like to examine the way in which a matrix of racialist matter is implicitly linked to the series of nodes connected through associative links that we have already explored in the work.

How does one identify an implicit link? As with defining the nature of links, the issue is a linguistic one. For communication to take place, there must be a shared content; inner material must be outwardly manifested, as Voloshinov observed in the case of the expression. The outward manifestation will necessarily require an adjustment from the exact form of the inner conception. We are inhibited psychologically, socially, politically, economically, and probably in other ways from producing the raw expression as it comes to mind. All of these inhibitions are mediated through space and history, so that the kinds of pressure they exert change over time and in different places. Any text will produce linguistic cues of variation from the reader's norm; indeed, the realization of these is part of the pleasure of reading. But there are always words and phrases in a text which tug at one's sleeve, begging one to understand more than they ostensibly imply. Sometimes, one realizes that such materials represent nothing more than a shift in the exact inhibitions which regulate the social space where a text is read. Sometimes, something more seems to be going on. The text is not merely obeying the social demands inhibiting it; rather, it is privileging the effect of one of the kinds of inhibitions above others. That is the place where the reader is alerted to an implicit link.

In *Adventures of Huckleberry Finn*, there are forty-two mentions of snakes, snake-skins, and the like. The references repeatedly privilege the status of the animal, by making it the instrument of Pap's tortures while suffering *delerium tremens*, by putting Jim in danger of dying when a snake bites him, by creating almost a subplot of 'bad luck' based on Huck's having brought back to camp the slough of a snake, and by being considered an important form of torment while Jim awaits his mock-escape at the Phelps' farm. The word 'horse', on the other hand, occurs fifty-one times in the book, but the references never enlarge the animal's social or psychological niche within the culture. I would argue that an implicit link exists in the book between snakes and a complex interpretational matrix dealing with superstition and economic status, and the parts of the text which explore these relationships are nodes in which 'snake' is tagged to make that link. There are other areas where I would look for implicit links, too. A representation of the verb 'to read' appears eighty-two times in the book, and I suspect that the word is tagged for implicit linking within a matrix of ideas about literacy and literature. Governance, the river, masculinity, femininity, etc. might all be tracked as implicit links in the work.

It is in the form of material implicitly linked to *Huckleberry Finn* that racial matters in the book are best analysed. The word primarily tagged to represent this link is the highly charged word, 'nigger', which appears in the text 212 times. The inhibitions against the use of this word today are sufficiently strong in the USA that journalists have long debates over when and under what circumstances it can be printed or spoken on broadcasts. Today, the word arouses almost all of the inhibitions possible against its use,[63] but a measure of the degree to which the epithet was tolerated within the memory of many is to be found in Ernest Hemingway's famous remark on the book in *Green Hills of Africa*. Hemingway says, '[i]f you read [*Huck Finn*] you must stop where the Nigger Jim is stolen from the boys'. It was possible in 1935 to use the word in a document produced for the dominant culture, into which category Hemingway's book falls, without arousing anger—at least, without arousing the opprobrium of the dominant culture of the time. However, the linguistic codes which determined exactly how that word was used during the period of the Civil War had apparently been forgotten.[64] It may be impossible now to save *Huck Finn* from the charge that it is a racist work *for us today* because the links express what has become inexpressible, and the matrix to which they link the text has to be reconstructed through painstaking scholarship which will not be read by those who will seek to have it removed from school libraries and curricula.

It is in the nature of implicitly linked material to create difficulties of interpretation because access to a given cultural matrix will necessarily change over time, whereas the links themselves are 'hard-wired' into the material text. This is a very significant distinction. Whatever the links meant to readers at the time of the original publication of the book is now mediated by their present signification. Still, we have to grapple with all that is implied by a work like this one, because it is a central text of the American canon, and that implies a work which the dominant forces of the culture have found to be supportive of their agenda and in which emergent forces might find the seeds if not the roots of whatever oppresses them. Homi Bhabha comments upon the problem of reconstructing the racialist implicit links for *Huck Finn* when he observes, '[c]ulture only emerges as a problem, or a problematic, at the point at which there is a loss of meaning in the contestation and articulation of everyday life, between classes, genders, races, nations'.[65] It is interesting that, when Mark Twain's book was published, the articulation of matters of everyday life between races in America was much more stable from the point of view of white society than it is now, albeit everyday life was often more repressive to African Americans than it is now, both economically and socially. Consequently, the racialist implicit links in *Adventures of Huckleberry Finn* seem to have allowed the reader at the end of the last century to view Jim as a man of some power, and certainly as a man to be respected, although now—as Jane Smiley's reading suggests—the same text often seems so patronizing.

Of the 212 uses of the word 'nigger' in the work, I want to look at three of them as implicit links to the interpretational matrix of racial issues with which Mark Twain would have been familiar. In each of these cases, the speaker uses the phrase, 'good nigger'. In Chapter 18, Jim reveals that he has made friends with the slaves on the Grangerford plantation: 'Dey's mighty good to me, dese niggers is, en whatever I wants 'm to do fur me I doan' have to ast 'm twice, honey. Dat Jack's a good nigger, en pooty smart' (p. 151). In Chapter 23, Huck describes how Jim cries at night over the loss of his family: 'He was often moaning and mourning that way nights, when he judged I was asleep, and saying, "Po' little 'Lizabeth! Po' little Johnny! it's mighty hard; I spec' I ain't ever gwyne to see you no mo', no mo'!" He was a mighty good nigger, Jim was' (p. 201). It is also relevant that Huck uses the term in his appearance in *The Adventures of Tom Sawyer* when he tells Tom that he helps Uncle Jake, the Rogers' family servant, in exchange for a place to sleep in the Rogers' hayloft: 'I tote water for Uncle Jake whenever he wants me to, and any time I ask him he gives me a little something to eat if he can spare it. That's a mighty good nigger, Tom. He likes me, becuz I don't ever act as if I was above him.'[66] The phrase is important because it points to Mark Twain's most significant ideological statement about the potential for an African-American 'community' which is never fully explored among the imagined communities the book describes. The bits of text quoted above exhibit aporia around the concept of the 'good nigger'. Whatever the phrase might have meant in the world at large, Mark Twain uses it as a way of admiring a virtuous slave, which we must suspect was its common usage (interestingly enough, the phrase does not appear in *Uncle Tom's Cabin*), but what counts for Mark Twain as virtuous might well subvert the common usage of the phrase.

When used by whites, at least, the phrase appears to be centred about the virtues of hearth, family, and hospitality, which are of considerable consequence. The point is made in great detail indeed in Chapter 42 after Tom has been shot, and the doctor reports how Jim gave up his attempt to escape in order to come to Tom's aid. Here, however, the doctor resorts to litotes ('he ain't a bad nigger') in his speech before the men. I believe that the ironic form is required because the doctor is making a rather formal oral defence of Jim. The negation de-sentimentalizes the phrase in the masculinist context. The positive form of the phrase we have been examining is always used intimately, and the point seems to be that the doctor realizes that he cannot call Jim 'good' among these men, but he must instead imply his goodness by saying that he is not 'bad'.

'Don't be no rougher on him than you're obleeged to, because he ain't a bad nigger. When I got to where I found the boy I see I couldn't cut the bullet out without some help, and he warn't in no condition for me to leave to go and get help; and he got a little worse and a little worse, and after a long time he went out of his head, and wouldn't let me come a-nigh him any more, and said if I chalked his raft he'd kill me, and no end of wild foolishness like that, and I see I couldn't do anything at all with him; so I says, I got to have help somehow; and the minute I says it out crawls this nigger from somewheres and says he'll help, and he done it, too, and done it very well. Of course I judged he must be a runaway nigger, and there I was! and there I had to stick right straight along all the rest of the day and all night. It was a fix, I tell you! I had a couple of patients with the chills, and of course I'd of liked to run up to town and see them, but I dasn't, because the nigger might get away, and then I'd be to blame; and yet never a skiff come close enough for me to hail. So there I had to stick plumb until daylight this morning; and I never see a nigger that was a better nuss or faithfuller, and yet he was risking his freedom to do it, and was all tired out, too, and I see plain enough he'd been worked main hard lately. I liked the nigger for that; I tell you, gentlemen, a nigger like that is worth a thousand dollars—and kind treatment, too. I had everything I needed, and the boy was doing as well there as he would a done at home—better, maybe, because it was so quiet; but there I was, with both of 'm on my hands, and there I had to stick till about dawn this morning; then some men in a skiff come by, and as good luck would have it the nigger was setting by the pallet with his head propped on his knees sound asleep; so I motioned them in quiet, and they slipped up on him and grabbed him and tied him before he knowed what he was about, and we never had no trouble. And the boy being in a kind of a flighty sleep, too, we muffled the oars and hitched the raft on, and towed her over very nice and quiet, and the nigger never made the least row nor said a word from the start. He ain't no bad nigger, gentlemen; that's what I think about him.' (pp. 352–4)

The phrase is repeated at the beginning and end of the speech, and the reader is left with exactly the kind of site in a hypertext to which an implicit link is most productively drawn. It is a little node, neatly framed at beginning and end, and containing a full narrative with its own beginning, middle, and end. '[T]he boy was doing as well there as he would a done at home—better, maybe, because it was so quiet', the doctor says in summary of Jim's skills as a nurse. The ideology inherent in this node is implicitly linked to a matrix of ideas about race and class, wherein goodness identifies the domestic ideal.

The word 'nigger' occurs in many other contexts too numerous to analyse here. All of these uses are linked to the same interpretational matrix, and through an examination of these links, we can begin to build a full sense of the racial ideologies the work espouses. So far, we have seen that the work values most highly a level of tranquility and perhaps equality among people of both races. We should not be surprised that a more heroic code is not advanced, because heroic actions are what motivate Tom Sawyer who is roundly ridiculed in *Adventures of Huckleberry Finn*.

When examined as a hypertext, Mark Twain's *Adventures of Huckleberry Finn* offers exceedingly rich readings, wherein basic notions about creating a national character, a national ethics, and a national poetics appear to come together in one book, and that book suggests that such cultural work might be undertaken by the most marginal of marginalized people, a runaway slave and the orphaned son of a drunkard. A residual colonialism affects the dominant American culture in this work, and as we follow the parts of the hypertext, we discover Mark Twain's constant effort to close off and to circumscribe dominant ideals through a variety of discursive strategies, and to raise up and privilege basic and universal cultural elements through a complex interaction of associative and implicit links in and around a series of nodes into which the concept of community and simple domesticity are continuously reinscribed.[67]

NOTES

1. Mark Twain, *Adventures of Huckleberry Finn*, ed. Walter Blair and Victor Fischer, in *The Works of Mark Twain*, viii (Berkeley: University of California Press, 1988), p. 362. Subsequent citations of this text are to this edition.
2. It was subsequently published by Walter Blair (ed.), *Mark Twain's Hannibal, Huck & Tom* (The Mark Twain Papers; Berkeley: University of California Press, 1969), pp. 81–140.

3. See Hugh Kenner, *The Mechanic Muse* (Oxford: Oxford University Press, 1987), *passim*. Mark Twain himself was also interested in the technologies of writing, and was among the first American writers to use a typewriter during composition; his investment in the Paige typesetting machine, a complex engine for composing and distributing cold type, led him into bankruptcy when Otto Merganthaler invented the hot-lead Linotype machine which eclipsed Paige's temperamental contraption. Mark Twain's passion for the invention, however, was due in large measure to his desire to see the effects of a fully mechanized printing process on communications and the publishing industry. See Justin Kaplan, *Mr. Clemens and Mark Twain* (New York: Simon and Schuster, 1966), pp. 329–36, 354–60.

4. For the first narrative reference to Huckleberry Finn, see Mark Twain, *The Adventures of Tom Sawyer; Tom Sawyer Abroad; Tom Sawyer, Detective*, ed. John C. Gerber, Paul Baender, and Terry Firkins, in *The Works of Mark Twain*, iv (Berkeley: University of California Press, 1982), p. 73.

5. In fact, Huck is used as the narrator of all of Tom's subsequent adventures, including *Tom Sawyer Abroad; Tom Sawyer, Detective*; 'Huck Finn and Tom Sawyer among the Indians'; 'Doughface'; 'Tom Sawyer's Gang Plans a Naval Battle'; and 'Tom Sawyer's Conspiracy'. The last four of these texts are edited by Walter Blair in *Mark Twain's Hannibal, Huck & Tom*; see n. 4, above, for editions of *Tom Sawyer Abroad* and *Tom Sawyer, Detective*. It is of interest in this context to note that on the title-page of *Tom Sawyer Abroad* Mark Twain listed the author as Huck Finn and himself as editor (p. 255), and describes *Tom Sawyer, Detective* 'as told by Huck Finn' (p. 357).

6. I have used the searchable electronic version of *Adventures of Huckleberry Finn* at The Huck Finn Homepage <URL: http://etext.virginia.edu/railton/ huckfinn/huchompg.html> and checked the text given there against the authoritative University of California edition.

7. Clemens used the initials G.G. to signify General Ulysses S. Grant on several occasions, but it is not clear why he would have thought Grant's name appropriate here. See *Adventures of Huckleberry Finn* (pp. 372–3).

8. Mark Twain more specifically and at greater length attacked Sir Walter Scott's work in *Life on the Mississippi*.

9. See 'Explanatory Notes', *Adventures of Huckleberry Finn*, p. 418.

10. See Kathryn Sutherland, 'Waiting for Connections: Hypertexts, Multiplots, and the Engaged Reader', in Susan Hockey and Nancy Ide (eds.), *Research in Humanities Computing*, 3 (Oxford: Clarendon Press, 1994), pp. 50–1.

11. Mark Twain, 'In Defense of Maxim Gorki', *New York Sun, Tribune, World* (1906), cited from *Mark Twain Quotations* <URL: http://www.tarleton.edu/ activities/pages/facultypages/schmidt/Mark_Twain.html>.

12. See Laura J. Murray, 'The Aesthetic of Dispossession: Washington Irving and Ideologies of (De)Colonization in the Early Republic', *American Literary History*, 8 (1996), p. 206.

13. Homi K. Bhabha, 'DissemiNation: Time, Narrative, and the Margins of the Modern Nation', in Homi K. Bhabha (ed.), *Nation and Narration* (London: Routledge, 1990), p. 311.

14. Julia Kristeva, *Language—The Unknown: An Initiation into Linguistics*, trans. Anne M. Menke (New York: Columbia University Press, 1989), p. 287.

15. See Raymond Williams, *Marxism and Literature* (Oxford: Oxford University Press, 1977), p. 185.

16. V. N. Voloshinov (*Marxism and the Philosophy of Language*, trans. Ladislav Matejka and I. R. Titunik (New York: Seminar Press, Inc. 1973), p. 96) uses 'genre' in a similar sense in speaking of illocutionary speech acts as 'these little behavioral genres'. In I. R. Titunik's 'Appendix 2. The Formal Method and the Sociological Method (M. M. Baxtin, P. N. Medvedev, V. N. Voloshinov) in Russian Theory and Study of Literature' (ibid., pp. 183–4), 'genre' is defined ideologically in contrast to a formalist definition. I have tried to use 'primary form' or 'form' when dealing with structuralist or formalist concepts, and to reserve 'genre' for 'that area where construction and theme meet and fuse together, the area precisely where social evaluation generates forms of that finalized structuredness . . . which is the very *differentia specifica* of art' (Titunik, ibid., p. 184).

17. A hypertext may, however, contain as members of its discursive inventory any of the other primary forms. Which of the four primary forms can contain others is interesting in the light of the way each of the four forms is coupled with a discursive technology. Poetry, which we very often view as the mode most basic to oral origins of literary discourse, cannot subsume any of the other modes.

18. The concept is schematic, not historical. The drama, for instance, appears to have had an oral phase, and prose may be more clearly linked to content than to the form of production. Nevertheless, the technologies of textualization are each coterminous with what becomes a high-status form of textuality for a particular technology. The technology of spectacle, dialogue, and presentation—that is, of theatre—is the most complex of all, and once lost in its classical form, did not begin to be supported until late in the Middle Ages when a new theatrical technology was developed. That development has continued to undergo radical change, embracing cinema, radio, and television successively. It is true that hypertext once again offers a new form at the time a new technology of textualization has appeared, but it remains to be seen whether developments in virtual reality will not reinscribe the dramatic and theatrical as the status form again. It is more likely, however, that virtual reality will create a fifth form, one which will embrace both an enhanced theatricality and hypertextuality as well.

19. J. C. Nyíri, 'Electronic Networking and the Unity of Knowledge', in Stephanie Kenna and Seamus Ross (eds.), *Networking in the Humanities: Papers in Honour of Michael Smethurst for his 60th Birthday* (Proceedings of the Second Conference on Scholarship and Technology in the Humanities, held at Elvetham Hall, Hampshire, UK, 13–16 Apr. 1994; London: Bowker-Saur, 1995), pp. 274–6.

20. Patrick W. Conner, 'Hypertext in the Last Days of the Book', *Bulletin of the John Rylands University Library of Manchester*, 74 (1992), 9–11, 21–2.

21. See J. David Bolter, *Writing Space: The Computer, Hypertext, and the History of Writing* (Hillsdale, NJ: Lawrence Erlbaum, 1991), pp. 132–9.

22. I expect to develop the argument through application to major works by Washington Irving, Herman Melville, Walt Whitman, William Faulker, and

others in addition to Mark Twain in *Hypertext, Ideology, and the American Canon* (forthcoming).

23. See Lawrence Buell, 'American Literary Emergence as a Postcolonial Phenomenon', *American Literary History*, 4 (1992), 411–42.

24. Albert Memmi, *The Colonizer and the Colonized*, tr. Howard Greenfeld (New York: Orion Press, 1965), p. 91.

25. See below, n. 56.

26. The phrase will be recognized from Benedict Anderson, *Imagined Communities: Reflections on the Origin and Spread of Nationalism* (London: Verso, 1983).

27. 'It is instructive that the Declaration of Independence in 1776 speaks only of "the people", while the word "nation" makes its debut only in the Constitution of 1789.' Anderson's note 53, citing Aira Kemiläinen, *Nationalism: Problems Concerning the Word, the Concept, and Classification* (Jyväskylä: Kustantajat, 1964), p. 105.

28. Anderson, *Imagined Communities*, pp. 51–2, 65.

29. Ibid., p. 46.

30. Economic competition among communities was often grounded in competing commodities, e.g. the range wars of the late 19th century pitted cowmen and sheep farmers against each other for the available range land; the so-called oyster wars in the Chesapeake Bay between Maryland and Virginia at the turn of the 20th century shows a similar thing occurring between larger communities denominated as states.

31. Nor were all of these English-speaking communities. Before the First World War, there were numerous German, Swedish, Norwegian, Spanish, and French communities springing forth, and maintaining a shared culture in the United States.

32. Lucien Febvre and Henri-Jean Martin, *The Coming of the Book: The Impact of Printing 1450–1800* (New York: Verso, 1976), p. 211. See also Geoffrey Bennington, 'Postal Politics and the Institution of the Nation', in Bhabha (ed.), *Nation and Narration*, pp. 121–32.

33. Edward W. Said, *Culture and Imperialism* (New York: Alfred A. Knopf, 1993), p. 215.

34. Ernest Hemingway, *Green Hills of Africa* (New York: Scribner, 1935), p. 22.

35. Jane Smiley, 'Say it ain't so, Huck: Second Thoughts on Mark Twain's "Masterpiece" ', *Harper's Magazine*, 292 (Jan. 1996), 61.

36. See Rachel Bowlby, 'Breakfast in America—*Uncle Tom's* Cultural Histories', Bhabha (ed.), *Nation and Narration*, pp. 209–10.

37. I reject George Landow's (*Hypertext: The Convergence of Contemporary Critical Theory and Technology* (London: Johns Hopkins University Press, 1992), pp. 106–7) reading of Hayden White to suggest that ideology and morality adheres in the linearity of narrative. White (*The Content of the Form: Narrative Discourse and Historical Representation* (London: Johns Hopkins University Press, 1987), p. 14) writes, '[i]f every fully realized story, however we define that familiar but conceptually elusive entity, is a kind of allegory, points to a moral, or endows events, whether real or imaginary, with a significance that they do not possess as a mere sequence, then it seems possible to conclude that every historical narrative has as its latent or manifest purpose the

desire to moralize the events of which it treats.' The structure White would moralize is the 'fully realized story, *however we define that*'. White's work on narrative discourse and historical representation strikes me as germane in many ways to issues raised by the conjunction of hypertext and ideology.

38. See Williams, *Marxism and Literature*, pp. 75–8.

39. Louis Althusser, 'Ideology and Ideological State Apparatuses (Notes towards an Investigation)', in *Lenin and Philosophy and Other Essays*, trans. Ben Brewster (New York: Monthly Review Press, 1971), pp. 143–50.

40. Landow, *Hypertext*, p. 2; Kathryn Sutherland ('Looking and Knowing: Textual Encounters of a Postponed Kind', in Warren Chernaik, Marilyn Deegan, and Andrew Gibson (eds.), *Beyond the Book: Theory, Culture, and the Politics of Cyberspace* (Oxford: Office for Humanities Communication, 1996), p. 15) observes, '[c]oherence, argues the deconstructionist critic, may be merely a matter of co-optation; there is value in incoherence.'

41. Williams, *Marxism and Literature*, p. 54.

42. For the full text of United States District Court for the Eastern District of Pennsylvania, Civil Action no. 96–963 (American Civil Liberties Union, *et al.* vs. Janet Reno, Attorney General of the United States) and an archive of materials on the case, see American Civil Liberties Union, 'ACLU Freedom Network' homepage, <URL:http://www.aclu.org/> under menu item 'In the Courts', sub-item 'ACLU vs. Reno'.

43. See Kathryn Jones, 'Candidates Seek Votes On Line But Largely Avoid Internet Issues', Cybertimes Section, *New York Times*, 12 Mar. 1996, <URL: http://www.nytimes.com/>.

44. For an excellent archive of materials associated with the production and marketing of *Adventures of Huckleberry Finn*, see Virginia H. Cope, *Mark Twain's Huckleberry Finn: Text, Illustrations, and Early Reviews*, <URL: http://etext.lib.virginia.edu/twain/huckfinn.html>.

45. In previous centuries, the circulating library, however, was accorded a much greater power to affect society than we are apt to imagine today, particularly with regard to the dissemination of the novel; the banning of *Adventures of Huckleberry Finn* by the Concord Public Library has to be seen in that context. See Sutherland, 'Looking and Knowing', in Chernaik, Deegan, and Gibson (eds.), *Beyond the Book*, pp. 19–21.

46. Williams, *Marxism and Literature*, p. 80.

47. On materiality and the ideological, see Althusser, 'Ideology and Ideological State Apparatuses', pp. 166–8.

48. This is clearly demonstrated in pseudo-Cicero's *Ad C. Herennium de Ratione Dicendi*, ed. and tr. Harry Caplan, Loeb Classical Library (London: William Heinemann, Ltd., 1968), pp. 107, 113.

49. Conner, 'Hypertext in the Last Days of the Book', p. 15.

50. See Voloshinov, *Marxism and the Philosophy of Language*, pp. 84–5.

51. Associative links have been defined by Stephen J. DeRose ('Biblical Studies and Hypertext', in P. Delany and G. P. Landow (eds.), *Hypermedia and Literary Studies* (Cambridge, Mass.: MIT Press, 1991), p. 191) as links which 'attach arbitrary pieces of documents to each other, like strings tied from one place to another. In general, they can represent any concept their creator desires.

Because of this, they cannot be replaced by retrieval algorithms, or even by unilateral creation on the part of a system "author" '. See also Conner, 'Hypertext in the Last Days of the Book', pp. 13–14.

52. Stephen J. DeRose ('Biblical Studies and Hypertext', p. 194) observes that structure-representing links 'form the basis for linearizing the text, i.e. for presenting it as a sequence of elements'. Indeed, it is these links which are generally realized in cybernetic versions of works which were not created in a computing environment. For example, most of the texts provided in The Electronic Text Center at the University of Virginia <URL: http://etext.lib. virginia.edu/uvaonline.html> are linked to a TOC (table of contents) file in which the chapters and sections are each accorded links to the respective parts of the text. Illustrations whose captions are a part of the text are linked to those captions. Otherwise, there is little or no analysis of the hypertextual structure of the texts found there. This is appropriate and defensible, in that the sort of hypertextual analysis I am providing here for *Adventures of Huckleberry Finn* involves textual interpretation of the sort editors have eschewed. A new area of literary work may be upon us, however, which I should call 'hypertextual modelling'. Practitioners of this work will mount their texts online appropriately linked in order to model a hypertextual theory applied to the text in question. If the resulting discussion about such models focuses on the ideological core each model emphasizes rather than merely demonstrating structural data, textual studies will be much advanced.

53. Voloshinov, *Marxism and the Philosophy of Language*, p. 86.

54. Ibid.

55. See *Adventures of Huckleberry Finn*, ed. Victor Doyno (New York: Random House, 1996), pp. 66, 376–7, for further information on the identification of the house as a brothel; Mark Twain altered some of the details before publication, apparently to reduce the raw description of his original manuscript in this place.

56. Mark Twain, 'A Defense of General Funston', *North American Review*, 174 (May 1902). <URL: http://web.syr.edu/~fjzwick/twain_html/deffunst.html>, in Jim Zwick (ed.), *Anti-Imperialism in the United States, 1898–1935*, <URL: http://web.syr.edu/~fjzwick/ ail98-35. html>.

57. DeRose, 'Biblical Studies and Hypertext', p. 198; see also Conner, 'Hypertext in the Last Days of the Book', pp. 15–16.

58. See Frederic Jameson, *The Political Unconscious: Narrative as a Socially Symbolic Act* (Ithaca, NY: Cornell University Press, 1981), pp. 29–32.

59. Voloshinov, *Marxism and the Philosophy of Language*, p. 84.

60. Ibid., p. 85.

61. See Carroll Stuhlmueller, 'Psalms', *Harper's Bible Commentary*, ed. James L. Mays (London: Harper & Row, 1988), pp. 433–4.

62. Frederic Jameson's notion of the 'ideologeme' is rather similar to my use of 'matrix'. See *Political Unconscious*, p. 87.

63. In searching the World Wide Web for the word, I determined that it is found only in academic papers and similar discussions of language and racism, in the lyrics of songs which express anger about racism, in online versions of literary texts such as *Adventures of Huckleberry Finn* and Joseph Conrad's

'Nigger of the Narcissus', and in patently racist material, such as neo-Fascist homepages. See Keith Woods, 'An Essay on a Wickedly Powerful Word', Poynter Institute for Media Studies, Nov. 1995. <URL: http://www.poynter.org/poynter/ec1195b.html>; also Keith Woods, ' "NIGGER": A Case Study in Using a Racial Epithet', ibid. <URL: http://www.poynter.org/poynter/ec1195a.html>. An excellent discussion of the word also occurred on the listserv discussion group, 'Critical Issues in African American Life and Culture', at <AFROAM-L@HARVARDA.HARVARD.EDU> whose archives can be found at <URL: http://www.afrinet.net/~hallh/afrotalk/afrosep95/0434.html>.

64. Blair and Fischer report ['Explanatory Notes', *Adventures of Huckleberry Finn*, p. 376] that public use of the word in 1884 was a sensitive matter, and tended to be avoided in the interests of 'good taste'.

65. Homi K. Bhabha, *The Location of Culture* (London: Routledge, 1994), p. 34.

66. Mark Twain, *The Adventures of Tom Sawyer*, p. 193.

67. I have enjoyed the support of my colleagues in the Department of English at West Virginia University in undertaking this study. In various specific ways, I have been aided by the particular kindnesses of Elaine Ginsberg, Matthew McCrady, Brian McHale, Jonathan Myerov, Vance Smith, David Stewart, Timothy Sweet, and Linda Yoder. I am, of course, responsible for any errors I may have made here or elsewhere in this essay and am in no one's debt for those.

Distribution of Links and Nodes in
Adventures of Huckleberry Finn

Node IDs and Chapters	Imagined Community	Link from	Links to
First I–IV	Community of adolescents (Tom Sawyer and his pirate gang) vs. community of adults (Miss Watson, Judge Thatcher, and 'sivilizing' institutions of school, religion, and law).	[Assoc. Link] When I lit my candle and went up to my room that night, there set Pap, his own self! (p. 22)	[Pap Node] Pap's negative community which he defines as himself in opposition to the nation or 'govment'.
Pap V–VII	Pap's negative community which he defines as himself in opposition to the nation or 'govment'.	[Assoc. Link] There was a little gray in the sky, now; so I stepped into the woods and laid down for a nap before breakfast. (p. 44)	[Jackson Island Node] Establishment of Huck and Jim as a mutually pledged pair bound by the knowlege of each other's past and reliance on each other's support on the river.
Jackson Island VIII–XV	Establishment of Huck and Jim as a mutually pledged pair bound by the knowlege of each other's past and reliance on each other's support on the river.	[Assoc. Link] We slept most all day, and started out at night, a little ways behind a monstrous long raft that was as long going by as a procession. (p. 106)	[Rafters' Node] Community of raftsmen, based on shared braggadocio and story-telling.

Node IDs and Chapters	Imagined Community	Link from	Links to
Rafters XVI	Community of raftsmen, based on shared braggadocio and story-telling.	[Assoc. Link] It was one of these long, slanting, two-mile crossings, so I was a good long time in getting over. I made a safe landing, and clum up the bank. (p. 131)	[Feud Node] Community of warring clans of Grangerfords and Shepherdsons.
Feud XVII–XVIII	Community of warring clans of Grangerfords and Shepherdsons.	[Assoc. Link] Then we hung up our signal lantern and judged that we was free and safe once more. I hadn't had a bit to eat since yesterday; so Jim he got out some corn-dodgers and buttermilk, and pork and cabbage, and greens—there ain't nothing in the world so good, when it's cooked right—and whilst I eat my supper we talked, and had a good time. (pp. 154–5)	[Frauds Node] Community defined in representative incidents of rural southern communal behaviour, including camp meeting, circus, the Duke and King's 'Shakespearean Revival' and 'The Royal Nonesuch', and Colonel Sherburn's public murder of Boggs and subsequent aborted lynching.
Frauds XIX–XXIII	Community defined in representative incidents of rural southern communal behaviour, including camp meeting, circus, the Duke and King's 'Shakespearean Revival' and 'The Royal Nonesuch', and Colonel Sherburn's public murder of Boggs and subsequent aborted lynching.	[Assoc. Link] Next day, towards night, we laid up under a little willow towhead out in the middle, where there was a village on each side of the river, and the duke and the king begun to lay out a plan for working them towns. (p. 203)	[Peter Wilks Node] Community defined in incidents of private behaviour, centred about the Peter Wilkes funeral.

Node IDs and Chapters	Imagined Community	Link from	Links to
Peter Wilks XXIV–XXX	Community defined in incidents of private behaviour, centred about the Peter Wilkes funeral.	[Assoc. Link] We dasn't stop again at any town, for days and days, kept right along down the river. We was down south in the warm weather, now, and a mighty long ways from home. (p. 265)	[Silas Phelps Node] Community of adolescents defined by Tom Sawyer in his ludicrous attempt to free the already freed Jim.
Silas Phelps XXXI–XLIII	Community of adolescents defined by Tom Sawyer in his ludicrous attempt to free the already freed Jim.	[Assoc. Link] But I reckon I got to light out for the territory ahead of the rest, because aunt Sally she's going to adopt me and sivilize me and I can't stand it. I been there before. (p. 362)	Mark Twain's unpublished sequel, 'Huck Finn and Tom Sawyer among the Indians'.

5

Out of Praxis: Three (Meta)Theories of Textuality

ALLEN RENEAR

INTRODUCTION

Many different crafts and disciplines concern themselves with texts, books, documents, and the like. Some, such as literary criticism and the philosophy of art, are recognized as intrinsically involved, at least in part, in developing a theoretical knowledge of textuality. Other more practical activities, such as publishing, office automation, textual editing, engineering text processing software, managing publishing systems, and developing textbases and digital libraries, while quite intimately involved with text, are typically not only not thought of as being sources of much theoretical insight into textuality, but may seem to have little theoretical content at all.

This essay focuses on one of these latter practical pursuits: computer text processing, and, more specifically, computer text encoding. I hope to show two things. First, that the particular community which has been designing and configuring computer text-processing and encoding systems has evolved a rich body of illuminating theory about the nature of text—theory that is useful not only to anyone who would create, manage, or use electronic texts, but also to anyone who would, more generally, understand electronic textuality from a theoretical perspective. Second, and more ambitiously, I hope to suggest that the significance of this body of theory and analysis extends well beyond the specific concerns of text processing and text encoding and contributes directly to our general understanding of the deepest issues of textuality and textual communication in general.

In fact, computer text processing and text encoding provide, I think, a much needed fresh perspective on textuality, a perspective which is deeply interdisciplinary, and which is largely driven by very practical problems and projects. For the most part however I will focus in what follows on understanding these theorizing practitioners in their own terms, so that when we do attempt to bring together all the strands of theorizing about texts and textuality we will understand our theories from the inside.[1]

Jerome McGann has said that between poets and information technologists (both, professions whose engagement with textuality seems to be pre-eminently practical), poets understand texts better. Perhaps, but let's see what the information technologists have to say.

TEXT ENCODING: SOME REPRESENTATIONAL STRATEGIES

In this section I describe the domain of text processing and text encoding, discuss several representational strategies involved in text processing, and then close with an extended treatment of a particular representational strategy—content-based encoding—that has been generally recognized as both the most successful strategy, and as the fundamentally 'correct' way of representing text. Then in the following section I take up the specific theoretical attitudes towards text that evolved as practitioners reflected on this strategy.

(It might be said that the 'representational strategies' discussed in this section are themselves *theories* of textuality (and in fact elsewhere we have called them 'models' of text) and that the so-called theories presented in the subsequent section are actually *metatheories*—second-order attitudes towards first-order theories. There is some plausibility in this view: the theories of the next section—Realism, Pluralism, and Antirealism—do seem to be theories about theories. But for now I sidestep these questions and treat the representational strategies of the current section as pre-theoretical practices and the three 'theories' of the next section as increasingly metatheoretical attitudes towards textuality.)

The Domain of Text Processing and Text Encoding

Computer text encoding may be characterized simply, although with no pretensions to theoretical perspicuity (we cannot take up all the hard problems of representation at once), as the representation of textual information on the computer. The purpose of this representation is to facilitate the use of computer hardware and software in creating and processing text, which is typically in the form of documents such as letters, reports, scientific papers, novels, etc. Some familiar examples of 'processing' include editing (correcting and revising), formatting, printing, typesetting, indexing, retrieval, analysis, and so on.

The process of computer text encoding (still speaking informally) consists of storing, in the computer's memory, codes that represent the linguistic content (typically alphabetic characters and punctuation) and additional information related to this content, such as intended or observed formatting or layout effects and explicit identification of sections of text as being footnotes, titles, paragraphs, etc. A text-encoding *system* is the system of codes which effect such a representation.

The very earliest text-encoding systems simply composed lines of alphabetic characters, but by the 1960s, as text-encoding systems became widely used commercially to support publishing and computer typesetting, techniques for controlling traditional formatting and page layout devices evolved. With the early *batch* systems, a compositor would typically prepare a data file consisting of 'markup' (computer codes specifying formatting information) and 'content' (codes specifying the linguistic items of the text, such as alphabetic characters and punctuation). This file would then be processed by formatting software, creating another data file of formatted text and printer codes which would then be transferred to a printer or typesetting machine to produce printed pages of text. Although markup codes originally only indicated formatting procedures, the preferred principled approach would later be to use markup to identify the type of textual element (e.g. title, chapter, paragraph, verse, extract, equation, proof, etc.) and then indicate formatting, or other processing, indirectly.

In the 1980s *interactive* word-processing systems came to dominate text processing. Although these systems were typically and misleadingly referred to as WYSIWYG systems ('what you see is what you get'), the essential characteristic of interactive systems was that the editing software (used to create and modify the text) also immediately and automatically formatted the text more or less as it would be arranged when printed. Although these systems also depended on encoding systems (that is, on markup), the computer codes in interactive systems were typically hidden from users even during composition. In interactive systems the user had neither a sense of specifying markup codes nor saw any explicit indications that they had created such codes. Typically the user would indirectly, and unknowingly (by key stroke, menu selection, or other devices), cause codes to be covertly inserted into the data file; these codes were then immediately acted upon by the software and the text was immediately formatted into visible pages and rendered with traditional layout (with leading, font changes, indentations, and so on).

Naïve users of interactive systems were quick to assume that since they did not keyboard any markup codes, and did not see any markup codes, that therefore, unlike previous text-processing systems, there were not any codes involved in the process at all—that they were somehow being given direct and 'transparent' access to 'the text itself'. This, of course, was not true. Whether (directly) visible or not there was still a complex system of encoding that represented the features of the text and supported both display and editing. Like the Molière character who did not know she was speaking 'prose', all users of computer text processors are unavoidably involved in computer text encoding, whether they are aware of it or not.

Most text processing involved creating and maintaining new texts, such as office documents, technical manuals, etc. In such cases an individual or corporate author definitively determines the document's content and structure. But almost from the very beginning of modern computing text encoding has also been used to represent already existing texts, such as literary works. Here transcribers attempt to accurately represent the content or structure of a text that already exists, typically without access to an author who could adjudicate uncertainties about structure or content. Both the complexity of literary encoding, and its descriptive, rather than performative, nature, stimulated theoretical reflections of text encoding.

Orthographic Strategies

Perhaps the simplest and most natural representational strategy treats text as a sequence of linguistic entities (such as the alphabetic characters of Western writing systems), and a few closely related paralinguistic items that are part of the writing system narrowly construed, such as punctuation marks, blanks, and horizontal and vertical white space.

Such an encoding system does in fact identify critical linguistic elements and make them available for processing. But as a general purpose encoding system it is very impoverished. There is no way to indicate or generate the rich array of layout and graphic devices that are critical aspects of textual communication, and no way to explicitly represent the structure of editorial elements, such as titles, chapters, verses, quotations, addresses, signatures, enclosures, etc. Orthographic representations not only can neither record nor produce (upon processing) the layout devices that are part of robust textual encounters, but they do not represent the critical structural features (a text's organization into, e.g. chapters, sections, verses, etc.) which are made evident by page layout devices and which are critical not only for taking advantage of the computer for advanced processing (analysis, retrieval, special views, and navigation, etc.), but even for understanding the text.

This representational strategy is interesting to us for several reasons. First, it is plausibly the earliest and simplest sort of computer text encoding, and as such seems to initiate, with its inadequacies, the dialectic of progressively more and more adequate, and more theoretically significant, representational strategies.

Second, a preference for orthographic representation continues to represent a perennial reactionary response to the sophisticated text-encoding systems described below. At issue here is not the creation of new texts, but cases where one is concerned with the representation of already existing texts, over which one has no (individual or corporate) authorial authority, as is the case for instance where the representation of already existing literary works is concerned. The reaction sees most text encoding as both dangerously interpretative and avoidable, with orthographic representation possibly presenting the 'text itself', unburdened by the interpretations of the transcriber. Populist examples abound, and are typically motivated by the belief that more elaborate encoding is unnecessary. More subtle versions of this reaction, motivated by the view that text encoding is unnecessarily interpretative, are arguably latent in some of the criticisms of the Text Encoding Initiative.[2]

The questions raised here are: (1) whether an orthographic representation is sufficiently functional to be a practical representation strategy, (2) whether orthographic representations can be plausibly said to represent 'the text', and (3) whether orthographic representation avoids interpretation. In fact, practitioners found that orthographic representations are far too thin to support the functionality we expect from text-processing systems; theorists doubt that orthographic representations can adequately represent 'the text'—or even what McGann calls the 'linguistic codes' of a text;[3] and, finally, it is doubtful in any case if interpretation can be avoided.[4] Purely orthographic strategies for representing texts are now rarely used.[5]

Pictorial Strategies

Pictorial representations, such as bitmaps or other digital images, are a natural representational strategy and typically, at some point, a part of every text-processing system. Such representations resolve an image of a document into an array of points, black and white, shaded, or coloured. To some, pictorial strategies seem to be a case where representation approaches perfection, allowing the full renditional detail of a particular document to be directly conveyed, in full detail and without any interpretative transformations.

However, pictorial representations obviously cannot be easily 'word processed', reformatted, searched for words or phrases, indexed, etc. In a sense they are arguably not *textual* at all: as far as the computer tools are concerned there are no accessible words, letters, punctuation marks, chapters, founts, or anything else of that sort present in the representation. So although generating such pictorial representations is useful for special purposes, this approach has almost nothing to recommend it as a practical representation of text.

(As with orthographic representations, we note that pictorial representations continue to have a natural role in the ecology of computer text processing, even when the dominant representation strategy is otherwise. When images are rendered on computer monitors, or laser printer drums they are bitmaps, pictorial representations rendered by resolving text and layout into pixel values.)

Format-Based Strategies

From the 1950s to the late 1970s, most text-processing systems used format-based representations of documents as their key representational strategy. In these systems a data file would be prepared and then processed into formatted page images. This data file typically consisted of (1) the linguistic character content (e.g. the letters of the alphabet, punctuation marks, digits, and symbols) of the text to be rendered and (2) interspersed codes indicating formatting information about that content. For instance, a code might be mnemonic expressions such as '.skip 3;' for 'skip three lines' or '.indent 5;' for indent five columns. Delimiters such as the indicated use of '.' and ';' would allow the computer to distinguish computer markup from text content.

Content-Based Strategies

Content-based representation strategies evolved naturally out of format-based strategies and reflected software engineering's growing ideology of structured design, modularity, and 'indirection'.

In the normal course of things during format-based encoding certain patterns of formatting codes will obviously tend to repeat. Prose extracts for instance will typically be preceded by whatever specific formatting commands secure the required formatting, for instance: '.skip 2;. indent 5 -5;.singlespace;.fountsize 9;'. Software designers could consequently simplify the creation and maintenance of the data file by allowing abbreviations for regularly occurring sequences of formatting codes. The abbreviations would then be automatically expanded into their corresponding formatting codes during computer processing. This had many advantages, but most obviously it not only simplified data entry but also made it easier to maintain and revise formatting, since abbreviation expansions were stored in a single revisable, and even replaceable, style sheet.

Although in a few instances these abbreviating codes were identified closely with a particular set of formatting commands and given arbitrary names such as '.format17;', in the thoughtful systematic use of such codes there was a natural tendency to identify a code not with its formatting effects, which could vary, but rather with a type of textual entity which was identified at the editorial, not typographical, level. This approach was supported by the use of mnemonics which suggested the specific identity of the element. For instance, '.prose extract;' would be used exclusively to identify portions of text as a prose extract and would only be indirectly associated with its typical formatting effects. This separation of format and content would turn out to be nearly revolutionary in its practical benefits.

Taxonomies of markup were developed in order to explain and theorize these practices. Codes such as '.prose extract;' were called *descriptive markup*, because they described or classified an interval of text. Commands such as '.skip 2;' were classified as *procedural markup*, because they specified procedures (typically formatting) that were to be followed by a formatter or other software program. Layout devices such as white space, leading, fount changes, etc. were also, in some systems, considered markup: *presentational markup*.[6]

The interplay between these three categories of markup during a typical textual encounter (e.g. formatting) both reveals that they mark salient aspects of text processing and suggests a certain priority for descriptive markup. *Descriptive markup*, which marks relatively stable and permanent (perhaps we could say intrinsic) features of the document, is mapped to selected *procedural markup*, which varies with the circumstances (different software, printer, occasion of printing, etc.) in order to produce, through the processing of that *procedural markup*, the *presentational markup* (fount shifts, white space, composed lines, etc.) desired for that particular instance of formatting. But, conversely, *presentational markup*, during a reading encounter, provides the visual cues that support a rapid grasp of text structure, allowing the text to be comprehended.

Responding primarily to this new appreciation of the significance of descriptive markup and the textual features or 'objects' that markup was used to identify, a standardization effort began in the early 1980s and eventually resulted in an international standard for defining descriptive markup systems: ISO8879: *Information Processing—Text and Office Systems —Standard Generalized Markup Language (SGML)*. SGML specifies a machine-readable format for defining markup tags that identify text objects ('elements' in SGML terminology), and for specifying what objects are allowed in a document and what the syntax of each object is—that is, what structural arrangements of objects are allowed or required. SGML is not itself a particular set of markup tags for specific textual objects, but rather it is a *meta-grammar* for defining sets of markup tags. The technique used by SGML for specifying these syntactical constraints is similar to the production rule meta-grammar developed by Noam Chomsky to describe natural languages.

SGML is used to define element grammars for classes ('Types') of documents. For example, an SGML 'Document Type Definition' for the document type *Verse* might define a syntactically valid poem (of a particular kind) as consisting of exactly one title followed by exactly one body; a body as consisting of at least one stanza, a stanza as consisting of at least one line, and a line as consisting of exactly two half lines. Different document types (e.g. Report, Memorandum, Letter, Contract, Task Order, etc.) would have different elements and syntax rules. The formal nature of definitions of this sort has been extensively explored in linguistics and mathematics.

This approach to text encoding and text processing turned out to have many practical advantages. In the 1970s several different groups of software designers and computer scientists reflected on these advantages and came independently to the conclusion that the best way to design efficient and functional text-processing systems was to base them on the view that there are certain features of texts—such as titles, chapters, paragraphs, lists, and so on—which are fundamental and salient, and that all processing of texts (such as authoring, editing, formatting, browsing, and analysis) should be implemented indirectly through the identification and processing of these features rather than by inserting formatting codes, or other processing codes, directly into computer files. These features have been called 'content objects' and this approach to text processing could be called 'content-based text processing'.[7]

Although content-based representations were developed in the 1970s and were recognized as superior to format-based representations, when the first interactive systems were released in the early 1980s they continued to use format-based representations, although, of course, the codes themselves were hidden from the user. Proponents of content-based systems argued that the important thing was being content-based, and that content-based systems could be (although at that time they were not) just as interactive as format-based systems. Partisans of format-based interactive systems argued that their systems had 'no codes at all' *a fortiori* no format codes. Efforts to elucidate the situation reminded theorists of just how elusive the problems of representation, textual identity, and the phenomenology of textual production and consumption are. In the end, although individual users could claim that format-based interactive systems were adequate for their purposes, publishers and managers of large documentation systems remained with content-based systems, eventually taking advantage of new systems that were both content-based and interactive.

Summary of the Advantages of Content-Based Text Processing

Because it is content-based text processing's extraordinary success at securing diverse practical advantages that provides the most compelling evidence for its implicit view of textuality (and recommends content-based representational strategies over the alternatives), it is useful to summarize these advantages in order to get a sense of their range and importance.[8]

First, from the point of view of an author, compositor, or transcriber, the process of *creating* a text, or a representation of a text, is substantially simplified and enhanced by content-based text processing; in particular:

Composition is simplified. With content-based text processing, formatting considerations make no claims on the attention of the author or transcriber during composition: rather than needing to remember both (1) the required style conventions relevant to the text being produced and (2) the formatting commands used by the software in order to format the text according to those conventions, an author or editor instead simply identifies each text element, perhaps by choosing a name from a menu, and the appropriate formatting takes place automatically. In the jargon of software engineering, content objects let the author or transcriber deal with the document at the 'level of abstraction' appropriate to their roles: identifying a text object as a quotation, paragraph, or verse line is an authorial task, while making decisions to italicize or centre a title is the task of a typesetter or designer.

Writing tools are supported. Content objects support 'structure-oriented editors' and other composition tools. These are software tools that 'know' about the syntax of the special editorial objects that are found in the author's document and so can intelligently support the author in entering, editing, and manipulating these objects. For instance, they will allow an author to perform operations such as moves and deletes in terms of these natural meaningful parts (words, sentences, paragraphs, footnotes, sections, etc.) rather than relying on the mediation of accidents: line displacements, numbers, or arbitrarily marked regions. Again, this kind of support allows the author to address the document in terms appropriate to the authorial role—that is, in terms of content and structure.

Alternative document views and links are facilitated. A familiar example is outlining software that takes advantage of the identification of the hierarchy of the major editorial content objects in a document. A more sophisticated and selective display of portions of documents can be effected using discipline-specific content objects in the document—for instance, one could specify a view that contained only the verse quotations or only the dialogue lines spoken by a single character in a script.

A very wide range of advantages are also provided to publishers, editors, and typesetters:

Formatting can be generically specified and modified. As we have seen, formatting of all instances of content objects can be easily and systematically controlled from one location, the rules file for object types, without altering the text file itself at all.

Apparatus construction can be automated. Apparatus such as indices and appendices can be much more fine-grained and their creation can be automated. For instance, if stanzas and verse lines are explicitly identified, the creation of an index of first lines of stanzas (or second lines or last lines) can be automated.

Output device support is enhanced. When internal coding is based on logical role rather than appearance, output device specific support for printers, typesetters, video display terminals, and other output devices is maintained separately, both logically and physically, from the data with the convenient result that the data files themselves are *output device independent* while their processing is efficiently *output device sensitive.*

Portability is maximized. Files that identify content objects are much easier to transfer to other text-processing systems or computers. They are relatively system- and application-independent.

Finally, the various sorts of advanced navigation and retrieval tools that it has always been imagined would be a part of computer-supported research and writing are facilitated by content-based encoding:

Information retrieval is supported. The content objects model treats documents and related files as a database of text elements that can be systematically manipulated. Using the text elements as if they were fields can support a variety of finding aids and even allow one to construct queries that locate very specific texts using discipline-specific features: for instance, one could select definitions of 'text' which contain the word 'intention' in one *clause* of the *definiens.*

Intelligent navigation and specialized views are supported. The content object model facilitates the generation of specialized discipline-specific views and supports advanced navigation strategies and intelligent hypertext.

Analytical procedures are supported. Similarly, much automated analysis (stylometrics, content analysis, statistical studies, etc.) is not possible unless features such as sentences, paragraphs, stanzas, dialogue lines, stage directions, and so on have been explicitly identified in a manner that is reliably tractable to machine processing.

Not only did content-based text encoding seem to have all these advantages, but, most importantly, it seems that *only* content-based encoding could deliver this functionality.

THREE THEORIES OF TEXTUALITY

With the emergence in the early 1980s of content-based text processing as the dominant principled approach to text processing and text encoding came a natural interest in articulating theoretical accounts of text that would explain and predict experience, regulate practice, and provide a rationale for changes in system or project design strategies. Idealizing somewhat, it might be said that this theorizing about text fell into the following three historical phases, which I will call Platonism, Pluralism, and Antirealism. These phases recapitulate a familiar dialectic of epistemological and metaphysical attitudes.

Platonism

The Platonistic view is that texts simply *are* hierarchical structures of certain sorts of objects—and, specifically, of *editorial* objects such as chapters, titles, paragraphs, stanzas, and the like. To the extent that this view is arguably implicit in the earliest efforts to promote the use of descriptive markup in the design of text-processing systems, we may say that Platonism, as a theory of textuality, was developed by a community consisting largely of publishers and editors managing publishing projects, software engineers designing text-processing and typesetting systems, and the systems analysts and programmers who were configuring and managing these systems.

Characteristic sorts of texts for this community are office documents, technical documentation for industry, government documents, and commercial publishing. The content and structure of such documents are for the most part authoritatively determined by the individuals or organizations creating and maintaining them—the authoritative text was under the control of its individual or corporate author. For this group of practitioners text encoding was *performative* and expressed the constitutive intentions of the persons, authors and editors, who in creating and maintaining documents determined their structure and content with complete and definitive clarity and authority. For the most part the authoritative version of a document was the electronic version; paper print-outs, books, and manuals being relatively ephemeral derived products.

In these circumstances texts were conceptualized as a single logical hierarchy of recognizably 'editorial' elements (e.g. chapters, sections, paragraphs, extracts, stanzas, equations, titles, etc.). Different genres might have different editorial objects—letters would have one set, memoranda another, technical reports a third—but each document instance would have a single 'logical' hierarchical structure which would consist of these genre-based editorial elements arranged in a combination that conformed to the syntactical rules of the genre. The SGML standard articulates and codifies this approach to textuality.

Of course the early arguments for the content-object approach to text processing were not intended to make a theoretical point about 'what texts really are'. They were intended rather to help engineers, systems analysts, editors, and others promote a particular approach to system design and encoding practice as being more efficient and functional than the competing alternatives. Nevertheless it turned out to be natural for the practical persons engaged in this dialogue to go on to claim that the deprecated alternative representational practices were inefficient and without functionality precisely because they were based on a misunderstanding of the nature of text, a false understanding that is, of *what text really is*.

The issue was eventually put in baldly ontological terms—'What is Text, Really?' and given an equally ontological answer: 'text is an ordered hierarchy of content objects', an 'OHCO'.[9] The thesis is that in some relevant sense of 'book', 'text', or 'document' (perhaps *qua intellectual objects*) these things simply *are* ordered hierarchies of content objects. A book on this account, simply *is* a sequence of chapters, each of which is a sequence of major sections, each of which in turn is a sequence of subsections, and so on; then within the lowest level subsections are objects like paragraphs, sentences, prose quotations, verse quotations, equations, proofs, theorems, and the like. This structure is *hierarchical* because these objects 'nest' inside one another without overlaps. It is *ordered* because there is a linear ordering of objects. And they are *content objects* because they structure the text into elements which are essentially connected with textual meaning and communicative intention.

Once the theoretical thesis was articulated, corroborating arguments of various kinds were adduced. In the conversations and writings of the text-encoding community in the 1980s and early 1990s I have observed at least these five broad categories of arguments to the conclusion that text is an ordered hierarchy of content objects:

Pragmatic/Scientific. These arguments observe that there are many practical advantages (as detailed in the preceding section) to modelling a text as an OHCO rather than using one of the alternative representational strategies; they then go on to claim that the comparative efficiency and functionality of treating texts *as if* they were OHCOs is best explained by the hypothesis that texts *are* OHCOs.

Empirical/Ontological. These arguments note that content objects and their relations figure prominently in our talk about texts, and specifically in our descriptions, explanations, theories, hypotheses, and generalizations about texts. For instance, our theories and conjectures about literature make use of terms for chapters, titles, sections, paragraphs, sentences, footnotes, stanzas, lines, acts, scenes, speeches, etc. Such things, then, would appear to be the stuff of which literature is made; they are in any case, as values of bound variables, the apparent ontological commitments of our theories about text.

Metaphysical/Essentialist. If a layout feature 'of a text' (such as leading or typeface) changes, we feel that the 'text itself' still remains essentially the same, but if the number or structure of the text's content objects changes, then we are no longer inclined to consider it 'the same text'.

Productive power. Here one finds a special, if obscure, significance in the fact that an OHCO representation of a text can mechanically generate other competing representations (e.g. an OHCO representation can be formatted into a bitmap image, plain orthographic text, or format-based representations) but none of these other representations can mechanically generate a corresponding OHCO representation.

Conceptual priority. Understanding and creating a text (i.e. reading and writing) appear to require grasping the OHCO structure of a text, but do not essentially involve grasping any other structure—and therefore it is the OHCO structure, but no other structure, that is essential to textuality.

If the foregoing arguments are good ones, then the thesis that *text is an ordered hierarchy of content objects*[10]

(1) explains the success of certain representational strategies;
(2) is logically implied by many important theories about text;
(3) matches our intuitions about what is essential and what accidental about textual identity;
(4) is richer in relevant content than competing models; and
(5) matches our intuitions about what is essential of textual production and consumption.[11]

Pluralism

The second theoretical approach to textuality, *Pluralism*, emerges in the mid- to late 1980s in a community quite different from the one responsible for Platonism. The community that developed Pluralism as an approach consisted of literary scholars and humanities computing specialists, rather than engineers and publishers. These scholars were not primarily concerned to create, print, and manage *new* texts (such as aircraft manuals and office memoranda), over which they had definitive performative authority as authors, but rather to represent certain culturally significant existing texts in order to create digital libraries, support analysis, facilitate the publishing of critical editions, etc. Much of this community was involved in developing and testing an SGML application, known as the Text Encoding Initiative (TEI), which was a markup system specifically intended for representing already existing literary texts. But as these literary researchers began using SGML in its TEI form to represent texts, the implicit assumption in SGML that every document could be represented as a single hierarchical structure, with a grammar of elements determined by its genre, quickly created real practical and theoretical problems.[12] The SGML community of editors and text-processing system designers had assumed that the 'logical' structure of a text could always be represented as a single hierarchy of non-overlapping editorial objects. But encoders transcribing literary texts identified many overlapping objects: a verse drama, for instance, contains dialogue lines, metrical lines, and sentences, but sentences and metrical lines obviously can overlap (enjambment); similarly, when a character finishes another character's sentence or metrical line, dialogue lines can overlap with sentences and metrical lines.

The problem seems rooted in the fact that SGML assumes that it is the hierarchy of editorial objects, as determined by genre or document type, which is constitutive of a text's logical structure. This is what determines what objects (elements) and grammatical arrangements are available to the text (SGML defines the central notion of *Document Type* thus: 'A class of documents having similar characteristics; for example, journal article, technical manual, or memo', ISO8879 4.102).

TEI researchers, however, found that there seemed to be many hierarchies that had equal claim to be 'logical', and thus constitutive. Where the original OHCO Platonists, and the designers of SGML, took the editorial hierarchy of *genre* or *document type* to be the original principle of decomposition, the literary scholars of the TEI took the disciplinary and methodological perspective being deployed as determining encoded structure. In a sense a play might seem to be, fundamentally, a hierarchy of acts, scenes, and speeches; but it also consists of a linguistic hierarchy of phrases and sentences, a prosodic hierarchy of stanzas, metrical lines, and feet, and other hierarchies as well—none of which could be assumed to be capable of assimilation into a single hierarchy of non-overlapping objects.

Literary encoders came to see texts not as single ordered hierarchies, but as *systems* of ordered hierarchies. Each hierarchy corresponds to an *aspect* of the text as revealed by what might be called an 'analytic perspective'—roughly, a natural family of methodology, theory, and analytical practice. Each analytical perspective on a text—e.g. prosodic, linguistic, dramatic—does seem typically to determine a hierarchy of elements. This principle seems in turn to reflect actual text-encoding practices in the literary and linguistic text-encoding communities: usually when text encoders find overlapping objects they assume that they pertain to different aspects of the text.

But does every perspective really determine a hierarchy of non-overlapping content objects? Arguably not: discussions of many sorts about texts are filled with characterizations, descriptions, and hypotheses that explicitly relate text objects from different perspectives—chapters and themes, speaker and metre, narrative and paragraphing. Moreover there are even technical terms, such as 'enjambment' and 'caesura', that specifically refer to relationships between objects from overlapping families. Because a technical vocabulary can be plausibly considered a sign of an analytical perspective, the existence of this terminology suggests that some analytical perspectives contain overlapping objects.

One might attempt to accommodate this result by allowing that analytic perspectives may have objects that sometimes have overlapping instances, but maintaining that whenever this is the case the analytic perspective in question can be decomposed into more basic component analytic perspectives, none of which contains both offending objects. The logic-chopping complexity of such manoeuvres is suspicious, however, and the objective —retaining some sort of hierarchical structure to text—seems excessively formalist. But more decisively, as Huitfeldt has pointed out, not only is there no *a priori* assurance that decomposition into sub-perspectives will separate overlapping objects, but there is a well-populated class of counterexamples: possible element tokens in some perspectives clearly overlap with other element tokens *of the same type*. Examples of this are strikeouts, versions, and phrases (in textual criticism), narrative objects in narratology, hypertext anchors and targets, and many others. Decomposition will not save us here.

Whatever may be said for hierarchy as a tendency, it does not seem to be, even in its perspective-contingent form, an *essential* aspect of textual structure. A defensible Pluralism, it would seem, can perhaps treat texts as systems of structures of objects, each structure corresponding to an analytic perspective, but it should not require that these structures be hierarchical.

Antirealism

Antirealism, the third and final theoretical phase, emerged among the most theoretically inclined members of the scholarly text-encoding community and seems to respond to the 'contradictions' of Pluralism much as Pluralism responded to the failures of Platonism.

Pluralism explicitly recognized the critical role that disciplinary methodologies, theories, and analytic practices play in text encoding. And consequently Pluralism acknowledges that what structure is actually articulated in an encoded text is at least as much the result of contingent facts about human interests, the current state of methodological practice, and specific judgements of the historically and theoretically situated encoder, as it is a function of an independently existing text. To an unabashed Pluralistic *realist* like myself there are no contradictions here, and no dialectical momentum: texts are complicated; they have many different aspects; what we find depends in part on how we search; encoding is a historically situated human activity. No profound epistemological insights here, and no reason to give up the common-sense view that texts do have an objective structure independent of our methods and theories about them.

But others have responded differently. Pluralism's foregrounding of methodological practice and historical contingency leads some theorists to see the contingent method-driven nature of text encoding as revealing, or confirming, the radically constitutive role of all textual representation, justifying scepticism about the very notion of a text which exists independently of our theories and practices.

This view, although not rare in conversation among encoders, has only recently been explicitly articulated in print. Some examples from the writing of Claus Huitfeldt and Alois Pichler:

I have come to think that these questions [e.g. What is a text?] do not represent a fruitful first approach to our theme . . . The answer to the question what is a text depends on the context, methods, and purpose of our investigations.[13]

'devising a representational system that does not impose but only maps linguistic structures' (Coulmas 1989) is impossible.[14]

Machine-readable texts make it . . . clear to us what texts are and what text editing means: Texts are not objectively existing entities which just need to be discovered and presented, but entities which have to be constructed.[15]

Pluralistic *realism* allows many perspectives on a text, but assumes that texts do have structures independently of our interests, histories, theories, and practices. The *Antirealist* trend in text encoding, which is consistent with post-structuralist epistemologies, rejects this view, seeing texts as in some sense the product of the theories and analytical tools we deploy when we transcribe, edit, analyse, or encode them.

What specifically are the positive arguments in favour of the Antirealist view of texts? Huitfeldt and Pichler are typical in emphasizing two particular claims about text which they seem to believe imply Antirealism. The first claim is that our understanding (representation, encoding, analysis, transcription, etc.) of a text is fundamentally interpretational:[16]

there are no facts about a text which are objective in the sense of not being interpretational.[17]

The second is that there are many diverse methodological perspectives on a text:

a text may have many different kinds of structure (physical, compositional, narrative, grammatical).[18]

But exactly what these claims amount to, whether and in what sense they are true, and how and whether Antirealism follows from them are all far from clear.

The Antirealism presented above is *ontological*, a view of the nature of text, a general account of *what text is*. But Pichler is typical of ontological Antirealists in also endorsing a companion *semantic* Antirealism, a view about the nature of our knowledge of texts and our representations of text:

the essential question is not about a true representation, but: Whom do we want to serve with our transcriptions? Philosophers? Grammarians? Or graphologists? What is 'correct' will depend on the answer to this question. And what we are going to represent, and how, is determined by our research interests . . . and not by a text which exists independently and which we are going to depict.[19]

Our aim in transcription is not to represent as correctly as possible the originals, but rather to prepare from the original text another text so as to serve as accurately as possible certain interests in the text.[20]

Semantic Antirealism thus seems to follow from ontological Antirealism: if there are no objectively existing text structures, then transcriptions cannot be commended as 'true' in virtue of correctly representing those structures. (Pichler also offers an independent argument for semantic Antirealism in the form of a competing analysis of the objective of transcription: 'Our aim in transcription is . . . to prepare from the original text another text so as to serve as accurately as possible certain interests in the text.'[21])

Antirealism in text encoding certainly resonates with the contemporary mood of poststructuralist and postmodernist theory, and it is perhaps that current *episteme*, as much as any manifest evidence, which is eliciting from practice this third phase of theory (or metatheory?). But however up-to-date this view is, and however nicely it seems to continue the dialectical momentum that began with Platonism and continued through various troubled Pluralisms, we should still ask if there is any positive merit to the argument for Antirealism, semantic or ontological, with respect to texts. I have argued elsewhere that Pluralistic realism is a stable defensible view of textuality, and that we have not yet been given good reasons to abandon it.[22]

CONCLUSION

Poets undoubtedly do know much about texts and textuality, but I hope I have shown that information technologists, working in practice-grounded interdisciplinary areas such as text encoding, have also provided, and will continue to provide, many valuable insights. This is a good thing—for I would say that despite the considerable work that has already taken place, we seem still to be at the very beginning of a theoretical understanding of textual communication.

NOTES

This essay draws very heavily on ideas and analyses developed collaboratively over the last ten years with James Coombs, Steve DeRose, Elli Mylonas, and David Durand. In addition, it also owes much to conversations with Claus Huitfeldt, Michael Sperberg-McQueen, Alois Pichler, Lou Burnard, and Julia Flanders. A more technical philosophical discussion of some of these topics, and a critique of the arguments for Antirealism, is contained in Allen Renear, 'Theory and Metatheory in the Development of Text Encoding', a target paper submitted for the electronic issue of *The Monist*; a summary of that paper and the ensuing electronic discussion is contained in Michael Biggs and Claus Huitfeldt, 'Discussion of "Theory and Metatheory in the Development of Text Encoding"' (forthcoming). As always, I must thank the Text Encoding Initiative and its sponsors, funders, and participants, for creating a truly extraordinary environment for thinking about texts and textuality.

1. Of course that is not to say that all these bodies of discourse and practice intend the same thing by 'text', or attempt to accompish the same objectives in theorizing—we cannot assume at the outset that the 'text' of the software engineer, or publisher, is the same as the 'text' of the literary theorist. After all, there is not even a univocal sense of 'text' within literary studies: Barthes's 'text' can hardly be Tanselle's 'text'. Not that all these uses of 'text', by theorists, bibliographers, editors, engineers, and programmers, are merely distant homonyms (like 'bank' the financial institution and 'bank' the slope of a river)—they all are efforts to understand textual communication. However, I think that taxonomies of sense are best deferred until after we have a better understanding of actual theory and practice.

2. Paul Fortier and the TEI Literature Working Group, 'The TEI Guidelines (version 1.1 10/90): A Critique' (1995). Available from the TEI listserv server, TEI-L, as document AI3W5 DOC. These issues are also periodically taken up on the HUMANIST listserv discussion group and was the topic of a panel, chaired by Richard Giordano, at the joint meeting of the Association for Literary and Linguistic Computing and the Association for Computing in the Humanities, Bergen, 1996.

3. Jerome McGann, *The Textual Condition* (Princeton: Princeton University Press, 1991), p. 87.

4. Because markup is unavoidable, and 'Markup reflects a theory of a text' (C. Michael Sperberg-McQueen, 'Text in the Electronic Age: Textual Study and Text Encoding, with Examples from Medieval Texts', *Literary and Linguistic Computing*, 6: 1 (1991) 34–46); an important paper in text-encoding theory.

5. But even if orthographic representations by themselves are inadequate, they are important for two reasons: first, because they are an essential part of almost all text-encoding systems, and second because they also raise the issues, even at the level of character and alphabet, of textual identity. Most text representation strategies (pictorial representation strategies, discussed below, are the exception), regardless of how minimalist or ambitious they are, must somehow represent the linguistic atoms of the text, such as alphabet characters.

     This, surprisingly, for such an apparently simple project, immediately raises its own unique set of illuminating problems and issues. For example, suppose we decided to limit ourselves to a 'literal transcription of the linguistic text of a physical document'—no bibliographic codes, no layout features, no interpretive or analytic encoding (see Allen Renear, 'Theory and Practice: The Textbase Methodology of the Brown Women Writers Project', *SCMLA, The Journal of the South Central Division of the Modern Language Association*, 11: 3 (1994), 113). We record the exact orthography of the given document, including compositor's errors, diacritical marks, capitalization, abbreviation, etc. But as we are only transcribing the linguistic codes, we ignore layout and graphic devices (as well as incidental anomalies such as worm holes and stains). We might also ignore typographic ligatures, reasoning that they are merely ornamental 'renditional variants' of the linguistic text, chosen according to the whim and capabilities of the individual typesetter. But what of, say, the Œ and Æ digraphs? These are ligatures, typographically, but they also correspond directly to a phonemic entity, a diphthong—so perhaps they are not merely a typographic variant, but a linguistic entity as well? Other such examples are easily found.

6. This taxonomy is from a more comprehensive theory developed by James Coombs which is in turn an extension and generalization of Charles Goldfarb's earlier division of text-processing markup into procedural and descriptive. (For references, see the Bibliography.)

7. Steven J. DeRose, David Durand, Elli Mylonas, and Allen H. Renear, 'What is Text, Really?', *Journal of Computing in Higher Education*, 1: 2 (1990), 3–26.

8. This section is based on the analysis in DeRose *et al.*, 'What is Text, Really?', which in turn is based on James S. Coombs, Allen H. Renear, and Steven J. DeRose, 'Markup Systems and the Future of Scholarly Text Processing', *Communications of the Association for Computing Machinery*, 30: 11 (1987), 933–47.

9. DeRose *et al.*, 'What is Text, Really?'.

10. Earlier versions of this account of the arguments for OHCO Platonism were first presented in Allen Renear, David Durand, and Elli Mylonas, 'Refining our Notion of What Text Really Is', in Nancy Ide and Susan Hockey (eds.), *Research in Humanities Computing*, 4 (Oxford: Clarendon Press, 1996), pp. 263–80.

11. To be sure, nothing about this view is uniquely motivated by text encoding; versions which are entirely independent of any interest in computing

applications can be discerned in the rhetoric of the 'parts of a book' which has been prevalent in style manuals and bibliography handbooks for some time (see Allen Renear, 'Representing Text on the Computer: Lessons for and from Philosophy', *Bulletin of the John Rylands University Library of Manchester*, 74 (1992), 221–48).

12. David T. Barnard, Ron Hayter, Maria Karababa, George Logan, and John McFadden, 'SGML-Based Markup for Literary Texts: Two Problems and Some Solutions', *Computers and the Humanities*, 22 (1988), 265–76.

13. Claus Huitfeldt, 'Multi-Dimensional Texts in a One-Dimensional Medium', *Computers and the Humanities*, 28 (1994), 235. Huitfeldt is director of the Norwegian Wittgenstein Archives at the University of Bergen and is a major figure in the development of text-encoding system; both he and Alois Pichler, a researcher at the Archives, are making substantial contributions to the theory of text encoding.

14. Ibid., p. 236.

15. Alois Pichler, 'Advantages of a Machine-Readable Version of Wittgenstein's Nachlass', in K. Johannessen and T. Nordenstam (eds.), *Culture and Value: Philosophy and the Cultural Sciences* (Austrian Ludwig Wittgenstein Society, 1995), p. 774.

16. Although Huitfeldt presents these claims as criticisms of the view implicit in views of SGML and TEI text encoders, in fact they have also been articulated explicitly from within the mainstream TEI community (e.g. by C. Michael Sperberg-McQueen) and are endorsed by many who would not consider themselves Antirealists (see Sperberg-McQueen, 'Text in the Electronic Age').

17. Huitfeldt, 'Multi-Dimensional Texts', p. 237.

18. Ibid.

19. Alois Pichler, 'Transcriptions, Texts, and Interpretations', in Johannessen and Nordenstam (eds.), *Culture and Value*, p. 690.

20. Ibid., p. 691.

21. Ibid.

22. I criticize the arguments for Antirealism in a target paper, 'Theory and Metatheory in the Development of Text Encoding', for electronic discussion conducted by *The Monist*. An edited version of the paper and discussion has been prepared by Michael Biggs and Claus Huitfeldt (forthcoming).

6
The Body Encoded: Questions of Gender and the Electronic Text

JULIA FLANDERS

The etymological meaning of the word 'virtual' implies the possession of a power or virtue without formal entitlement: one is virtually king by exercising a royal power without occupying the throne. This meaning has nearly been lost as 'virtually' has slid, with 'practically', towards the position of 'almost'; by contrast, the original meaning emphasized not the missing title but the power that was effectually present. The notion of the virtual which the electronic world has brought to popularity thus hovers in an odd state: 'virtual reality' could mean 'not-quite-reality' or 'reality in every important respect'. In fact the salient experience of virtuality is imagined as one of lack; the virtual, electronic world is set over against the real world as an inadequate, sketchy version of it, rather like a computer rendering of a landscape, with spiky mountains and preternaturally smooth surfaces. What is most importantly lacking is the body: virtual objects and activities appeal or perplex by the friction they set up between themselves and their ordinary physicalized original. Thus a comic strip shows a young woman doing 'virtual shopping', floating effortlessly through the air and buying things by pointing to them; her accidental purchase of a forklift is funny both because the machine's physical awkwardness is immaterial in the virtual world, and because its gigantic price tag ends the fantasy by being irreducibly 'real'.

Electronic texts are implicated with peculiar force in this notion of the virtual, because our understanding of textuality originates in the same philosophical crux as our ideas of physicality and representation. The electronic text's lack of, or freedom from, a body is a crucial focus for the anxieties and hopes which attach to the new medium. If the body, the physical book, is construed as providing a grounding for the text that it carries—both in the sense of offering a stable object of reference, and in the sense of securing its cultural authority in familiar terms—then the loss of that body can seem like the severing of the bonds between meaning and its foundation, the opening up of the doors of chaos. We might term this formulation the elegiac version of events; it takes the creation of the virtual as an occasion to imagine, for mourning purposes, a lost world of cultural meaning and readership in which the book was a central and emblematic cultural object, now more or less vitiated. The more enthusiastic version construes the virtual as a postmodern space, in which the loss of the body is a severance of the bonds between the sign and the signified, the loss of a referent which was never really there to begin with. In this formulation, the body is a fetish on which we mistakenly pin our hopes for meaning and certitude and authority; the virtual space is a space of freedom from such imaginary grounding.

Elegists and enthusiasts alike focus their assessment of the political and cultural influence of the electronic text on its virtuality. Working as I do with a large database of early modern women's writing,[1] I must ask daily what a theory of virtuality—or alternatively, a theory of the body—has to say about gender politics. Reciprocally, what insights can an analysis of gender issues offer into the workings of the electronic text? And what practical consequences can we discern for our work in developing electronic resources? The politics of the traditional text and its production have always had a great deal to do with gender, though not always in an obvious manner. In order to understand the deep-rooted implication of gender in our textual beliefs and practices, it will help to take a brief excursus into the history which has produced our notion of the 'traditional text'.

GENDER IN EDITING

Scholarly editing is now undergoing a renaissance of interest from non-practitioners, thanks in part to the issues raised by electronic texts and their production, though the discipline still seems quite arcane to the large majority of academics. Yet however peripheral it may now appear to the main current of literary enquiry, it began with nothing less than the construction of a new cultural space for the study, preparation, and transmission of texts—one within which those activities could be understood as of paramount cultural and even political importance. The roots of these activities as practised today lie in the medieval manuscript tradition, and in the humanist recovery and study of classical texts. Stephanie Jed, for instance, marks early republican Florence as one locale for the development of a rhetoric of textual criticism, showing how this rhetoric supported a theory of the republican state and in fact shared with it a lexicon of crucial ideological terms.[2] The humanist text, as the bearer of the cultural authority of the new state, required editorial treatment that would fit it for this role; scholar and text together were defined so as to give their relationship maximum importance for the project of building a republic. The organizing terms of this relationship revolve around a familiar binary of body and spirit: each physical text, the manuscript or printed book, is a particular, concrete carrier of a universalized and disembodied textuality, the 'text of the author' which may be fully represented in one physical object, in many, or in none at all. Within this schema the physical object, in a manner familiar to any student of neoclassical aesthetics, is subject to corruption and debasement, its very physicality and particularity drawing it towards the realm of the monstrous and the deviant. The task of the scholar and editor, then, is to discern the universal text within the various documents which instantiate it, and by patient study and labour produce a new—but also originary and authoritative—witness which perfectly transmits the 'text of the author'. In Jed's example, these texts are the foundational documents by which republican Florence was to construct a public ideology based on an assertion of lineage from ancient republican Rome (p. 75).

Jed's account of the invention, as it were, of traditional textual editing is extremely revealing, but nowhere more so than in its attention to the gender politics of this crucial activity. Again, anyone familiar with neoclassical aesthetics will have already predicted that in the body–spirit dynamic we are confronting, the body will be gendered female and the spirit male.[3] Thus the error-ridden manuscript is figured, in the rhetoric of the humanist scholar, as an unchaste female body which has suffered 'corruption' (p. 59) as a result of sexual attack. The violation of the physical text's accuracy is thus an adultery, an adulteration. The remedy is a 'castigation'—literally, a making chaste—whereby the scholar restores the true readings, measuring the document against the authorial, universal text and eliminating deviancy; both the standard of reference and its champion are male agents within this dynamic. What is most important here is the fact that this castigation creates a fiction: a text which manages to escape the economy of the physical altogether and trace its origins straight back to an authority which does *not* rely on any particular textual exemplar. In producing a new, chaste text, the scholar claims to be *undoing*, restoring a lost wholeness, but he does so by further intervening in the text and altering it yet more so as to cover over the places of its corruption. The entire endeavour, seen within the theoretical economy which it insists on, at once repudiates and relies on the particularity of the individual witnesses; it requires the element of female unchastity, with the correction thereby called forth, as a way of supplying access to the always already lost original. One might take this a step farther and say that the myth of the lost original is a pretext for an activity essential because of what it enables: the construction of a position of cultural authority for the editor and the text he produces.

Although Jed's work focuses on manuscript, the issues raised extend to the editing of printed texts as well. This is not the place to detail the development of editing and philology through the eighteenth and nineteenth centuries, the editing of biblical and classical texts, and the vast cultural importance these activities came to assume. As an example, though, of the applicability of Jed's model to the editing of English printed books, we have only to look at Samuel Johnson's *Preface to Shakespeare*, in which he too is attempting to establish the triple importance of a literary, a textual, and an editorial tradition. Johnson offers Shakespeare as 'one of the original masters of our language',[4] who found the English nation and its literature 'yet struggling to emerge from barbarity' (p. 81). In claiming for Shakespeare 'the dignity of an ancient' (p. 61), Johnson is not so much interested in Shakespeare's merits in themselves, as in establishing Shakespeare as the anchor and origin for a national literary tradition, one which begins in barbarity and ascends to refinement. Johnson's production of Shakespeare as a rough ancestor of genius is famous and needs no repetition here; mirroring that history, though, is that of the texts themselves. 'Mutilated' and 'printed without correction of the press', they remained in this state 'because the editor's art was not yet applied to modern languages, and our ancestors were accustomed to so much negligence of English printers, that they could very patiently endure it' (p. 93). The history that occupies the latter half of Johnson's account is a history of editing, the gradual process by which Shakespeare's true text is freed from the encumbrance of poor editions and made fit to occupy the foundational position it deserves.

Johnson's language throughout this account echoes that of Jed's Florentine humanists in its reliance on metaphors of sexual violation and physical corruption. It is the 'licentiousness' (p. 94) of the early press that has 'corrupted' Shakespeare's text (p. 95), and Hanmer is praised for editing with 'the least possible violation of the text' (p. 97). Johnson speaks of his own efforts to distinguish between the true, authorial text and its subsequent, deviant incarnations thus: 'These corruptions [by previous editors] I have often silently rectified; for the history of our language, and the true force of our words, can only be preserved, by keeping the text of authours free from adulteration' (p. 105). His chastity with respect to the textual tradition is figured as a true self-restraint; conjecture, he says, 'I have not wantonly or licentiously indulged' (p. 106), though '[t]he allurements of emendation are scarcely resistible' (p. 109). The psychodynamic of 'danger hid under pleasure' (p. 109), which the text offers the editor, is what constructs the activity of textual criticism as empowerment and challenge; this tightrope act of restoring integrity while not committing further violation is designed to elicit the judgement and discretion that measure the refinement of the age possessed of them.

The sexual drama latent in Johnson's language becomes more apparent as we consider the way modern editorial theory conceptualizes the roles of author and editor *vis-à-vis* the text they work to produce. The identification and recovery of the author's true text relies on a belief in the centrality of intention—the ability to will and to perform one's will—to the production of textual meaning. Intention here is defined in opposition to the realm of the involuntary, the physical body which compromises the spiritual man. These terms are polarized by gender: in the traditional economy of body and spirit which goes back in Western culture at least as far as Plato, matter is a female principle which needs to be infused with the masculine spirit in order to take form and meaning. Editorial theory draws implicitly on this binary by locating formal control—the will, the origin of textuality proper—in the notion of the author, who is the quintessence of the willing being, a source of intention sufficient to preside over every detail of a work that is to be considered a work of literary art. The book is an embodiment—feminized, as we see in Jed's work—of this intention; its physicality is a clog on the meaningfulness of which textuality is capable, and yet is also a necessary condition of making textual meaning at all. In effect, the relation between the two is conceptualized as a sort of marriage in the name of art: the feminized principle of embodiment carries the text into sensuous, particular being, but also brings into play the possibility of deformity, monstrosity, corruption, if not sufficiently controlled.[5] Sexual conquest is thus the paradigm for the production of the kind of meaning that counts: authorially intended meaning is achieved within an eroticized theatre of sexual domination, in which the subordination of the material to the authorial will is cast as a feminized sexual submission. The position of the editor, as curator of the author's text, is to preserve the propriety of this relationship: making certain that the physical medium is subordinated to the textual meaning, and that its potential for infidelity is kept under control.

The central practices of modern textual editing, though they foreground the physical document, do so in a way which confers an ironic lack of value upon it. In preparing a critical edition, the editor identifies the important previous editions and manuscript sources, and reconstructs their relationship to each other and to the author's intentions.[6] A copytext is chosen as the basis of the new edition according to its proximity to these intentions, and then variants from other versions may be substituted where they are deemed more authorial than the readings from the copytext. Other variants—those with a lesser claim to the author's stamp—may be recorded in the margins (literally and figuratively) of the text. This minute attention to the documentary history treats textual detail like a fetish: something which stands in for the real object of desire, displacing it and reifying it. Establishing the sequence of documents that has carried the 'author's text' is not a way of valorizing that tradition, but of disciplining it and in the end nullifying it: overcoming its material resistance, correcting its deviancies and corruptions, and forcing it to testify submissively to the authorial meaning. The textual variants which are introduced by successive manuscripts or printed editions, being evidence of the material existence of the author's text in the world, are not of value except insofar as they enable the editor to determine which are the true carriers of the author's meaning. Solving their mystery means making the document transparent to this meaning, thinning out its substance until the author speaks across time unimpeded by the interference of printers, editors, and the physical, historical world. The real object of desire is thus the always already lost original: the imaginary text the author would have produced if he had never had to write his text into material existence.

There are, however, alternatives to this approach and its assumptions, whose implications may open up in turn the possibility of a different gender dynamic. Some theorists—notably Jerome McGann—have already argued extensively against the centrality of authorial intention in editorial practice, pointing out instead the 'dialectic between the historically located individual author and the historically developing institutions of literary production'.[7] McGann's assertion that in many cases authorial intentions 'may not exist, may never have existed'[8] counts most not as a denial that such intentions *can* exist, but as a dislocation of intention from the ontological position in which its history has placed it. What his dialectic most crucially allows us to see is that the idea of authorial intention is part of the historical development of the institutions of literary production: with Malone's generation in the early nineteenth century, scholarly editing becomes a strategy for identifying the author's interiorized thoughts and intentions as the correlative of textual meaning and artistic value, just as Romantic authorship applies the same paradigm to the production and consumption of literary texts.[9] When we turn from the realm of intention *per se* to the 'historically located individual author' and his or her relationships with literary institutions, we can see how the category of intention functioned within those relationships, and thus get a purchase on how it may have functioned differently for male and female authors.

McGann also reminds us that art need not depend on complete domination of the textual space by the author's will, invoking William Morris's observation that 'you can't have art without resistance in the material'.[10] This model of artistic production, based not on the subordination of the material but on the potential meaningfulness of its autonomy, helps diversify our sense of what counts as meaning and where we look for it: not just authorial meaning but social meaning; not just in the author's production of language, but in the cultural incarnations of that language. This paradigm allows for the inclusion of numerous other agents and influences—editors, printers, readers, libraries—which, as McGann points out, also play determining roles in the production of textual meaning. It is only according to the sexualized drama of authorship that we must cast these as corrupters or adulterators.

In more concrete terms, the reconsideration of these premises of editorial theory points to some possible changes in practice as well.[11] One of the most important of these is the treatment of variants. In the reconstruction of the authorial text, the emendation of the copytext using variants from other editions results in a text that never existed before, though it invokes one which is supposed to have existed all along. The resulting new edition proposes to be ideal for the study of the text as a literary work: an art object, the product of the author's genius. It may or may not be so; in the case of a text which exists in substantially varying forms, the editor's decisions about which are the more authorial, more artistically valuable readings will in the nature of such things be open to debate. But more importantly, it is not necessarily an ideal edition at all for studying the text from other standpoints. If one wishes to think of the text not as an art object but as the record of a particular textual event— something which was produced and consumed at a particular moment in history—then the synthetic edition could be misleading. As linguistic or historical evidence, the synthetic text is potentially even more limited. One might say in response that linguists and historians do not generally use such sources; this is certainly true of traditional literary editions (and for good reason), but if one is constructing, for instance, an electronic resource to have wide utility and long life, it is important to anticipate as wide as possible a range of users and uses. Thus an edition based on a single original, with relevant variants provided as part of the apparatus if necessary, would be data of better quality for many purposes.

Having said this, I note that the treatment of the variants in the apparatus is a problem in its own right. The consignment of variant readings to the margins of the text gives them a diminished status, regardless of their actual importance. This is a logistical problem resulting from the technology of the book, but it can matter a great deal when the text—a manuscript, for instance—contains multiple readings whose differences affect the reading of the text substantially. The reading which is placed among the variants becomes precisely that: a variation, a deviation from the text proper. Its placement in the margin serves as evidence of the editedness of the text from which it has been banished, but may do so in disproportion to its importance or interest relative to the chosen reading. What begins as a problem of technological limitation thus becomes embedded in larger theoretical issues.

Editorial emendation which actually seeks to correct the text based on the editor's judgement rather than on existing textual exemplars is yet another problem, and one which plays even more into the theoretical problems I have been discussing.[12] Emendation of this sort ranges from the correction of 'obvious printer's errors' (turned, uninked, or wrong-fount letters, omitted punctuation, obvious misspellings, and the like) to the regularization or normalization of textual features such as capitalization and fount shifts, to the improvement of authorial punctuation, wording, and lineation (most famously in the instance of Emily Dickinson). Emendation of the first kind is clearly an outgrowth of the assumptions about the relationship between the text and its physical incarnation, but since what it obliterates is a record entirely of inadvertencies, it arguably damages the text for only a very limited range of uses. The second kind of emendation addresses itself more to the presumed irrelevance of the physical text than to its corruptness; it assumes that no meaning of any interest is carried in the details of the text which were intended by someone other than the author: the printer, the compositor, the culture that trained them. Altering these features makes a significant difference not only to the kind of data that the edition provides—which could be important to a number of users—but also to the kind of message the edition sends to the reader. By minimizing, instead of foregrounding, the historical distance between the text and the present, the edition gives the text a specious comprehensibility and familiarity, encouraging us to imagine it as a transhistorical message of universal value. The last kind of emendation compounds these difficulties by enlisting the editor as a surrogate author who is empowered to hypothesize the author's intentions and write them more firmly into the text. Although in respectable editions such changes are recorded in the apparatus, the emendation nonetheless becomes a part of the text in a way that the original reading—now, ironically, a form of variant—is not. Additionally, in bringing the text into greater conformity with the editor's expectations, these changes generate a circular argument for the familiarity and regularity of the indicators of textual meaning. The text is corrected on the basis of assumptions about how texts should be punctuated, spelled, arranged—assumptions which in turn appear to be based on how texts actually are punctuated and so on. But this appearance, in part created by the very process of correction which it serves to substantiate, obscures not only the diversity of means by which a text might communicate, but also the uniqueness and unpredictability of the meanings it might contain. This point is of particular importance when we are dealing with a group of non-canonical writers—for instance, women—whose texts have not necessarily been a formative part of our expectations about textual meaning.

However clear these difficulties may be to modern editors, they remain almost impossible to solve adequately within the limitations of the printed book. In most cases the solution requires a substantial increase in the quantity and complexity of the information presented to the reader, and in a physical book—however easy to take to the beach or the bathtub —this information is impossible to present lucidly. The advent of the electronic medium, with its profoundly different technologies of storage, management, and display of information, offers different approaches and possible solutions to some of these challenges. However, some of these approaches, when we investigate them, may resemble less solutions to old problems than new cruxes in their own right. What, for instance, are the defining limits of the 'edition'? How little editing can it contain and still be recognizable? If one of the possibilities of the electronic edition is to provide a new space for the reader's own judgement and experimentation, how do the editor's and reader's roles intersect? In considering these questions we must constantly remind ourselves of our true goals: not to protect the idea of the edition itself, for its own sake, but to create textual resources which fulfil the purposes which we care most about.

THE NEW WORLD: ARE WE BRAVE ENOUGH?

The most important feature of the electronic medium is its ability to present different sets of information, or different views of the same information, quickly and flexibly. Given the proper encoding, an electronic text can be stored in numerous versions, complete with variants; readers can view the text in any configuration that is appropriate to their needs. If, for instance, a text existed in three different versions, each of which derived from a manuscript original laden with revisions, the reader could view any of the versions separately, move from one to the other to compare particular readings, read transcriptions of the manuscript sources (viewing them either with all revisions presented in some convenient manner, or with only final revisions or initial readings visible), examine scanned images of the original sources, or read any one of a number of collated editions prepared by expert—and perhaps interestingly differing —editors.

With this logic of abundance at work, it is no wonder that electronic editions have tended to be conceived on a grandly inclusive scale. The *Canterbury Tales* Project, for instance, aims to include images and transcriptions of all extant manuscripts of the *Tales*, a truly massive undertaking. (See the essay by Peter Robinson in this collection.) To an extent, such a collection is simply the fulfilment of the aims of any comprehensive edition: to take account of all the textual phenomena pertinent to the publication history of a given text. Where the traditional edition for reasons of space can only record the places where the witnesses differ (and often only those differences which are considered most interesting), the electronic edition can splurge and give more scope to its display of the information, showing each witness in its entirety. The addition of facsimile images likewise can be construed as the logical indulgence—given the new availability of space—of the longing awakened by the few plates illustrating the traditional edition. The mood of demonstrations of new electronic editions is heady, flush with the copious fulfilment of what the traditional edition, at its most comprehensive, has always wanted to be.

But this abundance comes to mean more than just an arrival at the editorial land of milk and honey. The desire to increase readerly access to primary data, paired with a now frequent questioning of the nature of the editor's role, impels the electronic edition increasingly towards inclusiveness as a way of avoiding editorial intervention. The collection of witnesses and the preservation of information aims to set the reader up as an independent intelligence, equipped with the data and the tools to manipulate it, and supplying his or her own critical and editorial acumen. In what sense, we may then ask, is this an edition? And what pressure does the term 'archive'—now increasingly used to describe large collections such as the Rossetti Archive or the Wittgenstein Archive—put on the conceptualization of the 'edition'?

These terms seem to pull in opposite directions, and must do so as long as we think of them in terms of mutual inadequacy: the archive as a failure to provide an editorial synthesis; the edition as a failure to provide access to all the evidence. But the more we work with both, and the more indigenous they become to the electronic world, the more I think it will be useful to see them as converging. If we define the electronic archive by its chief aim—to provide large bodies of primary data—we will find it nonetheless drawn towards the condition of the edition simply by virtue of being prepared, encoded, and to some inevitable degree selected. This editedness cannot be evaded or hidden, though it can be usefully distinguished from the more explicit editing which aims actually to alter the text. Similarly, if the electronic edition is above all an attempt to articulate and document a theory of the text, the ample documentation which is now called for will seem to pull the edition towards the status of an archive. Where the edition seems most threatened by its slide in this direction is in the heart of its cultural power: its presentation of an ideal text, its persuasiveness in convincing the reader that the ideal text is more real than any of the individual witnesses, its insistence on pulling that text out from amid the morass of other possibilities. When this ideal is withheld, we feel the threat of disorientation, a sort of textual agoraphobia, but we should not accord this feeling the status of a legitimate complaint about our surroundings. The cacophony of data which can at first seem overwhelming in even as well-organized a collection as the *Canterbury Tales* Project—which records scores of manuscripts, several different categories of variants, multiple letter forms—is no creation of the archive, but the true realm of textuality from which, through the traditional edition, we seek to protect ourselves. The electronic edition, when it exploits the power of the medium to record this abundance of information, both preserves and mitigates this cacophony. In the best electronic editions, those which use a text-encoding system like SGML,[13] the data itself has qualities of intelligence,[14] in the sense that each textual phenomenon is explicitly identified in its relationship to the entire textual system being recorded: as a variant, a printer's error, a witness, a conjectural reading. Thus, while the amount and complexity of data is overwhelming, it comes to us in a manageable form: we can focus on the problems that interest us most and hold the rest in abeyance.

The evidentiary value of the information thus preserved is critically important, but the electronic edition—like its traditional counterpart—has also the capacity to create for the reader a textual space from within which one feels the representational power of the text, not as an assemblage of data but as a meaningful, coherent universe. The ideological power of the text depends on this space, not just on its projection of textual meaning, but also on the means used—words, spelling, layout, and the cultural connotations of these things—to achieve that projection. It is in this context, therefore, that we can register the real effects of editorial encoding on issues like gender. The Women Writers Project, in determining its approach to the encoding of early modern women's writing, has had to consider not simply scholarly usefulness—though this is obviously crucial—but also the ways in which our electronic texts will be read, the kinds of readings they may encourage and discourage, from the standpoint of gender. The choice of what and whether to modernize, for instance, alters the effect the text has on the reader profoundly. The process of modernization is a way of minimizing the text's difference, making it seem to speak a familiar language. This process also works to diminish our awareness of the text's presence in history, as witnessed by its physical presence in the world and that of the readers to whom it once did speak familiarly.[15] Eliminating this difference, this component of materiality, confirms us in our tendency to read the text as a timeless expression of the author's mind and genius, rather than as a socialized production with many participants and a contemporary reading audience. As a technique of scholarship it underpins a view of literary writing which has helped, I think, to produce our current misconceptions about the role of women in the history of our literate culture. The question of how much of the text to transcribe—whether to regard the 'work' as the unit of meaning, or to include the entire document as it originally circulated, including title-pages, advertisements, prefaces, and the like—must be addressed in the light of the same considerations. To isolate the literary component of the document like a gem from its setting is to locate it solely within the ideologic: ' space of our existing version of literary history, and to preclude any contextualization which might enable a different reading. The Women Writers Project addresses these issues by avoiding modernization, and by regarding the printed document, in whatever form it originally circulated, as the unit of transcription. Phenomena such as printers' errors, brevigraphs and abbreviations, and early typography are preserved both in their original form and in a corrected or expanded form, so that the original details are retained but a version more suitable for searching and analysis is also available. Given the practical need to provide a resource which people will find useful for the kinds of work they currently do, as well as one which will challenge them to work in new ways, the ability of the encoded text to preserve these multiple versions of the data is crucial to the Women Writers Project's enterprise.

The ease and flexibility of this kind of text encoding, which enables us to avoid in some measure the previous obliteration of the historical body of the text, seems ironically to be gained by losing the body of the text altogether. But has this really happened? We think of the physical book as the body of the text because the logic of this relation has a long history; the computer is fetishized, culturally, as the emblem of the new virtuality, filled with representations of things but not the things themselves: the quintessence of lack. This preoccupation with the thingness of a book, though, obscures the fact that it too is a representation: it is *an* object, but not *the* object. Our desire for it to be *the* object stems from the same fruitless search for origins that motivates the scholarly editor's attempt to reconstruct a lost manuscript original that can finally ground an entire textual tradition. The preoccupation with the electronic text's virtuality expresses not its profound difference from the book, but the anxiety generated by the loss of the earlier fetish: the book's supposed body, its supposed substantiality.[16]

Thus with all the potential advantages described above, electronic texts nonetheless provoke fears of various sorts. These fears begin with the practical: concerns over the accuracy of electronic texts, their derivation from an accurately documented source, and the proper way of cataloguing them or citing them as references, all of which are legitimate issues at this early stage in the development of electronic text technology. Other concerns seem to begin with the practical and move towards something less identifiable. Questions of accuracy and documentation, for instance, are complicated by uncertainty about what kind of electronic text one has in hand. In the electronic world the familiar markers identifying different kinds of texts are lacking, and new systems of customary practices have not yet developed fully. With conventional books, one knows that a colourful embossed paper cover is not likely to house a scholarly edition, but how can one distinguish the scholarly electronic text from the random production of an enthusiastic typist? In this unfamiliar terrain, the fear of being taken in—of unwittingly using a corrupted text—is magnified far beyond the comparable fear in the realm of the printed book. In fact, the vouchers of accuracy are not much better, if at all, in print; conventional books—even scholarly editions—may contain numerous typographical errors, and the source text is not always identified satisfactorily. But these flaws are taken in stride, affecting the assessment of that particular book but not seen as indicating a profound untrustworthiness in the medium itself.

It is easy to show, by turning on the lights and opening the closet door, that there are no monsters within, but anxiety does not yield reliably to such comforts—instead it has recourse to artificial reassurances. In the electronic medium, these quite often involve re-establishing a relationship between the electronic text and the conventional book, supplying the missing physical referent by symbolically invoking it. Thus one strategy for positioning the electronic text in a safe relationship to traditional books is to maintain as many similarities as possible between the two, avoiding the more un-booklike potentialities of the new medium. Just as there is a certain kind of vegetarian cuisine that tries to make vegetables look and taste like meat—often a strategy that appears in cookbooks aimed at converting the non-vegetarian—so there is a corner of the electronic world which focuses on making 'electronic books' look and function as much as possible like paper books. This includes sound effects which mimic the turning of pages, screen borders which resemble paper corners, and an interface which offers the reader a linear progression through the text, page by page, by means of arrows which move the pages forward or back.[17] Not surprisingly, these details have not won over the book fans, for whom the appeal of the book lies elsewhere, but they are interesting as an indication of a felt need: they attempt to reassure the user that this is a familiar textual space.

Along similar lines, the Women Writers Project often receives queries regarding the visual fidelity of our electronic transcriptions to the original books. It is clear that there is some component of our user population who want our electronic texts literally to re-produce the book, to provide as exactly as possible the same experience of reading and study. This is understandable, given that one of our stated functions is to facilitate access to texts which are otherwise difficult to get; in some sense we present the text as—if not a substitute—at least a stand-in for the 'real thing' which is the ultimate object of desire for the researchers. Visual fidelity, in this context, would be again a marker and guarantee of the familiarity of the textual space; the fact that for these researchers it may be the very thing they are studying means only that their study of the text is rooted in this textual space and in the technology of the book. Fidelity here works against precisely what is textual about this material; it moves along an axis at whose endpoint lies the holy grail of exact visual reproduction. This goal is impossible to achieve; but the digital image which attempts it is no longer, properly speaking, a *text* from the computer's point of view, and is completely cut off from any textual existence in electronic form. The specious comfort provided by these appearances of familiarity comes at the cost of what can really be achieved by the electronic text when it no longer tries to be a substitute book.

What ties the electronic text to the book is in some sense the need for legitimacy, but for texts already under the mark of illegitimacy the issue becomes more complex.[18] The texts in the Women Writers Project corpus have typically remained unedited and unread for the last hundred years. Their existence as archival materials rather than as continuously transmitted texts is closely bound up with their non-canonicity: these are not the texts whose textual meaning is regarded as transcending its history and its printed incarnation, the texts whose cultural importance warrants the preparation of editions that will erase their history and let the author speak to us directly. The Women Writers Project, in preparing these texts for classroom and research use, has no interest in performing such an erasure. However, the adoption of these texts for classroom use tends to require their presentation as 'real', 'legitimate' texts worth discussing alongside the other texts which already occupy a secure place in the syllabus. As long as they are offered for consumption as products of the electronic medium, without being inserted into the familiar cultural position occupied by the book, these texts carry a double stigma. Not only do they not function culturally as books (being printouts or xeroxes or some other more casual form of print), but they also do not function as idealized texts, in the sense that they have not been freed from their historical baggage: they pose their difficulties of spelling and layout and printing errors unchastened. As non-books they perplex because of their lack of a body, as it were—they seem to derive from a variable and inherently untrustworthy source. At the same time, ironically, as non-texts they seem to suffer from the reverse problem of being clogged by their physicality, their rootedness in history. Thus by traditional measures they fail twice to occupy the textual economy in which the body remains only just present to testify to the accuracy and primacy of the textual meaning it carries.

To address this seeming failure by courting legitimacy—publishing these texts as books, insisting that they share, as Sven Birkerts puts it, 'the authority of unambiguous origins . . . [a] verifiable historical existence'[19] —is to gain only a specious victory. The electronic medium is not irrelevant to such an approach; one of the practical virtues of a textbase is that it can be used to produce print editions, and the Women Writers Project has even experimented with a series of books.[20] But the legitimacy offered by the printed book depends on the very structures that kept women's writing in the archive in the first place, structures whose larger effects go far beyond the textual world. The psychic comfort of handling a book with footnotes and an introduction, of presenting it to a class as a warrant of the text's cultural importance, is purchased at a cost: the lost opportunity to examine precisely why the lack of these comforts seems so disorienting, so challenging. The attempt to legitimize the electronic text by making it perform like a book is a similar evasion. To use the electronic medium, for instance, to produce an 'electronic book' simulacrum of a scholarly edition would be equally to miss the real point: the possibility of reconstructing the relations between the editor, the text, and the reader.

There is nothing intrinsic, then, about the electronic medium that guarantees a radical departure from the habits of thought fostered by the culture of the book. Though it may seem like an obvious point, it is important to remember that habits this deeply rooted—not just at the level of reflex, but at the level of ideology—require a great deal of work to counter. The medium will not do this work for us: in designing and building a textbase we need to interrogate and exercise the medium and the facilities it offers, but at bottom the medium is only an instrument of our methodology, and remains limited by our conceptual horizons. How limited these horizons may be is indicated as much by how electronic texts are not used as by what they are used for. As long as they are seen primarily as vitiated books —books with all the sensual and cultural redolence removed—they are doomed to be used as if they really were just books with an extraordinarily unwieldy agglomeration of plastic and silicon in the way. Similarly, as long as they are constructed using the same intellectual methodology as traditional books, they will continue to perpetuate the conceptual limitations, and worse, that the traditional book culture has fostered.

NOTES

1. The Brown University Women Writers Project, which is creating a full-text database of pre-Victorian women's writing in English, encoded using Standard Generalized Markup Language (SGML).
2. Stephanie H. Jed, *Chaste Thinking: The Rape of Lucretia and the Birth of Humanism* (Bloomington and Indianapolis: Indiana University Press, 1989), p. 60. Further references are included parenthetically within the text.
3. For an illuminating and detailed discussion of this dynamic as it emerges in neoclassicism, see Naomi Schor, *Reading in Detail: Aesthetics and the Feminine* (New York and London: Routledge, 1987), pp. 11–79.
4. Samuel Johnson, 'Preface' to *The Plays of William Shakespeare* (1765), in *Johnson on Shakespeare*, vol. vii of *The Yale Edition of the Works of Samuel*

Johnson (New Haven and London: Yale University Press, 1968), p. 70. Further references are included parenthetically within the text.

5. So, for instance, Thomas Tanselle, distinguishing between the idealized 'work' and the physical 'text', asserts that '[t]hose texts, being reports of works, must always be suspect'; this idea recurs more emphatically when he speaks of 'human creativity liberat[ing] the soul from its bondage to human flesh' (*A Rationale of Textual Criticism* (Philadelphia: University of Pennsylvania Press, 1989), pp. 69, 92). The linkage between embodiment and deformity is not limited to the textual realm; it is a conceptual paradigm with broad influence on Western cultural theories. Thus, for instance, Sir Joshua Reynolds in the Third Discourse speaks of an ideal of perfect beauty, 'that central form . . . from which every deviation is deformity', and asserts that every embodiment of this form does in fact so deviate: 'All the objects which are exhibited to our view by nature . . . will be found to have their blemishes and defects' (see Reynolds, *Discourses* (New York: Penguin Books, 1992), pp. 106–7). Schor's *Reading in Detail* discusses the gender implications of embodiment and deformity in greater detail (see pp. 11–20).

6. Whether first, final, or some other intentions varies with particular circumstances, but this makes no difference to the basic approach.

7. Jerome J. McGann, *A Critique of Modern Textual Criticism* (Chicago: University of Chicago Press, 1983), p. 81.

8. Ibid., p. 90.

9. See Margreta de Grazia, *Shakespeare Verbatim* (Oxford: Clarendon Press, 1991), p. 206 and ff. As discussed above, the distinction between the authorial work and the physical document goes back much further than this; what is new in the 19th century is the particular potency that intention and originality take on as determinants of authorial meaning.

10. Jerome J. McGann, 'Composition as Explanation', in Margaret J. Ezell and Katherine O'Brien O'Keeffe (eds.), *Cultural Artifacts and the Production of Meaning: The Page, the Image, and the Body* (Ann Arbor: University of Michigan Press, 1994), p. 136.

11. I am not talking of the production of mass market editions, which in any case are not usually prepared using careful textual criticism. I am referring rather to the editions which are intended for the use of literary scholars, students, and others who are interested in actually studying the text.

12. In a sense, editorial emendation as discussed below can be classed with other aspects of the history of textual production: just as the compositor, printer, and early editors collaborate with the author in producing the text for circulation in culture, so the modern editor's reproduction of the text is a culturally meaningful act. Seen from this standpoint, the modern editor's emendations have the same ontological status as the work of the author's contemporaries, and could be valuable evidence for posterity concerning our assumptions about texts. This does not mean, however, that the assumptions themselves deserve preservation.

13. Standard Generalized Markup Language (SGML) is a text-encoding system characterized by extraordinary power in recording textual structure, content, and appearance, including multiple variations on all of these. Since it

separates the presentation of textual information (e.g. printed output, an on-line browser, and so forth) from the preservation of the primary data about the source text, it is especially well suited for editorial work; information about variants, original spelling and typography, and the like can all be preserved and then expressed or suppressed as appropriate in a given situation.

14. What I have called 'intelligence' here does not of course originate in the data; the editor-encoder adds it by an act of interpretation. Although it is strictly true that this, like the traditional procedures of emendation, is a form of cooking which intercedes between us and the raw data, I think in this context it is more useful to emphasize the differences between the two, particularly since we never really get our data raw in any case. However, the interpretive nature of encoding is an important consideration when designing an electronic edition.

15. I remember hearing, as a justification for modernizing the spelling in an edition of a Renaissance woman writer, that the standard edition of Philip Sidney (with whom she would be taught) was modernized, and to leave her text in its original spelling would create the impression that she was uneducated. The deeper problem here is that the canonical male authors already occupy a space in our culture which is ahistorical.

16. The response to this supposed loss need not be anxiety; enthusiasm for the potential of the virtual text derives equally from this fetishization of the book as origin. Where the anxious response sees the book as a crucial source of grounding without which there can be no meaning, the enthusiastic response sees it as a crucial impediment to the free play of textuality and readerly power.

17. Voyager Books, for instance, use an interface which relies on such presentational details.

18. For a discussion of this issue inflected through the concept of the text's authenticity, see Kathryn Sutherland, 'Challenging Assumptions: Women Writers and New Technology', in Warren Chernaik, Caroline Davis, and Marilyn Deegan (eds.), *The Politics of the Electronic Text* (Oxford: Office for Humanities Communication Publications, 3, 1993), pp. 53–67.

19. Sven Birkerts, 'The Book as Emblem: The Besieged Stronghold?', *Journal of Scholarly Publishing*, 26: 1 (Oct. 1994), p. 4.

20. The *Women Writers in English, 1350–1850* series, published by Oxford University Press; at the time of writing, at least twelve titles are in print.

7
New Directions in Critical Editing

PETER M. W. ROBINSON

It is a topos of discussions of the impact of computers on textual editing to invoke the ghost of Gutenberg, only to bury him with some such statement as 'We believe that the most fundamental change in textual culture since Gutenberg is now under way.'[1] For textual scholars, there is a more relevant assertion. We are, in fact, involved in the greatest change in textual scholarship since Aldus Manutius. As we prepare to plunge into the new world of electronic editions, it is instructive to look back on what Aldus achieved in the two decades from 1495 in his new world of printed books.[2]

Before Aldus began work, around 1494, although many Latin texts had been printed, in the whole of Western Europe there were barely a dozen volumes printed in Greek.[3] Aldus changed that completely. In the space of twenty years, up to Aldus' death in 1515, the Aldine press published the first printing of nearly all the classical Greek authors.[4] In just two years, from 1502 to 1504, his press published the first editions of Sophocles, Euripides, Herodotus, Thucydides, and Demosthenes. Indeed, in the five years beginning 1501, the Aldine press published a new edition of a classic text about every two months: thirty volumes in all in sixty months. Nor did Aldus just publish major Greek authors: among authors rarely read, he published Herodian, Pollux, Stephanus of Byzantium, and Philostratus' *Life of Apollonius*. This last is particularly interesting, as Aldus declared in the preface to this Philostratus that it was the worst book he had ever read.[5] Besides Greek texts, Aldus found time to publish the italic edition of Vergil, the *Canzoniere* of Petrarch, and Dante's *Divine Comedy*.[6]

There are some interesting lessons for us in this astonishing record. Aldus was, without doubt, a most capable scholar by the standards of his time, but he could not have done all this if he were only a scholar, or if he were working on his own. He was many things: a businessman, a determined visionary, a page and fount designer, a diplomat, an entrepreneur, as well as a scholar. Also, Aldus had help: he chose to establish his press in Venice, where more than anywhere else he could find four things he needed: money, manuscripts, printers, and scholars. And especially this last: most of the editing work was not done by him, but by individual scholars. Aldus used to insist that the scholars stayed in his house while they worked for him; one of these scholars was Erasmus, who complained bitterly in later life about the miserable food in Aldus' house.[7] In many respects, Aldus' printing house and his scholars were more like a club than a business: indeed, around 1502 Aldus set up what he called the Neakademai, a club for the promotion of Greek, including his scholar-editors among its members.[8]

Making electronic editions will require of us much the same combination of skills and circumstances as Aldus had. In these pioneering days, the editor of the electronic edition has to be many things besides an editor: a perpetual grant applicant and entrepreneur, a software designer and (perhaps) writer. And, at this moment in the history of editing as the old gives way to the new, the editor must be a collaborator: part of a shared enterprise. We who are now making electronic editions are our own club, our own Neakademai: we share ideas about encoding, about software, about presentation, about editing. We are part of a floating world-wide conversation about editing and computers. In place of chance meetings on the Rialto, we have electronic mail; for talk over Aldus' meagre dinner table, we have rolling meetings at text encoding initiative meetings, at seminars and workshops, and at conferences.

Above all, the electronic editor has to be an optimist. Electronic editors have to live in hope: hope that the long-awaited standards for encoding texts for the computer will arrive; hope that they will be workable; hope that software will appear to handle these texts; hope that all the scholars of the world will have computers which can drive the software (which does not yet exist) to handle the texts (which have not yet been made) encoded in standard computer markup (which has not yet been devised). To hope for all this requires a considerable belief in the inevitability of progress and in the essential goodness of mankind. In 1493 an Italian printer, not Aldus, published the editio princeps of the Greek text of Isocrates. This sold so slowly that 42 years later, in 1535, the publisher was able to issue a new edition just by binding a new title page into the unsold volumes.[9] Aldus must have known that no Greek text printed before he started had sold more than a few hundred copies, not at all enough to sustain a press.[10] Yet, he persevered: he, certainly, was an optimist.

The single most impressive fact about Aldus is this: he printed between a thousand and three thousand copies of each of his editions.[11] Just to put this into perspective: the average print-run of any printed book at the time is thought to have been around 250.[12] Cambridge University Press have a print run of 800 for their new critical edition of D. H. Lawrence.[13] Furthermore, there simply cannot have been two thousand people in the whole of Western Europe in 1500 who could read classical Greek and could afford Aldus' editions (which were not cheap).[14] Selling copies of a Greek text to people who cannot read Greek is rather like us trying to sell electronic editions to people without computers. How did Aldus do it?

Many people around 1500 must have bought volume after volume of Aldus' Greek texts without being able to read a single word. The great French bibliophile Jean Grolier, for example, had little Greek but bought not just one but several copies of many of Aldus' editions.[15] Why? It appears that the reason is that the latest copy of the latest classic Greek text was part of the essential equipment of the smart humanist of around 1500. To have any street credibility as a humanist, you had to have your shelves stocked with Aldus' Greek volumes. It was a sort of humanist designer accessory, the equivalent of today's personal digital assistant. The fact that you could not read the books did not matter: it was enough to own them.

There is a lesson for us in this. Aldus identified the wave of enthusiasm which arose when the new humanist scholarship, offering new eagerness for old texts and new texts to edit, encountered the new technology of printing, offering new ways of distributing these texts. Aldus guessed that many people would be so swept up with this wave of enthusiasm that they would buy scholarly texts they otherwise would not dream of buying. That is exactly what happened. Aldus exploited this enthusiasm to have texts edited that otherwise could not have been—and, perhaps, should not have been, as in the case of the appalling Philostratus *Life of Apollonius*. In the same way, the great potential of computers for scholarly textual work has woken interest from people who would otherwise never think of manuscripts and editions. In the next few years, we have the chance to convert that interest into new scholarly work, work that could not otherwise be done.

COMPUTERS AND NEW TOOLS FOR EDITORS

Just as around 1500 the new horizons of humanist scholarship met the new means of distribution made possible by printing, computer methods now offer not only cheaper means of distribution but also open new possibilities in the making of editions. In fact, the advent of printing did not of itself much alter the way in which scholars made editions, though greatly changing the dissemination of what the scholars made. Many early printed editions were achieved by nothing more than the publisher giving a manuscript to the printer and saying: 'print that'. Many of Aldus' editions are just this, as was Caxton's first printing of Chaucer's *Canterbury Tales*.[16]

In contrast, computer methods may change what scholars do far more than this.

Computer methods may touch every aspect of what scholars do: they may change how we acquire and view images of primary sources (manuscripts, first printed editions, etc.) and what we look for in them; how we transcribe the sources; how we collate the transcriptions; how we analyse the collations in search of a rationale for the history of the text; how we compile glossaries and research word-use and spelling in the text. We are still years away from the full realization of these methods, with many of them still under development or dependent on changes in the computing environment in which we work. Hope has to be our constant companion in this work. For example, fundamental advances are still necessary in computer storage and network technology before high-resolution manuscript images can become widely available. But enough has been done for us to see what we can do now and what will be possible soon. The *Canterbury Tales* Project, for which I am joint general editor, is using many of these methods and most of the examples I give are drawn from that project.[17] Over a ten-year period we intend to issue computer images and transcriptions of all 84 manuscripts and of the four pre-1500 printed editions of Chaucer's work, amounting to around 30,000 computer images and six million words of transcription.

Most textual editing begins with a primary text: a manuscript, a printed first edition, printer's proof, etc. Here I concentrate on primary texts in manuscript form, but most of what I have to say applies equally to printed first editions and the like. For a primary text in manuscript form, unless you are lucky enough to be editing a text in just one manuscript, with that manuscript available to you in a local library, you will have to work from a reproduction of the manuscript, and not the manuscript itself. Indeed, it is likely that even where the manuscript itself is available librarians will not be happy to allow the lengthy access to the manuscript itself that editing might require. Almost invariably, the manuscript reproduction will be based on microfilm: either the library will provide a copy of the microfilm itself, or it will provide (as do the Bodleian and British Libraries) paper prints from the microfilm. Machines are now available which can convert entire microfilms into computer images, so that one can view a manuscript page not on a microfilm viewer, or on a printed page, but on a computer screen. This process is very cheap, very convenient where microfilm copies already exist, and the resulting computer files can be made sufficiently small as to be easily distributed.[18] The Bibliothèque de France is in the process of putting millions of pages of printed texts into computer form using just this process. Libraries and microfilm companies have already shown considerable interest in this technology, and most of the manuscript page images on the first *Canterbury Tales* Project CD-ROM, containing 1,200 page images for all the surviving fifty-four manuscripts and four pre-1500 printed editions of the Wife of Bath's Prologue, are so derived from microfilm.[19]

One can expect that in the near future libraries may offer microfilm images in scanned computer-readable form as well as in film or page forms. At present, acquisition of manuscript reproductions is a lengthy process. Typically, one must write to the library to enquire about availability and cost; await a reply; then pay for the reproductions; finally wait for them to be sent. Even under ideal conditions this may take several weeks, and several months is more usual. Distribution of computer images by network will allow this to be telescoped into a few minutes, or even seconds. Indeed, the manuscript images might not be distributed at all: a scholar might dial into the library, or archive, from his or her computer and view the image within the archive, with obvious advantage to the library as it keeps control of the image.

The convenience alone of this distribution of microfilm-based computer images may be a considerable boon. But computer methods may offer much more than this. Microfilm is actually a very poor method of reproducing a manuscript. Modern high-contrast microfilm is very well suited to archiving of printed materials, with plain black text on white paper, but is very poor for reproduction of manuscript materials. Manuscripts may have fading brown ink on darkening parchment, with different hands writing in different inks, with different pen-pressure for punctuation and calligraphic flourishes, with scribal rubrication and ornamentation in various colours. Scholars are increasingly aware of the importance in a manuscript of not only the letter forms made by the scribe but their disposition upon the page: the use of colour, as emphatic, or structural, or decorative device; the layout of scribal signs upon the page (including signs other than letters); a hierarchy of scripts within the inscribed text; indications of correction, annotation, or deletion; the physical characteristics of the manuscript itself.[20] Much of this is lost in high-contrast microfilm; colour reproduction can capture a far higher proportion of this information. However, colour photography and reproduction are extremely expensive, so much so that there is only one colour facsimile of any complete Middle English manuscript of Chaucer—and this facsimile costs some $7,000 in its cheapest state.[21] The advent of digital photography, with devices such as the Kontron ProgRes camera demonstrating that images of astonishing clarity may be made rapidly and cheaply, may change all this.[22] The images made by this and similar cameras are at least as good as those available from large-format transparencies (60 mm, or 10 by 8, etc.), and to the viewer are equivalent to seeing the manuscript under full daylight. A single CD-ROM, costing around £5 for the physical medium and its pressing, could contain a complete colour record of a whole manuscript.[23]

Colour images of this quality will give scholars detail about the manuscripts hitherto available only to those fortunate enough to work in the great research libraries. In itself, this may revolutionize textual scholarship.[24] The possibility of this new means of cheap distribution of high-quality facsimiles will itself present new and difficult choices to the editor. Indeed, why stop here? Why not include not just every page of every different edition, but every page of every separate printed copy that you can find? Already, I know of projects where it seems to me that digitization is in danger of running amok. It is very tempting to digitize everything in sight. Most dangerously, it seems that digitization might actually substitute for scholarship. Why bother reading, transcribing, and editing a document when all you have to do is photograph it, put the photograph on a CD-ROM or a network and flood the world with copies of undigested, undifferentiated, and unedited images?

An editor who does no more than accumulate and distribute quantities of such images will not deserve the name of editor. To begin to unlock the information in them, one must transcribe the manuscripts from these images. There is a simple rule for editors of electronic editions who are contemplating digitizing vast quantities of primary materials. The rule is this: no digitization without transcription. If you think the image is worth distributing so that others can read it, then read it yourself before you do. If you are really serious about helping others read it, and really want to make sure that you can read it, then transcribe it. The computer provides new possibilities—and difficulties—in the process of transcription. It offers possibilities, for the low cost of computer distribution means that one can 'publish' the computer transcriptions themselves, with the transcriptions linked by 'hypertext' software to the images. It offers difficulties, for there is a fundamental difference between transcription for the computer and transcription for a traditional scholarly edition. When one is transcribing for a traditional edition, the choices are bounded by the characters available in the printer's fount; furthermore, the end of the transcription is its printing, and not its distribution in electronic form. But one can expect a computer-readable transcription to be searched, analysed, and edited in ways not possible with a printed transcription. Thus, when making a computer transcription one must consider the possible uses of this transcription by other scholars and let this weight decisions about what to include, what not to include.

This suggests that manuscript transcription for the computer is a complex business, with many subtle choices having to be made. It is far from the mechanical affair that it is sometimes thought to be, as instanced by the recurrent discussion on scholarly electronic discussion groups about possible machine systems for 'reading' manuscripts. Computer transcription, with its special requirements of consistency across a possibly huge body of material, highlights what manuscript scholars have always known: that reading manuscripts might draw on all a scholar's training and knowledge. In essence, transcription is a series of acts of translation, from one semiotic system (that of the manuscript) to another semiotic system (that of the computer). Like all acts of translation, it must be seen as fundamentally incomplete and fundamentally interpretive.[25] After five years of work on the manuscripts of the *Canterbury Tales*, we are still uncertain about exactly what marks we should record, and how we should record them. It is hard to conceive that any supposed handwriting recognition system will ever produce a satisfactory transcription of a *Canterbury Tales* manuscript, indeed of any medieval manuscript.

In the 'Guidelines for Transcription', first prepared for the transcription of the manuscripts of the Wife of Bath's Prologue and now in use across the whole *Canterbury Tales* Project,[26] we identified four possible levels of transcription: 'regularized', with all manuscript spellings levelled to a particular standard; 'graphemic', with all manuscript spellings preserved without distinction of particular letter forms; 'graphetic', with discrimination of all distinct letter forms; 'graphic', with every mark in the manuscript represented in the transcription. The choice among these levels is not simple, and we have found that it is not possible to achieve a stringent conformancy to any one level in the course of a long transcription of many manuscripts. Thus, while we aim at a graphemic transcription such as will be useful to students of the language of the manuscripts, the uncertain graphemic status of many marks in the manuscripts (particularly, tails and flourishes) means that our transcription includes some graphic and graphetic elements. Exact documentation of what we have done is therefore vital if others are to use our transcripts. We have attempted to provide that in our 'Guidelines for Transcription' and recommend strongly that other scholars engaged in manuscript transcription for the computer also document their practice.[27] In addition, every one of the transcripts of the fifty-eight witnesses published on the *Wife of Bath's Prologue on CD-ROM* is prefixed by a 'transcriber's introduction', written by Elizabeth Solopova, which spells out the particular difficulties we found in the transcription of this witness, and thus the likely areas of uncertainty which might constrain scholarly use of the transcript.

One must also decide exactly how one does the transcription: what word processor, what computer, does one use? It is tempting to use one's favourite word processor and to devise an *ad hoc* markup system deploying the facilities most computer systems now provide for italics, underlining, special characters, and different founts, etc., to register various manuscript features.[28] This is convenient and satisfying for the transcribing scholar. But it will lead to problems when the transcript files are shifted to another system (or even, when the word-processor software is upgraded), or when one attempts to use the files alongside transcripts made by other scholars using different systems, or to use them with different software. There is a special compartment reserved in hell for scholars who devise their own *ad hoc* markup systems for use with their own favourite word processor. Scholars may escape from this compartment by use of a widely supported standard system of computer markup. This will make it far easier for the transcript files (representing a considerable investment of scholarly time and effort) to survive changes in computer systems, and will make them available to a wider scholarly community and amenable to different software packages.

One such standard system of markup is that specified for my computer collation program *Collate*: this is the system used by the *Canterbury Tales* Project, and by several other major editing projects.[29] Files using this markup can be collated by *Collate*, and also searched, indexed, and concorded by the Oxford Concordance Program. Though adequate for its immediate purposes, the *Collate* markup scheme (like all such specialized markup schemes) has severe limitations. For example, it does not handle gracefully very complex encodings of text rendition, with many tags nested inside one another. In particular, only the few programs which understand *Collate* style markup (essentially, those which can read the COCOA markup used by the Oxford Concordance Program) can manipulate *Collate* marked-up files just as they are.

There is a clear need for a standard system of encoding electronic humanities texts which will permit scholars to say all they want and yet will be transportable across any computer platform, including configurations as yet undreamt of. It was for this reason that, in the late 1980s, the three major humanities computing bodies (the Association for Literary and Linguistic Computing; the Association for Computational Linguistics; the Association for Computers and the Humanities) sponsored the Text Encoding Initiative (TEI). Over a five-year period and with considerable grant support from Europe and North America, the TEI developed an implementation of Standard Generalized Markup Language (SGML; itself a widely supported International Standard, ISO 8879) designed for encoding and interchange of humanities texts. The publication of the *Guidelines for Electronic Text Encoding and Interchange* in 1994 marked the end of the first cycle of its work.[30] There is a summary version of its recommendations touching on transcription of manuscripts in my *The Transcription of Primary Textual Sources Using SGML*.

Although at the time of writing the TEI *Guidelines* have been published little over two years, their rapid acceptance by many electronic text projects is one of the signal successes of humanities computing. The large collection of texts in the Electronic Text Centre at the University of Virginia, and many of those in the Oxford Text Archive, the one hundred million words of the British National Corpus, and the substantial electronic publications of Chadwyck-Healey and Cambridge University Press—somewhere in excess of the equivalent of several thousand printed volumes —have all already been encoded in an implementation of TEI markup. Furthermore, a variety of software is now available for presentation and manipulation of TEI-encoded text: thus the DynaText and Panorama browsers and the OpenText PAT search engine. The success of TEI encoding is such that for the present no scholarly transcription should proceed without some thought as to future translation of its files into SGML/TEI form. To pursue the analogy with Aldus Manutius one stage further: before Aldus published any Greek texts, he had a special fount cut, to ensure that his editions could appear as his editors wished and his readers expected.[31] The TEI *Guidelines* are to textual editors making electronic editions in the late twentieth century as Aldus' founts were to his editors in the late fifteenth century: the fundamental step which liberated solitary effort into scholarly communication.

EDITING A TEXT IN MANY VERSIONS WITH THE COMPUTER

Printed books and print culture altered far more than the distribution of books: they transformed the world. Already, for this editor at least, the small world of textual editing has been changed profoundly by the impact of computing. In this section, I wish to consider in more detail the effect of computing on the case of editing a text extant in many different versions. The discussion will be based on my experience of the use of computer methods in editing the fifty-eight fifteenth-century witnesses of the Wife of Bath's Prologue.

In essence, the techniques used by editors for preparing and presenting such a text have changed little since the scholars of the library at Alexandria sought to reconstruct the text of Homer. These techniques might be reduced, in summary form, to four steps:

Step One: The scholar identifies the different versions likely to be useful in the reconstruction.

Step Two: A conspectus is made of the variant readings in these different versions.

Step Three: A single text is made, by some process of selection from these variant readings combined with editorial emendation where deemed necessary.

Step Four: This single text is presented to the reader, with or without indication of the other readings available to the editor but rejected.

Every one of these four steps has been affected by the advent of computing. For Step One: the increasing availability over computer networks of manuscript catalogues and images of the manuscripts themselves (made using digital photography) will make it far easier for scholars to find and examine all the extant witnesses of any text. With only traditional tools, it can be very time-consuming and difficult to achieve this for a text in even a few witnesses. Indeed, of all the tasks faced by the *Canterbury Tales* Project, the apparently routine business of locating each manuscript, establishing where there are good copies (if any), writing to request these copies or arranging for new ones to be made, has proved the single most frustrating task we have had. We are still, after five years' effort, waiting for copies from some archives. Furthermore, the quality of many of the copies we have to use is often very poor: badly photographed microfilms, with text only intermittently readable. As more catalogues and images appear on the networks, it will be easier to find all there is, and there will be less and less reason for a scholar not to examine everything that is relevant, and not just those materials which are to hand—and it will be easier for readers to check that he or she has indeed done this.

In itself, this is revolution enough: this will make easy what has been difficult. But Step Two above, the identification of variant readings, is far more affected by computer methods. If one is collating 'by hand' (that is, by some process of transcribing variants from a more-or-less arbitrary base onto collation cards, or into rows and columns) one must apply some principle of selection, either in the choice of 'base text', or in variants recorded, or both together. But where one is editing a text in many manuscripts and has transcribed all the texts into electronic form, as outlined above, one can have the collation done by computer program.[32] There are considerable advantages in computer collation where one desires the most complete, word-by-word record of manuscript agreements and disagreements. One may experiment with collations with different levels of regularization, or with different master texts. For example, collation of the unregularized transcripts of the earliest manuscripts of the Wife of Bath's Prologue has shown remarkable agreements in spelling (as against substantive variation) between each of two pairs of manuscripts thought by many scholars to have been written by the one scribe.[33] Also, it is likely that computer collation will give a far more accurate and complete record of variation than is possible from manual collation. If the transcripts are accurate, then the collation will be accurate, and it is easier to check a transcript against a manuscript than to check a manual collation. In the first case, you are comparing just two things (the transcript and the manuscript); in the second you have to compare three things (the manuscript, the master, and the collation).

Computer collation on the model above, and as executed in our work for the Wife of Bath's Prologue, may generate far more information concerning all the variation in the manuscripts, both as 'substantive' variation, involving 'significant' variation affecting the meaning of particular lines, and as 'orthographic' variation, involving only the spelling or presentation of particular words and lines. Thus, for the Wife of Bath's Prologue we carried out two collations: a 'regularized' collation, presenting only substantive variation in the witnesses; and an 'unregularized' collation, presenting all information on variation of any kind preserved in our transcription. Between them, these collations contain a huge volume of information: around 700,000 items concerning the presence of particular readings in the fifty-eight witnesses.

In addition, as part of the regularization process for the Wife of Bath's Prologue, we created a complete record of every regularization of every word (or group of words, in the case of word division). For every spelling of every word, this record gave a headword form (typically, the infinitive form for verbs; the nominative singular for nouns), the part of speech, and the regularized and unregularized equivalents for every one of the more than 350,000 words in the fifty-eight witnesses. All these are sorted by headword form, part of speech, and spelling, and organized into spelling databases on the CD-ROM: fifty-nine spelling databases altogether, with one for each of the fifty-eight witnesses presenting only the spelling information for that witness and a single 'all-witness' spelling database which presents all the spellings in all the witnesses. For example, the 'all-witness' spelling database tells us that there are 172 different spellings of the thirty different parts of the verb 'to be' occurring in the fifty-eight witnesses. From this, one discovers that the Fitzwilliam manuscript spells the indicative present 3rd person singular of the verb 'to be' as 'ys' fifty-eight times, and 'is' three times, and that all of the 'is' occurrences occur in the last 150 lines of the Prologue (see Figure 4). A scholar could take this hint to explore the databases for further differences of spelling between the parts of the poem in the Fitzwilliam manuscript, to test a hypothesis about a shift of exemplar. Similarly, one might correlate the distribution of different forms with known facts about the provenance of individual manuscripts or about the geographical and historical distribution of particular forms and use the results to advance knowledge both about the manuscripts themselves and about the linguistic and dialectical variation they contain. This information will greatly facilitate studies such as those of Smith and Samuels into the 'orthographic layering' of manuscripts.[34]

It should be emphasized that, with the assistance of the computer, all this work proceeds far more quickly and easily than could be possible with any manual collation. The most time-consuming task is that of transcription. I estimate that the transcription of all the fifty-eight witnesses, each containing around seven thousand words of sometimes difficult-to-read Middle English, required about two thousand hours work, inclusive of at least four proof-readings of each transcript. Once the transcription was complete, the computer collation, including the classification of head-word form and part of speech for every one of the 350,000 words in the witnesses, took around 200 hours work, inclusive of two checks. Unques-tionably, one might have carried out a traditional selective hand-collation faster than this. But no hand-collation could have generated anything close to the amount of information we have been able to provide for the witnesses to the Wife of Bath's Prologue, with all the possible scholarly avenues this may open.

It may appear that the computer methods described above in Step Two of the processes of preparing an edition of a text in many witnesses are too successful: they identify far too much variation, and so make the editor's task in Step Three—the making of a single text from all this vari-ation—quite impossible. Indeed, it might be claimed that the electronic medium liberates editors from the need to create any single text. Why not just present every extant witness, perhaps in both transcript and image form, and perhaps with a collation showing variation in other witnesses relative to each witness, and have done with it?[35] As I suggest below, it is indeed likely that computer presentation may permit us to learn new ways to read multiple texts. But I believe that an editor may do far more than just collect and present multiple variant texts. In particular, one may turn once more to computer methods to interrogate the vast quantities of information provided by the processes of computer transcription and col-lation. One may have the computer sort, classify, filter, compare; point us where we might most usefully search; and so help us find the needle of significance in the haystack of variation. In our work on the Wife of Bath's Prologue we have used the computer techniques of cladistic and database analysis to search for patterns of variant distribution which might reveal the existence of family groupings of manuscripts, and thus provide the beginnings of an account of the development of the textual tradition.

I have discussed elsewhere in greater detail cladistic analysis and the reasons for its clear success with some textual traditions.[36] Cladistic ana-lysis is a technique developed in evolutionary biology to reconstruct the 'family tree' of related species by study of the characteristics they share and do not share. The success of cladistic analysis, working from manu-scripts' agreements and disagreements on particular words as generated by *Collate*, has been demonstrated on a variety of texts, particularly the forty-six manuscripts of the Old Norse narrative sequence *Svipdagsmál*.[37] Here, I will not say anything more about cladistic analysis except this: it works. That is the best theoretical justification available for any method.

For all its power, cladistic analysis cannot, of itself, explain exactly how each and every witness is related. It can suggest, by way of a 'first guess', that there might be a relationship between certain witnesses, but it cannot determine just what the relationship is: whether descent from a common exemplar, or one from another. Cladistic analysis may also be misled by contamination into thinking that manuscripts are much more closely related than they are. In order to determine exactly how manuscripts are related, one needs ready access to the variants themselves which evidence a relationship. One needs answers to questions like 'what variants are found in these two manuscripts, and in no more than three other manuscripts, but not in this manuscript'. This is precisely the sort of task at which a well-designed database can excel, providing in seconds what might take hours or days to discover manually. The *Canterbury Tales* Project uses a variant database facility built into *Collate* for just this purpose.

Cladistic analysis, supplemented by variant database analysis, is that rarest of phenomena: a completely new tool which offers fundamental advances far beyond what might be achieved simply by the refinement of existing methods. The availability of this technique was decisive in persuading us that it was possible to go beyond Manly and Rickert's analyses of the relationship among the manuscripts of the *Canterbury Tales*, and hence that the Project might be worthwhile.[38] Preliminary work, reported in my 'An Approach to the Manuscripts of the Wife of Bath's Prologue', suggests that this confidence is reasonably based.[39] A further test of the utility of a new scholarly method is its ability to enable new work, by other scholars. Already, my cladistic analysis of the witnesses to the Wife of Bath's Prologue has led to new work which could not otherwise have been done. The cladistic analysis revealed a remarkable link between five manuscripts among the fifty-eight witnesses. It appears that these five are united by a distinctive system of punctuation, and further that this distinctive system was introduced into the manuscripts by at least three different scribes, working independently of one another. The variant database, in a few seconds, revealed the exact lines in these five manuscripts which showed this distinctive punctuation. Elizabeth Solopova took up this information and compared the punctuation system in these five manuscripts (and some other manuscripts) to the rather different system found in the Hengwrt and Ellesmere manuscripts.[40] From close analysis of the two systems, she concluded that the system found in the five manuscripts was scribal, and not authorial, while that found in Hengwrt and Ellesmere appeared to be authorial: Chaucer's own punctuation, apparently not understood by scribes and replaced (in these manuscripts) with a scheme more familiar to them. Solopova's findings contradicted those of an earlier study by Killough.[41] A crucial factor in her work was the evidence of scribal punctuation given by these five manuscripts, evidence not available to Killough.

The example of cladistic and database analysis given above, and the use made of it in underpinning other original research, suggests that computer methods might help us to understand better some aspects of a given tradition. I suggest in my paper on 'Best-Text Historical Editing' that an editor might use this understanding to inform assessment of the relative weight to be given to various witnesses, and the readings contained within them.[42] From this, one might arrive at a reasoned determination of just what witness, and just what readings, are likely to stand closest to the author's original, and thus form the basis of a 'single-text' edition, exactly as provided in Step Three of the editorial schema given above. In this, it might appear that we have gone to all this effort to achieve no advance on traditional editorial practice, as embodied in five centuries of printed editions. These printed editions might present a single text; so too might the editor of an electronic critical text.

However, there is a considerable difference between the single printed text of any work compiled by traditional manual methods and that compiled by the electronic means outlined above: between, for example, the text presented in volumes three and four of Manly and Rickert's *Text of the Canterbury Tales* and the text we might present. A print editor must build the edition on more-or-less partial transcripts and collations; the processes of assessing the relative authority of the witnesses and thus fixing a text must be, at least in part, selective and intuitive. By contrast, an electronic edition may rest on comprehensive transcription, collation, and analysis. In fact, the differences between the editions made by these methods may actually be quite small, or even non-existent. Most editors using traditional methods try to be impartial and objective in their application of them; as the discussion of transcription above shows it is perfectly possible for editors using electronic means to introduce subjective elements into the data so that what appears 'scientific' may in fact be highly personal. The real difference between the processes of preparation of a printed edition and an electronic edition may be in their presentation. Because of the limitations of space in most printed editions, and because of the limitations of the medium itself, it is not possible for print editors to do more than include the results of their analysis, perhaps together with a summary of the processes of analysis. As a result, it is easy for critics of textual scholars—whether fairly or unfairly—to present their methods as partial or capricious (as for example Kane does in his critique of Manly and Rickert).[43] In contrast, an electronic edition may permit the editor to set out all the stages of analysis leading to the substantive conclusions of the edition. Furthermore, the editor of the electronic edition could provide the means by which the reader might re-create all these stages, test the evidence for each hypothesis, and use the same tools to explore a counter-hypothesis. Thus, a future release of the *Canterbury Tales* Project would permit a reader to follow through every stage of the cladistic and database analyses of the Wife of Bath's Prologue which underpin Solopova's arguments, and so be better placed to assess the force of the evidence for her conclusions. As an aside, one may doubt that editions of the *Canterbury Tales* based on the Ellesmere manuscript would still be in use if Manly and Rickert had been able to present fully the evidence for the superiority of the Hengwrt manuscript.

The possibilities for the presentation of the electronic edition, referred to in the last paragraph, bring us to Step Four of this summary of the potential differences between print and electronic media: the presentation of the text to the reader, with or without indication of variant forms of the text. As I note above, one might eliminate Step Three altogether, and simply present all the accumulated evidence for all the different states of the text. Indeed, the Wife of Bath's Prologue on CD-ROM goes some way towards this kind of edition. This CD-ROM does present transcripts and images of all the witnesses; it does present a full bibliographic description of each witness; it does give massively detailed word-by-word collations documenting all the variation in all the witnesses; it does set out all the different spellings of every part of speech of every word in every witness. This amounts to a quantity of information roughly equivalent to around one hundred printed volumes, and unimaginable in printed form. While it is our intention to present, ultimately, our own account of how we believe the textual tradition developed, it is also our intention (as explained above) to present the materials in such a way that the reader may test our conclusions and explore different hypotheses. The electronic medium permits us this freedom: we can present not just one text of the Wife of Bath's Prologue; we may present fifty-eight at once.

This possibility creates a new challenge for the editor, for the publisher, and for the reader: how does an edition present fifty-eight different texts at once? how does a reader read fifty-eight texts at once? The *Wife of Bath's Prologue on CD-ROM* presents the beginnings of an attempt to meet these challenges. In essence, we have used hypertext to link together the transcripts, images, collations, and spelling databases of all the witnesses on the CD-ROM so that the reader can compare any word or line in any witness with that in any other witness in an instant, with a few mouse-clicks. Thus, one can click on a word in any witness and see two full collations of every witness at that word. The first collation presents a 'regularized' collation: that is, presenting only substantive variation in the witnesses. Figure 1 presents the regularized collation for the word 'Experience', as it appears in *The Wife of Bath's Prologue on CD-ROM* when one clicks on this word, the first word in the first line of the Wife of Bath's Prologue. The second full collation is an 'unregularized' collation, presenting all information on variation of any kind. Figure 2 presents the unregularized collation for 'Experience', as it appears when one double-clicks on the icon next to the instruction 'Double-click the icon to the left to see the unregularized collation at this word' in the regularized collation window shown in Figure 1.

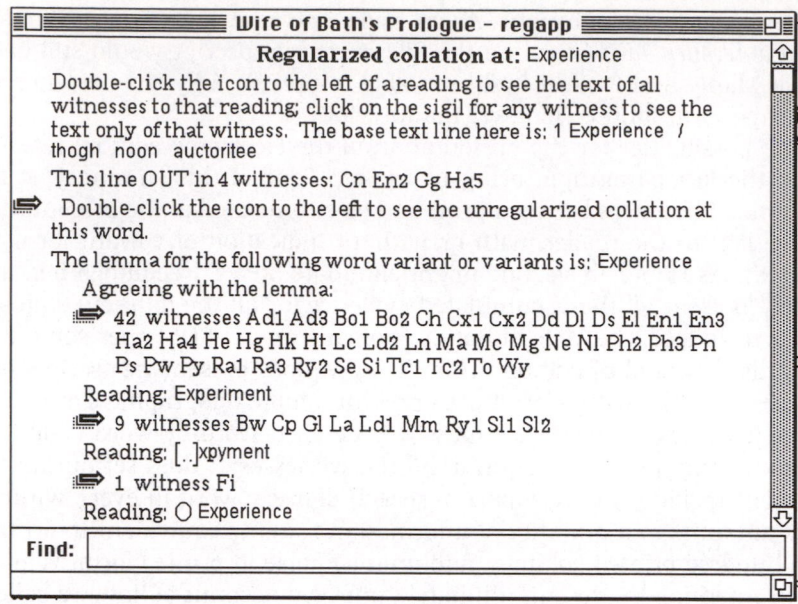

FIG. 1. Regularized collation of 'Experience', from *The Wife of Bath's Prologue on CD-ROM*, showing only substantive variation at this word.

Wife of Bath's Prologue - unregapp

Unregularized collation at: Experience

Click on the sigil for any witness to see the text of that witness. The base text line here is: 1 Experience / thogh noon auctoritee

⟹ Double-click the icon to the left to see the regularized collation at this word.

Experience Cx1 Ma; Experience Ad1 Ad3 Hg Hk Ra3 Se; [.e.]xperience Bo1 ; Expience Bo2 Dd Ry2; Expiment Bw; Expience Ch Ld2 Mg Ph2 Si To; EExperience Cx2; Experience Dl Ne; Experience Ds; Experience El; E xpience En1 Ht Pw; Experience En3 Ps Py; Experyence Ha2; Expiens Ha4; Experyence He; Expience Lc Mc; Expience Ln; Expimente Mm Ry1; Experiens Nl; [.e.]xperience Pn; Experyence Ra1; Eryment Ra2; Experience Tc1; Experyence Tc2; EXperyence Wy; ¶ + Cx1 Ma.

Experience...thogh Expiment þough Cp; ○ Experience though Ii; Experiment þough Ld1; Experyens thow3 Ph3; Experiment though Sl2.

Experience...noon [..]xpyment though none Fi; Experyment though none Gl; Expiment þouhe / none La; Experyment þough noñ Sl1.

Click on this line to see the variants on the next word

Find: |

FIG. 2. Unregularized collation of 'Experience', from *The Wife of Bath's Prologue on CD-ROM*, showing all variation of spelling and substantive variation at this word.

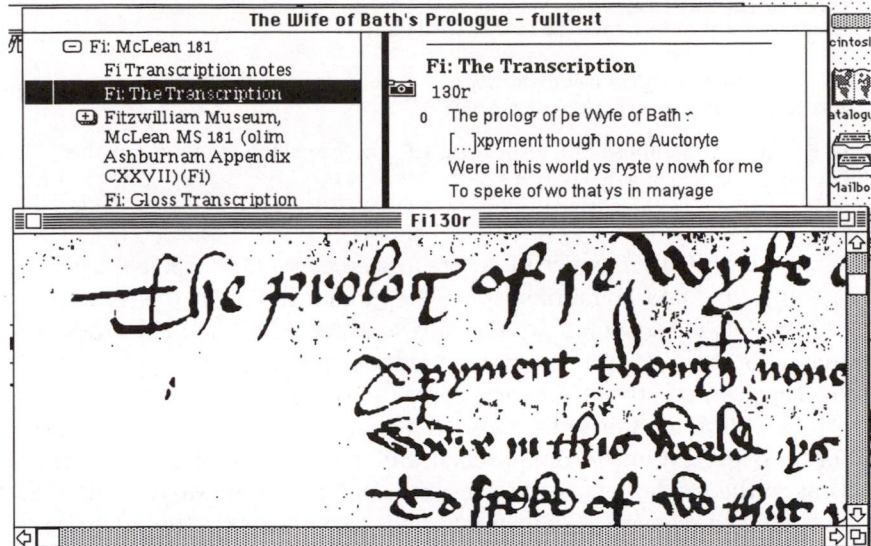

The Wife of Bath's Prologue - fulltext

Fi: McLean 181
Fi Transcription notes
Fi: The Transcription
Fitzwilliam Museum,
McLean MS 181 (olim
Ashburnam Appendix
CXXVII)(Fi)
Fi: Gloss Transcription

Fi: The Transcription
130r

0   The prolog' of þe Wyfe of Bath ·
    [...]xpyment though none Auctoryte
    Were in this world ys ry3te y nowh for me
    To speke of wo that ys in maryage

Fi 130r

FIG. 3. Transcription and image of the opening lines of The Wife of Bath's Prologue in Fitzwilliam Museum McLean MS 181.

One may move instantly from one collation to another, or one may move to that point in the full transcript for any witness just by clicking on the sigil for that witness in the collation, and then there are further links from each page of the transcript to the images of each witness page. For convenience, the transcript and the image of any part of the text may be placed in separate windows, as shown in Figure 3.

This provides access to the transcripts and images of the witnesses, and to information on all word-by-word and line-by-line variation across the witnesses. In addition, the CD-ROM also presents the fifty-nine spelling databases referred to above. From these, one can gain access to information about all the variation in spelling of every word across each witness and across all witnesses. I give the example above of the two forms of the indicative present singular 3rd person in the Fitzwilliam manuscript. The CD-ROM allows the reader, within an instant, to see all the fifty-eight lines in the transcript of this manuscript with the spelling 'ys' and the three with the spelling 'is'. Figure 4 shows the three spellings with 'is', and shows too that all these are found in the last 150 lines of the text. One may then (through yet more hypertext) move into the all-witness database, and survey the comparative frequency of 'ys'/'is' spellings across all the witnesses, once more with links from every citation of a word in a witness to the line in that witness. Effectively, this is a massive key-word-in-context fully lemmatized concordance. I noted above how all this is made possible

Click on any line to move to that line in the transcription. Number of occurrences of this spelling in this witness: (3)

683 And venus falleth þeɼ Mercurie is reysed

752 Betɭ is quoth he high in the Rofe to abyde

827 Do dame teɫ forth youɼ tale and þ t is best

FIG. 4. Spelling database entry showing the three spellings with 'is' in the Fitzwilliam manuscript.

by computer collation, which discovers and creates all the linkages between the transcripts and collations (some 1.9 million links on this CD-ROM), and by SGML/TEI encoding, which expresses all the links found by the computer collation. Now, the electronic medium makes it possible for all this to be represented attractively and conveniently on the computer screen.

This CD-ROM contains much else to help the reader read fifty-eight texts at once: hypertext links from Elizabeth Solopova's discussions of the transcripts to the transcripts themselves; more links to Dan Mosser's descriptions of the witnesses; to Stephen Partridge's transcripts of the glosses. Yet, an electronic edition could still do far more to present multiple versions of the one text. We intend that future *Canterbury Tales* Project CD-ROMs will include a collation module, so that scholars may have the program run collations on whatever text in whatever witnesses they wish, and view the collation in a variety of formats. Future CD-ROMs should also include a variant database module, so that scholars may have instant answers to complex queries concerning the distribution of the variants across the witnesses. There is also much work to be done on refining and elaborating the links between the transcripts and the images. On the CD-ROM of the Wife of Bath's Prologue, the links are one-way only, from each page of the transcript to each page image. There are no links from the image to the transcript, and no links from the image of one page to the preceding or next page. These links at the page level are coarse and inconvenient: one should like to be able to click on a line, or a word, in the transcript and have the corresponding line or word in the image highlighted: and also move in the reverse direction, from a line or word in the image to the transcript. Furthermore, we may expect that the application of pattern-matching techniques, identifying each letter form in every word of the images by comparison with the transcripts and then classifying them into databases by their shape, will open up new realms of palaeographic research.[44]

Work is under way on all these enhancements; and no doubt as these are implemented, yet further enhancements will suggest themselves.[45] Nor will editions of this kind be restricted to CD-ROM format. Many of the elements of this edition of the Wife of Bath's Prologue could already be made available on the World Wide Web over the Internet. There are still difficulties, both technical and administrative, in the way of full network publication of electronic editions of this complexity. However, we can expect that these difficulties will very soon be solved, and that editions of this kind will soon be routinely distributed over the Internet. Even with the current mode of CD-ROM distribution, and without the further developments outlined above, the CD-ROM of the Wife of Bath's Prologue is very different from a printed book. I have suggested above that every aspect of the preparation of an electronic edition by a textual scholar has been altered, in some aspects profoundly, by the impact of computing methods. Making an electronic edition is very different from making a printed edition. Using and reading an electronic edition will be very different from using and reading a print edition.

Compare, for example, the spelling databases on this CD-ROM with the 'linguistic profiles' in the *Linguistic Atlas of Late Middle English*.[46] These linguistic profiles are based on surveying comparatively few selected spellings in the manuscripts; in contrast, the electronic spelling databases present every spelling of every word in the manuscripts. Again, the wealth of information will require that the scholar master various computer-aided techniques, to mine useful insights from so much data. More significantly, this marks a shift from judgement based on selected and necessarily limited samples of information towards comprehensive analysis of all available data. Similarly, discussions of the textual tradition will not be based on partial and selective collations, but on complete word-by-word collations, with analysis again assisted by computer techniques.

ELECTRONIC TEXTS AND HUMAN READERS

We will be disappointed if only a few linguistic and textual specialists were to use the CD-ROM of The Wife of Bath's Prologue, in the manner outlined in the last paragraph. Central to our programme is the belief that scholarly texts are best read in a form as close to the original as possible. Hence, our emphasis on distributing images of the highest possible quality of the manuscripts of the *Canterbury Tales* in the later CD-ROMS. Up to the advent of computing, scholarship has been defined by physical access to primary materials. If all that is available is an old edition of Chaucer, then that is how you have to read Chaucer. If no women's texts of the English romantic period are available, then you cannot read them at all.[47] Libraries have jealously guarded their manuscripts. Only a few fortunate scholars a year could read *Beowulf* in the unique original manuscript, or Chaucer in the Ellesmere. For most readers, the primary source does not exist. The effects of this can be felt in every corner of scholarship. It can be felt in editions which are impoverished in detail because they have had to be based, at best, on microfilm, or, at worst, on other printed editions. It can be felt in critical studies which study the text as if it were written when it were printed, apart from the manuscript or other culture in which it was created. It can be felt in readings which forget the radical happenstance attendant on the birth of any text, evident in the catscradle of corrections found in authorial manuscripts.

The great power of digital methods to capture, preserve, and distribute scholarly resources—texts, sounds, images still and moving—will redress the balance of reading. A text will not be simply its latest printing, in black text on white paper. In the world of printing and self-proclaimed 'definitive texts', a poor microfilm of a manuscript appears only as a step along the way to the perfection of the text in its printing, a step which only certain unfortunate textual scholars might have to negotiate. Instead, the excellence of the images we can now create and distribute will encourage readers to see the primary source as another perfection too, with its own codes and values, and at least as worthy of attention as the printed text. Manuscript scholars, and buyers of deluxe facsimiles, have always known this. These fortunate few have always known that the printed text which, for so many readers and critics, is all the text they ever see, is a pallid shadow of the author's manuscript or the scribal copy. We have the means to make many others aware of it too.

Where, then, are these new directions in critical editing taking us? One of Aldus' contemporaries, the Venetian noble and diarist Domenico Malipiero, commented of attempts to find a proper home for the great library of Greek manuscripts collected by Cardinal Bessarion that these manuscripts 'were not worth much, since you could buy printed copies'.[48] We are reversing Malipiero's dictum: once we can see, through the magic of digital imaging, all that is in the manuscript, then it is the printed copy which is 'not worth much'. In electronic editions such as that of the *Canterbury Tales* Project we will be shifting the focus from the printed object back to the primary sources: to the manuscripts, to the first printed editions. As never before, scholars will be able to examine these in the images we provide, to read them in the transcriptions, to research them through the collations, databases, and analytic tools. Erasmus said of Aldus that he was producing a library which was not bounded by place or time, like the great libraries of the past, and knew no boundaries except the boundaries of the world.[49] The electronic editions we are making may open up the records of the past to many more people than can be fitted into the manuscript reading rooms of the Bodleian Library, or the British Library, or the Bibliothèque Nationale. There is no telling where this process might lead. In 1516 Bishop Richard Fox established Corpus Christi College in Oxford, dedicated exclusively to the study of theology in Latin, Greek, and Hebrew. In Corpus Christi's first library catalogue, 24 of the 33 Greek volumes were Aldine editions.[50] One may well speculate that if it had not been for Aldus providing these Greek texts, Fox would not have founded Corpus Christi. The *Canterbury Tales* Project intends to publish a full transcript and complete high-quality digital photographic record of Corpus Christi MS 198, preserved in that same library and possibly the earliest manuscript of the *Canterbury Tales*. If it had not been for Corpus Christi, this manuscript might have been lost; if it had not been for Aldus, there may have been no Corpus Christi. Of such links are the chains of knowledge constructed. In the next few years, we have a remarkable opportunity to make a new chain of knowledge, building it from electronic editions containing materials of unparalleled richness. This will need all the energy, enterprise, determination, and vision we can gather. Above all, we have to work together. If in the next twenty years we can achieve in this new medium half of what Aldus managed in the twenty years between 1495 and 1515, then we will have done well.

NOTES

A version of this essay was read at the Maison Française, Oxford, on 2 October 1993 during a conference on computing and textual scholarship. I am indebted to those present on that occasion for their comments, and particularly to Marc Fresko for his continued encouragement. Many of the ideas stem from frequent and lengthy discussions with Marilyn Deegan and Kathryn Sutherland: so much so that none of us could now say for certain who originated which idea. As will appear from the substance of the examples drawn from the work of the *Canterbury Tales* Project, I owe more than any acknowledgement can repay to the staff and associates of that project, and especially to my long-time collaborator on the Wife of Bath's Prologue, Elizabeth Solopova.

1. P. Delany and G. P. Landow (eds.), *The Digital Word: Text-Based Computing in the Humanities* (Cambridge, Mass. and London: MIT Press, 1993), p. 5. For the impact of printing on textual scholarship, see the accounts in L. D. Reynolds and N. G. Wilson, *Scribes and Scholars*, 3rd edn. (Oxford: Oxford University Press, 1991), pp. 154–8; and, in more detail, in D. C. Greetham, *Textual Scholarship: An Introduction* (New York and London: Garland, 1992), pp. 77–112.
2. The account of Aldus Manutius in this article draws on M. Lowry, *The World of Aldus Manutius* (Oxford: Blackwell, 1979).
3. Ibid., pp. 80–1, summarizes printing of Greek texts before Aldus.
4. Ibid., pp. 109–67, especially tables I, II, III; see also pp. 257–8.
5. Ibid., p. 148.
6. Brian Richardson, *Print Culture in Renaissance Italy* (Cambridge: Cambridge University Press, 1994), pp. 48–53, discusses Bembo's Aldine edition of Petrarch and Dante.

7. Lowry, *Aldus Manutius*, p. 94, citing M. M. Philips, *The Adages of Erasmus: A Study with Translations* (Cambridge: Cambridge University Press, 1964), pp. 67–8. The quotation from Erasmus is from his *Apologia adversus Albertum Pium*, printed by Froben at Basle in 1531 (pp. 55–60). Erasmus prefaces his remarks with 'I loved Aldus alive, and I would not harm him dead.' Elsewhere in his works, he expresses sincere admiration for Aldus, and his achievement: see n. 49 below.

8. Lowry, *Aldus Manutius*, p. 94, describes the conditions in Aldus' printing house amusingly: 'As far as we can reconstruct them, the conditions reflect a now-incredible mixture of the sweat-shop, the boarding-house and the research institute.' Those who have raced to complete an electronic edition to a publisher's deadline will not find this description incredible.

9. Robert Proctor, *The Printing of Greek in the Fifteenth Century* (Oxford: Oxford University Press, 1900), p. 71.

10. Lowry, *Aldus Manutius*, pp. 80–1.

11. Ibid., p. 257; also p. 174 n. 96.

12. Colin Clair, *A History of European Printing* (London: Academic Press, 1976), p. 121.

13. Personal communication, Cambridge University Press editorial staff.

14. Lowry, *Aldus Manutius*, pp. 115–16, compares the prices of several Aldine editions of Greek texts with those of other publishers. In general, Aldus' prices were double those of the other publishers.

15. Ibid., pp. 280–1.

16. See the discussion of Caxton's first printing of *The Canterbury Tales* in N. F. Blake, *Caxton and his World* (London: Andre Deutsch, 1969), pp. 102–5.

17. The *Canterbury Tales* Project is directed by Professor Norman Blake of the University of Sheffield, with myself as joint general editor and Elizabeth Solopova as principal transcriber. The project has received support from the Universities of Sheffield and Oxford, De Montfort University, and Brigham Young University, the British Academy, the Leverhulme Trust, and News International. The first major publication of the project was my *The Wife of Bath's Prologue on CD-ROM* (Cambridge: Cambridge University Press, 1996). The project has also published an *Occasional Papers* volume, edited by myself and N. F. Blake (Oxford: Office for Humanities Communication, 1993). A second *Occasional Papers* volume was published in April 1997.

18. There is an account of the possibilities for the making of computer images of manuscript and other primary sources in my *The Digitization of Primary Textual Sources* (Oxford: Office for Humanities Communication, 1993).

19. Robinson (ed.), *Wife of Bath's Prologue on CD-ROM*. During 1993, the British Library carried out tests with a Mekel microfilm scanner, and achieved typical digitization rates of twenty frames a minute with satisfactory resolution. In discussions with the author, the principals of several microfilm companies stated their intention to digitize some (at least) of their microfilms in the near future.

20. Many scholars, working in widely separated fields, have recently stressed the importance of the physical expression of primary texts. For medieval texts, see the discussion of the changes in manuscript presentation in the context

of the development of research tools in the 12th and 13th centuries in M. A. Rouse and R. H. Rouse, *Authentic Witnesses: Approaches to Medieval Texts and Manuscripts* (Notre Dame, Ind.: University of Notre Dame Press, 1991), pp. 191–258. For modern texts, see the work of Jerome McGann on 'bibliographic codes' (e.g. his 1991 article 'What is Critical Editing', *Text*, 5 (1991), 15–30); D. F. McKenzie, *Bibliography and the Sociology of Texts* (London: British Library Publications, 1986); and the summary discussion in Greetham, *Textual Scholarship*, pp. 291–4.

21. This is the facsimile of the Ellesmere Chaucer published in 1995 by Yushudo Publishing, Tokyo, and the Huntington Library, San Marino.

22. An example of modern colour printing of a high-quality facsimile is the process found necessary by Alecto Historical Editions for their photographic facsimile of the Domesday Book, in (for example) *The Lancashire Domesday*, ed. A. Williams and G. H. Martin (London: Alecto Historical Editions, 1991). Every page had to be photographed five times, with film of differing grains and sensitivity, each photograph developed and plates made, and then the facsimile made by overlay printing of the five plates with different colours onto specially chosen paper (personal communication, J. G. Studholme of Alecto Historical Editions). Compare the account of Griggs's printing of the colour pages of the 1911 Ellesmere facsimile in Ralph Hanna III, *The Ellesmere Manuscript of Chaucer's Canterbury Tales: A Working Facsimile* (Cambridge: D. S. Brewer, 1989), pp. 4–9. With, for example, the Kontron camera, one simply places the manuscript under the camera; the computer image appears on the screen within thirty seconds. Three colour plates in my *Digitization of Primary Textual Sources* are printed from manuscript photographs taken with the Kontron camera.

23. Thus, a single CD-ROM could contain around six hundred images of 10 by 7 inch pages captured at 300 dpi and 24 bit colour, compressed with JPEG to a megabyte of file storage for each image; enough for a full manuscript. Accordingly, the University of Michigan Press, in association with the Society for Early English and Norse Electronic Texts (SEENET), has announced publication of a full digital photographic record of Corpus Christi College Oxford MS 201, containing Langland's *Piers Plowman*, edited by Hoyt N. Duggan. The *Canterbury Tales* Project has contracted with Cambridge University Press for publication of two CD-ROMs presenting a full photographic record of two *Canterbury Tales* manuscripts, Corpus Christi College Oxford MS 198 and British Library Harley MS 7334.

24. There has been considerable excitement at the prospect of image enhancement techniques on digital photographs of manuscripts yielding new readings, and confirming or denying old ones. In fact, experiments so far have not confirmed this promise. Image enhancement appears a useful way of making a poor photograph better and is simply not needed (beyond basic magnification) when working with a high-quality image taken with appropriate lighting such as those provided by the Kontron or similar devices. See K. Kiernan, 'Digital Image Processing and the *Beowulf* Manuscript', *Literary and Linguistic Computing*, 6 (1991), 20–7; and my *Digitization of Primary Textual Sources*, pp. 55–9. For the effect of these on scholarship, compare the

intense study of manuscript detail for Chaucer and Langland found in the last decades in the work of Malcolm Parkes and Ian Doyle: for example, their seminal 'The Production of Copies of the *Canterbury Tales*', in M. B. Parkes (ed.), *Scribes, Scripts and Readers: Studies in the Communication, Presentation and Dissemination of Medieval Texts* (London and Rio Grande: Hambledon Press, 1991), pp. 210–48; and their essay on the Hengwrt manuscript in *The Canterbury Tales. Geoffrey Chaucer. A Facsimile and Transcription of the Hengwrt Manuscript*, ed. P. G. Ruggiers (Norman: University of Oklahoma Press, 1979). Research of this kind will become possible for a much wider scholarly community.

25. The interpretative nature of transcription is discussed in P. M. W. Robinson and E. Solopova, 'Guidelines for the Transcription of Manuscripts of The Wife of Bath's Prologue', in Blake and Robinson (eds.), *Occasional Papers*. This has also been republished, slightly revised, in Robinson, *Wife of Bath's Prologue on CD-ROM*.

26. Robinson and Solopova, 'Guidelines', in Blake and Robinson (eds.), *Occasional Papers*.

27. Instances of similar statements of practice for machine-readable transcription of manuscript materials are: *Möðruvallabók*, ed. A. Van Arkel (Leiden: E. J. Brill, 1987), for the great Old Norse manuscript Möðruvallabók; H. Fix, 'Production and Usage of a Machine-Readable Manuscript: A Report on the Saarbrücken Version of *Grágás Konungsbók*', in A. Gilmour-Bryson (ed.), *Computer Applications to Medieval Studies* (Kalamazoo: Western Michigan University, 1984), for the Old Norse *Grágás Konungsbók*; and *Beowulf: An Edition with Manuscript Spacing Notation and Graphotactic Analyses*, ed. R. D. Stevick (New York: Garland, 1975).

28. Several such 'home-grown' systems of transcription are surveyed in my *The Transcription of Primary Textual Sources Using SGML* (Oxford: Office for Humanities Communication Publications, 1994).

29. Peter M. W. Robinson, *Collate: A Program for Interactive Collation of Large Manuscript Traditions*, Version 2.1 (Milton Keynes: International Institute for Electronic Library Research, 1996).

30. C. M. Sperberg-McQueen and Lou Burnard (eds.), *Guidelines for Electronic Text Encoding and Interchange* (Chicago and Oxford: Text Encoding Initiative, 1994).

31. Lowry, *Aldus Manutius*, pp. 86–7.

32. Obviously, not all manuscripts of all texts are of such interest as to merit the full transcription here outlined, and proposed by the *Canterbury Tales* Project. One might carry out a full transcription only of samples of the text in all the manuscripts, or transcribe all the text only in some manuscripts. Whatever fractions of text are transcribed, the techniques here described hold good.

The scholar has a choice of many collation programs, including the widely used programs developed by Ott and Shillingsburg. For Ott's TUSTEP, a set of routines (including a collation facility) for editing and for processing of scholarly information, see the summaries in I. Lancashire, *Humanities Computing Yearbook 1989–90* (Oxford: Oxford University Press, 1991), pp. 407–8 and in *Literary and Linguistic Computing*, 4: 3 (1989), 235–7. TUSTEP is available from the Zentrum für Datenverarbeitung, University of Tübingen,

Brunnenstrasse 27, D-7400 Tübingen, Germany. For Shillingsburg's CASE, available on many different computer platforms and used, for example, in editions of Thackeray, Dreiser, Conrad, Hardy, and Carlyle, see P. L. Shillingsburg, *Scholarly Editing in the Computer Age: Theory and Practice* (Athens and London: University of Georgia Press, 1986). The program is available from the Department of English, Mississippi State University, Miss. 39762.

33. See the discussion in my 'An Approach to the Manuscripts of the Wife of Bath's Prologue', in I. Lancashire (ed.), *Computer-based Chaucer Studies* (Toronto: University of Toronto Press, 1993), pp. 17–47. The two pairs of manuscripts are: Hengwrt and Ellesmere; Corpus Christi Oxford and Harleian 7334, characterized by Parkes and Doyle, 'Production of Copies', in Parkes and Watson (eds.), *Medieval Scribes*, as written by 'hand b' and 'hand d', respectively. For a different view, see R. Vance Ramsey, 'The Hengwrt and Ellesmere Manuscripts of the *Canterbury Tales*: Different Scribes', *Studies in Bibliography*, 35 (1982), 133–54; and id., 'Paleography and Scribes of Shared Training', *Studies in the Age of Chaucer*, 8 (1986), 107–44.

34. For example, the essays collected in J. J. Smith (ed.), *The English of Chaucer and his Contemporaries* (Aberdeen: Aberdeen University Press, 1988).

35. One could, for example, follow the example of Michael J. Warren in his *The Complete 'King Lear', 1608–1623* (Berkeley: University of California Press, 1989). This presents facsimiles of the corresponding passages in the folio and quarto versions of *King Lear* side-by-side, with no commentary or explanations, avowedly to remove the editor's presence from the text. But even Warren admits that the editor cannot help but be present in the text, as he found himself having to order the text with the parallel texts placed first: 'Thus I who wish to avoid editing as far as possible find myself, incongruously enough, placing my version before the historical documents' (preface, p. vii). See too T. H. Howard-Hill's review of Warren in *Review of English Studies*, n.s. 43 (1992), 420–2, and especially his comment (p. 421) 'simply to place illustrations of the physical forms of the respective texts together amounts to an assertion of their physical relationship . . . *The Complete King Lear* seems to say that the physical forms of the later text may be explained by the physical forms of the earlier text, whereas that is a contention requiring examination'.

36. See my 'Computer-Assisted Stemmatic Analysis and "Best-Text" Historical Editing', in P. van Reenen and M. van Mulken (eds.), *Studies in Stemmatology* (Amsterdam: John Benjamins, 1996), pp. 71–103; and the articles I wrote with Robert O'Hara on cladistic analysis in 'Report on the Textual Criticism Challenge 1991', *Bryn Mawr Classical Review*, 3 (1992), 331–7 and 'Cladistic Analysis of an Old Norse Manuscript Tradition', in S. Hockey and N. Ide (eds.), *Research in Humanities Computing*, 4 (Oxford: Clarendon Press, 1996), pp. 115–37.

37. Robinson and O'Hara, 'Cladistic Analysis', pp. 125–8.

38. John Manly and Edith Rickert, *The Text of 'The Canterbury Tales'* (8 vols.; Chicago: Chicago University Press, 1940).

39. Robert O'Hara and I have used the cladistic program PAUP ('Phylogenetic Analysis Using Parsimony' developed by David Swofford) on NEXUS files

generated by *Collate* direct from the collation output. The Project edition of *Collate*, due for release on the Macintosh platform in July 1997, refines the interface between it and cladistic programs. A full survey of the results of my analysis of the textual tradition of the Wife of Bath's Prologue has been published in the second volume of the *Occasional Papers*.

40. The following sentences summarize Elizabeth Solopova's work as described in 'Punctuation in the Early Manuscripts of the *Canterbury Tales*', a paper presented at the York Medieval Texts conference in July 1996.

41. George B. Killough, 'Punctuation and Caesura in Chaucer', *Studies in the Age of Chaucer*, 4 (1982), 87–107.

42. Robinson, 'Computer-Assisted Stemmatic Analysis and "Best-Text" Historical Editing', in van Reenen and van Mulken (eds.), *Studies in Stemmatology*, pp. 96–9. Compare the method espoused by George Kane and Janet Cowen in their edition of Chaucer's *The Legend of Good Women* (East Lansing, Mich.: Colleagues Press, 1995), p. viii, where 'genetic relation' is one of a set of probabilities 'in a structure of related contingencies' which editors must assess in determination of the text.

43. George Kane, 'John M. Manly and Edith Rickert', in Paul G. Ruggiers (ed.), *Editing Chaucer: The Great Tradition* (Norman, Okla.: Pilgrim Books, 1984), pp. 207–29.

44. These techniques might lead to the development of 'scribal profiles' anticipated in Michael Benskin, 'The Hands of the Kildare Poems Manuscript', *Irish University Review*, 20 (1990), 163–93, based on analysis of the full repertoire of scribal choice of letter forms and potentially capable of distinguishing and identifying individual scribes and groups of scribes at work in different manuscripts.

45. The *Collate* program is already capable of both 'on-line' collation and variant database searches, as here outlined, on the Macintosh computer platform. A Windows version of *Collate* is in preparation, and this will enable integration of these tools into a network-capable browser running on both the Macintosh and Windows platforms. Similarly, one could use the software tools available in the system integrator's version of DynaText, the program used to present the Wife of Bath's Prologue CD-ROM, to have links from images to transcripts, or from image to image. The European Union funded BAMBI project is currently developing a full implementation of the image and text integration routines developed by Andrea Bozzi, of the CNI laboratory in Pisa. These promise the linkage of image and transcript at the word and line level here anticipated.

46. Angus McIntosh, M. L. Samuels, and Michael Benskin (eds.), *A Linguistic Atlas of Late Mediaeval English* (4 vols.; Aberdeen: Aberdeen University Press, 1986).

47. The Brown University Women Writers Project (http://www.wwp.brown.edu/) and the Oxford-based Project Electra are addressing exactly this problem, so far as women's texts of the English romantic period are concerned.

48. Lowry, *Aldus Manutius*, p. 230.

49. Ibid., p. 258, citing Philips, *Adages of Erasmus*, pp. 180–1. Philips is translating adage IV. VI. xxxv, on the proverb 'Festina lente'. This adage first

appeared in the 1526 edition of the adages, published as *Adagiorum Opus* by John Froben of Basle. Philips's translation of this passage (from the 1533 edition) is worth quoting in full: 'the man who sets fallen learning on its feet (and this is almost more difficult than to originate it in the first place) is building up a sacred and immortal thing, and serving not one province alone but all peoples and generations. Once this was the task of princes, and it was the greatest glory of Ptolemy. But his library was contained between the narrow walls of its own house, and Aldus is building a library which has no other limits than the world itself.'

50. Lowry, *Aldus Manutius*, p. 258, citing J. R. Liddell, 'The Library of Corpus Christi College, Oxford, in the Sixteenth Century', B. Litt. thesis (Oxford, 1938), summarized in *Transactions of the Oxford Bibliographical Society*, 18 (1938), 385–416.

8

Digital Archive as Expanded Text: Shakespeare and Electronic Textuality

PETER S. DONALDSON

INTRODUCTION

The materials relevant to the study of Shakespeare are extensive: they include the early folio and quarto editions, the literally hundreds of complete editions and the much greater number of editions of single works published since the seventeenth century, a vast body of critical and interpretive literature, a small library of sources and supposed sources, records of theatrical productions, including playbills, promptbooks, reviews, and other materials. Shakespeare's works have been copiously illustrated, documented, and interpreted in the visual arts, from the water-colour illustrations in promptbooks to etchings, engravings, oil paintings, and photographs. The film, video, and audio record is uniquely extensive. Shakespeare on film begins in the first years of the medium, with *King John* in 1899, Hamlet's 'death scene' performed by Sarah Bernhardt in 1900, and includes over 700 titles in the recent filmographies edited by Kenneth Rothwell and Annabelle Meltzer[1] and by Olwen Terris and Luke McKernan.[2] Shakespeare materials are of unusual cultural range and geographic distribution—there are translations into most major languages, long traditions of performance and interpretation in Germany, Scandinavia, most of Europe, and in all English-speaking countries; there are important Russian, Japanese, German, Swedish films, and a rapidly increasing number of video records of productions from every part of the world.

In 1992 the Shakespeare Electronic Archive was founded at MIT in order to explore the potential of emerging electronic technologies to enhance access to these materials. Our vision—first articulated in Larry Friedlander's plans for a 'living variorum' in 1988[3]—is of an electronic archive, eventually networked and available throughout the world, in which documents of all kinds—films, sound recordings, texts, digital facsimiles—would be linked in electronic form to one another and to the lines of text to which they refer or which they enact. There are substantial barriers to immediate implementation of such a scheme even in an age in which technology has evolved so rapidly: problems of institutional co-operation, copyright, video delivery, and others will take some time to resolve; but a substantial part of the 'Shakespeare docuverse' can be realized now. Our strategy has been to identify appropriate combinations of materials, emerging technologies, and institutional partners so that workable prototypes embodying major aspects of the overall vision can be built, tested, and used in the near term.

Our first project was a text-video system based on commercially available video laser discs. We began with one text, the Oxford Electronic Edition, based on *The Complete Works* edited by Stanley Wells and Gary Taylor, and 30 film adaptations of the plays on disc. The initial list included productions of *Hamlet* directed by Olivier and Franco Zeffirelli; the *Macbeth* films of Polanski, and Orson Welles as well as Kurosawa's *Macbeth* adaptation, *Throne of Blood*; Olivier and Branagh's *Henry V*; the Granada Television production of *King Lear* with Olivier in the title role, Kurosawa's *Lear* adaptation *Ran*; the Welles *Othello*, the Olivier *Richard III*, and others. Ian McKellen's recent *Richard III* and Branagh's *Othello* are now included, and the Baz Luhrmann *Romeo and Juliet* is being linked. As available, new titles will be added to the system. For each film, an extensive set of software links has been created so that any sequence of film can be located with precision from the corresponding place in the text. In the case of plays for which several films are available, the system makes it possible to select among them (see Figure 1). Additional linked resources—film and performance lexica, tools for integrating 'live' video citations into multimedia essays, and on-line commentaries—are also provided. The system has been actively used at MIT for two years and has provided us with a stable, robust environment for teaching and research. In the Spring of 1996, we began to use a networked version of the system for an experimental distance collaboration with Stanford, in which students could find and select video passages and post 'live' citations, with their comments, on web pages.

In the second phase of the project we are including digital facsimile images of the pages of early editions and works of art and illustration in an extensive system intended for installation at MIT and at the Folger Shakespeare Library. The Folger Archive will include high resolution digital facsimiles of all pages of the First Folio in corrected and uncorrected states, complete facsimiles of all individual copies of both *Hamlet* quartos, 1,500 works of *Hamlet* art and illustration, and several *Hamlet* films (see Figures 2 and 3). At the time of writing, all photography and digitization of images has been completed, as have several prototypes of a system for delivering these resources to the desktop.[4]

We are also currently taking the first steps towards a globally linked archive of Shakespeare documents on the World Wide Web. Several

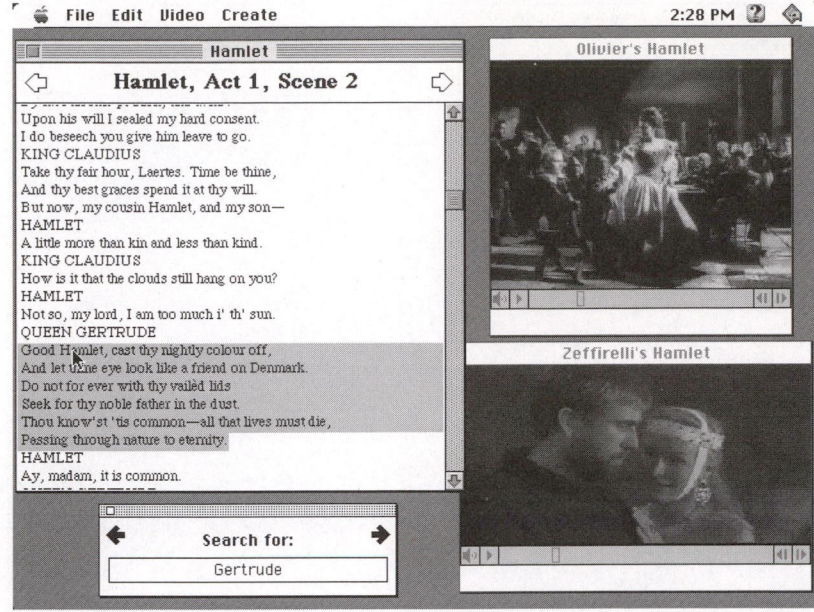

Fɪɢ. 1. User can compare two film versions of the highlighted text.

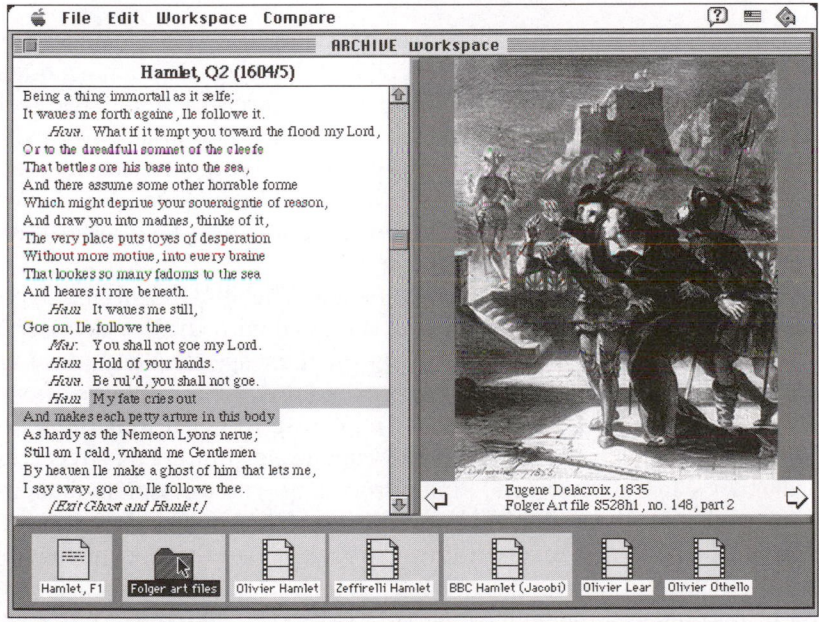

Fɪɢ. 2. 'My fate cries out'. Prototype interface showing juxtaposition of text and one of many illustrations of this passage.

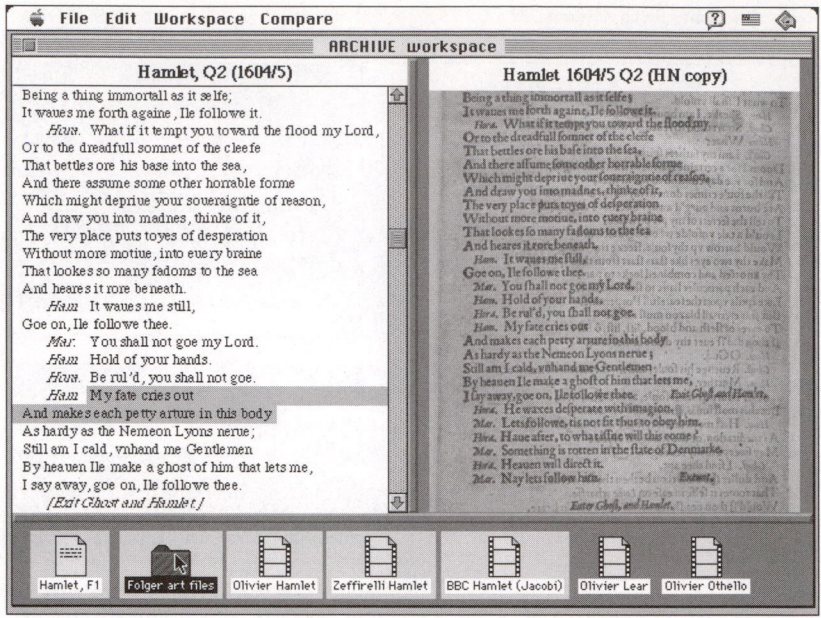

Fig. 3. 'My fate cries out'. Second Quarto in transcription and digital facsimile.

publishers and a number of libraries, including the Folger Shakespeare Library and the Henry E. Huntington Library, have agreed to make materials available for the construction of a prototype archive on a single scene of *Hamlet*. Each contributor's materials will be clearly marked, even when texts drawn from different libraries are juxtaposed on the same screen, and links to the home pages of the libraries will be included. As the 'one scene' global archive progresses, video materials and live performance records will be added from around the world.

While our projects are collectively known as The Shakespeare Electronic Archive, this essay will be principally concerned with these collections as text in several senses: first, by focusing on their specifically textual elements—electronic versions of modern edited text, transcriptions of early editions, facsimile texts—and then by exploring the idea that the whole archive constitutes a text, a large and expanding multimedia hypertext. Friedlander's 'living variorum', Philip Brockbank's dream of a 'mobile text' on optical disc, or the 'expanded book' format of the Voyager *Macbeth*, published on CD-ROM and incorporating illustrations and videoclips together with A. R. Braunmuller's New Cambridge text,[5] the Shakespeare Database being prepared for publication on CD-ROM by Joachim Neuhaus in Münster, or the recently published Arden 2 CD-ROM including full texts of all sources—all these can be regarded as digital archives, whether they reside on a small CD-ROM or on a large server, and they also can be thought of, equally appropriately, as a new kind of text—a multimedia hypertext —in which text in the conventional sense and digital reproductions of documents in other media are linked together.

Calling such a structure a text is only one way to name it; and, like the term 'archive', it is one that evokes distinctions that belong to the familiar world of printed text, bound books, and physical artefacts, distinctions that do not apply exactly in the domain of electronic texts and digital documents.[6] But pursuing the idea of the Shakespeare Electronic Archive as an expanded text can help to make certain aspects of the convergence of text and other media in hypertext more visible, and can also test the limits of 'text' as a metaphor for the new form. The degree to which media converge in the now familiar environment of the graphic user interface of a personal computer are impressive: texts and documents are presented in the same medium of display, they are searched, accessed, and manipulated by a suite of similar tools, and they are stored as bits of information and brought to the screen by the same means—the enactment of commands embodied in the 'script' or 'code' of a computer program. In a multimedia hypertext archive such as the one we are constructing, the relationship between text and document is even more intimate, for resources that originate in disparate media are not only linked, but comprehensively mapped to one another at corresponding points by software links so that they can be experienced not merely as related materials for study, but as dynamic transformations or versions. A line of *Hamlet*— for example, 'I am thy father's spirit'—may exist in an array of forms, each literally capable of evoking the others through the activation of the hypertext links. The 'textual' forms of this utterance include the Oxford Electronic Text of the passage and the transcription of the First Quarto, Second Quarto, and Folio texts. The 'documentary' forms include more than two dozen digitized images of book illustrations, engravings, etchings, and other interpretations in the graphic arts, and versions of the line as presented in the film versions of Olivier, Zeffirelli, Ragnar Lyth, Tony Williamson, and several others. The documents are not only accessed in the same way as the 'texts' but can be juxtaposed to them, so that the experiences of *reading* text, *comparing* versions, and *examining* documents in several media begin to converge. In such a structure, links embedded in words on the screen activate sound and moving image, creating what I have called elsewhere the 'enactment effect',[7] and pictures and film can similarly evoke their written counterparts, in what Nicholas Negroponte has called the 'transcoding' of one medium to another.[8] None of these elements, of course, simply replicates another—film does not 'become' text, even if a particular film version uses the words of a particular edition; and even transcriptions of early editions stand in a complex relationship to the early printed editions whose readings they transcribe—but all these versions can be brought into a common space that makes their similarities as well as differences salient.

Textual and documentary characteristics combine perhaps most inextricably and interestingly in the case of *digital facsimiles*, for these are both texts and electronic reproductions of the pages of specific copies of early printed books, and therefore discussion of the facsimile component of the archive—which at present includes all variant states of the First Folio and all copies of the *Hamlet* quartos—will be given special emphasis in this essay.

THE 'EXPANDED TEXT' IN SHAKESPEARE STUDIES, 1965–1996

What Shakespeare scholars and teachers mean by 'the text' of a Shakespeare play has changed, slowly but decisively over the last generation, expanding beyond the traditional boundaries of the single, authorial 'text' and beyond the confines of the printed book to include variant readings, and even performances, adaptations, and other forms of interpretation and 'reception' in its purview. These changes were partly independent of the electronic revolution, and in large part preceded the development of the technologies that now make it possible to embody the idea of the expanded text in multimedia hypertext systems.

For many people, 'the text' of Shakespeare calls up the image of a large book, a 'complete works' such as the *Riverside Shakespeare*, the Oxford Edition edited by Stanley Wells and Gary Taylor, the David Bevington edition, or an equally imposing series of single volumes—the Arden, New Cambridge, or Oxford. Despite the number of such texts (each slightly different from the others), the impression is given that there is a *single*, well-established text, corresponding to what Shakespeare wrote. Scholarly editors are aware, of course, how far from certainty their textual choices are, but there is a disparity between the way they present the complexity of the evidence in their notes, and the impression of finality conveyed by the appearance of a new edition of the collected works between the covers of an imposing and scholarly volume or as an 'authoritative' and comprehensive series lining the shelves of a library. Introductions, apparatus criticus, marginal, median and final notes, textual appendices—all these simultaneously acknowledge and minimize, by their 'specialist' format, the untidiness and uncertainty of the textual record. The impression left on readers and students is that the text has been established firmly, and that such variant readings as there may be can be safely ignored. If exceptions prove the rule, even the celebrated departure from the norm of the Oxford Shakespeare—the printing of two distinct texts of *King Lear* in full —has not altered the popular image much, and the Oxford text is widely thought of outside the scholarly world as yet another instantiation of the 'authoritative' or 'definitive' text—with doubts, anomalies, and complications banished even further from the sacred precincts of the authorial text by being consigned to a large, but less frequently purchased *Textual Companion.*[9]

No manuscripts of any of Shakespeare's plays have survived, unless one counts the debated revisions in 'Hand D' in one manuscript of *Sir Thomas More*, a play of composite authorship.[10] Otherwise there are no Shakespearean autographs, no 'foul papers', manuscripts on which to base a text. For about half the plays, the sole textual foundation is the text of the First Folio, collected by Shakespeare's colleagues in the theatre and published in 1623, six years after his death. Though the Folio claims to be based on the 'true originall copies',[11] it is often demonstrably based on earlier quarto editions rather than on manuscript, and for those plays whose folio text does appear to be based on manuscript, the nature of the manuscript—authorial, theatrical, corrected, uncorrected—must be assessed and the typical patterns of error and distortion conjectured or guessed on the basis of that assessment. For eighteen plays there are early quarto editions. For two plays, *Pericles* (1609) and *Two Noble Kinsmen* (1634), a Shakespeare–Fletcher collaboration, there is only the quarto, while for the other sixteen 'quarto plays' there is a Folio text as well. A number of plays were published in multiple quarto editions before the publication of the Folio, and several of these, the 'bad' quartos, diverge substantially from both the Folio and the 'good quartos' of the same play.

The effort to produce a single best text, or 'ideal text' begins as early as the Folio itself with its claim to have located original copy; since Alexander Pope's edition in the early eighteenth century,[12] editors have regularly compared Folio and quarto readings in order to select those closest to the author's intentions, correcting or emending when necessary. While the efforts of editors to stabilize the text have been partly successful, they remain in considerable measure speculative, and for many of the plays, both the fact of variation and its inherent interest now seem important not merely to recognize but to emphasize and to teach. Indeed, the differences among early printed editions can be major: in the case of *King Lear* the First Quarto contains three hundred lines not in the Folio and the Folio contains one hundred lines not in the quarto. In the case of *Othello*, First Quarto (1622) and Folio differ in more than a thousand readings of individual words as well as in the addition or omission of speeches. In the Folio, Desdemona's heart is 'subdu'd euen to the very quality of my Lord',[13] while in the First Quarto it is 'subdued, euen to the vtmost pleasure of my Lord'.[14] *Hamlet* exists in three distinct texts, a 'bad quarto' (1603) in which, for example 'To be or not to be' is followed not by 'that is the question', but by 'I, there's the point', and in which a scene between Gertrude and Horatio, absent in Second Quarto and Folio, makes unambiguous what is left doubtful or undecideable in the standard texts—that the Queen is Hamlet's knowing ally and co-conspirator in the final act.[15] The Second Quarto, by far the longest of the three, is the only text that contains the soliloquy 'How all occasions do inform against me', as well as Hamlet's meditation, just before the second appearance of the ghost on the ramparts, on the 'vicious mole of nature' or 'one defect' that can undermine a state or an individual's rational faculties, a passage that links the play (though how directly can be debated) to Aristotle's theory of tragic shortfall or *hamartia*.

Such variation may make it impossible to recover a single original—or it may be that there never was one. Shakespeare himself may have revised his work, leaving two or three originals, each imperfectly transmitted by the existing editions. Though revision theories have long had a minor place in Shakespeare studies, such theories have had greatly increased influence since the publication of E. A. J. Honigmann's *The Stability of Shakespeare's Text* in 1965, and the attempts by Steven Urkowitz, Michael Warren, Gary Taylor, and Stanley Wells in the late 1970s and early 1980s to argue for the authorial revision of *King Lear*. In the case of *Lear*, the revision theory led to perhaps the most visible breach to date in the tradition of publishing single 'best' texts in scholarly editions, the printing of complete edited texts of both the First Quarto and Folio versions, *The History of King Lear* and *The Tragedy of Kind Lear* in *The Oxford Shakespeare* of 1986.[16]

Even if his intentions were single, the collaborative nature of life in the London theatre in Shakespeare's time may give the variation among early texts more importance than the hypothesis of a single text 'corrupted' by alterations for the stage would suggest. Very few plays in any theatrical tradition enact an unchanging script, and differences among early versions may reflect creative or necessary modification in and for performance. Shakespeare wrote for the theatre, not primarily for publication, and the variety of the early textual evidence may reflect the fluid character of writing for the stage more accurately than the attempt to re-create a single conjectured original.

Theoretical considerations have also influenced the transition from single to multiple text. Contemporary literary theory has advanced several complications into the simpler view that a text is the unproblematic transcription of the intended meaning or utterance of an author. Beginning in the 1930s, the 'New Criticism' of I. A. Richards, Cleanth Brooks, René Wellek, and others played a pivotal and still influential role in the reframing of questions of authorship; for, while such critics tended to construe text in ideal terms, they disconnected it, to a certain extent, from authorial control and sponsorship with warnings against the 'biographical' and 'intentional' fallacies, and positive injunctions to attend to 'the words on the page' in preference to reasoning from assumptions about an author's meaning. More recent theory has, notoriously, been more radical, replacing the author with the theoretical construct of an 'author effect', as Foucault does in 'What is an Author?'[17] or, as in various cultural studies approaches, which ask us to understand texts as shaped by broad patterns of social discourse or to locate them as nodes in a web of related 'intertexts'.

The more expansive meaning of 'text' is one that has been evolving in literary and cultural studies for a generation. 'Text' can now refer not only to the characters printed in a book or written in a manuscript, but can refer to works of art of all kinds, and even, more broadly, to any social practice that can be closely read or densely described. In this extended sense, a cock-fight in Bali is a 'text' for anthropological analysis; a film is a text, and a Shakespeare play is a text—or, rather, a great many 'texts', for its discrete editions are all texts, as are its performances and their filmed records. In the work of a critic such as Barbara Hodgdon, the 'text' of *A Midsummer Night's Dream* extends beyond the literary and performance text to the cultural 'event' surrounding particular productions, and includes playbills, publicity, and reviews.[18] The 'reception text' is broad, capacious, hard to bound or delimit—and yet, in the usage I am describing here, it is still the text of a Shakespeare play. In a decisive shift of meaning, what used to be thought of as criticism, editorial work, production history, adaptation, reception, or *Nachleben* (afterlife) is now thought of not as part of the penumbra, periphery, or later history of a play, but as part of its text. Text, so understood, expands beyond the covers of a book, and becomes, in George Landow's apt phrase, a 'complex field of variants' in several media.[19]

Attention to performance as a kind of text in its own right and the related contributions of 'reception' studies have altered the model by which one thinks of an author's text as origin or source and theatrical performance or critical commentary as secondary phenomena. The 'text' of *Hamlet* may be read in ways that are shaped by the performance and interpretation of the play in the present. Freud's construction of *Hamlet* in his letters to Fliess; Ernest Jones's formalization of the Freudian view of the play in articles and books appearing between 1910 and 1949 in several languages;[20] the popularization of the Freudian approach by Olivier in

1937 in the Old Vic production, in 1947 in the film version, by Zeffirelli in the 1989 film (with a different emphasis), and countless other perform-ances and interpretations shaped in part by psychoanalysis create, it can be argued, a different 'text', even if the words on the page remain the same. In addition, a single performance can be regarded as a text, and its textual or text-like properties are greatly enhanced when performance is recorded or recast in a durable medium such as film or tape, so that it can be replayed, re-experienced, and closely read in ways that are analogous to the close reading of a poetic or literary text. Precise formulations of the shift from text as source to text in this expanded, performative, and his-torical sense differ widely. To choose a moderate but influential example, Philip McGuire has argued that Shakespeare's 'open silences'—places in the text in which an important character does not speak and yet must reveal an attitude towards the action or speech of others—is evidence of an open texture in the composition of the plays themselves that accounts for the viability of opposed interpretations. McGuire argues for a gener-ously defined 'family' of meanings,[21] and for the location of the value of Shakespeare's plays not in the discovery of one correct interpretation, but in the quality of the dialogue they have sustained with later times and cultures. Here later theatrical artists, critics, and ordinary readers are in a sense authors, contributing to an expanded cultural 'text'.

'The text', then, can be as capacious as all of its versions in all media and in all times and places. Such an expansion of the term has not, of course, been universally accepted and has not gone unopposed. Many have seen a danger of fragmentation, nihilism, and incoherence in the shift. It is true that the new ideas of author and of text have, in their ini-tial and still most sophisticated formulations in Derrida, Foucault, and DeMan, suggested not merely the expansion of the category of the author-ial text but its dissolution. But as such theories have taken hold, they have become detached from the cultural moment of their own origins and can sustain other uses, in which the blurring of boundaries is more generous, and, rather than casting doubt or disrespect on the achievement of authors, can offer a new model for it, one based not on a reader or audience's pos-session of a work created entirely by another but on participation in the process of its reception and transformation.

The revolution in electronic communication has, as noted earlier, also brought parallel changes in our understanding of 'text', by making text manipulable, migratory, and relatively unfixed and unstable in form, by making the boundaries between one text and another permeable in hyper-text, by extending text, more recently, from hypertext to 'hypermedia', an extension that closely parallels the inclusion of image and performance in the extended dramatic text, and most recently by making possible the global sharing of text, hypertext, and multimedia text on the World Wide

Web. As in the case of literary theory, these changes have also been feared as destructive of culture and meaning. This is especially true because electronic text is in fact an alternative to printed text, so that its growth can be seen as heralding 'the end of books', or 'the end of reading'.[22]

But electronic forms also have powerful syncretic and organizational potential, and can make it possible to articulate gracefully a profusion of versions of related texts and documents in several media, making them easier to juxtapose and compare, and even to read in new ways that combine the coherence, context, and sequence of what we now know as reading with an immediate awareness of alternative possibilities. And, like the theoretical loosening of the dead hand of the author, technology has the potential to extend greatly participation in the creative dialogue Shakespeare's plays have provoked since their first performance by making the text—even in its most extended, multimedia incarnation—available through international networks.

MODELLING THE VARIANT TEXT:
EARLY EDITIONS AS ELECTRONIC DOCUMENTS

The digital facsimile components of the Shakespeare Electronic Archive are an instance of the ways electronic forms can create new kinds of text that are both *variant* and *documentary*.

Variation among editions has been briefly discussed already—it extends, in the case of *King Lear* and *Hamlet* to the addition or omission of hundreds of lines, whole speeches, and even scenes. Books printed during Shakespeare's period also varied within an edition more than modern books do. The principal cause of variation was the practice of stop-press correction. Proofs were corrected while uncorrected pages continued to be printed, and complete copies were made up of unpredictable combinations of corrected and uncorrected sheets, so that, in the case of the First Folio, for example, no two copies are the same, and no one copy contains either all corrected or uncorrected states. Variations within an edition were also caused by the deterioration or movement of type during the process of printing, by too light or too heavy inking, and by damage, deterioration of the pages after they had been printed.

One way to represent all levels and types of variation in a digital collection would be to photograph all copies of all early editions, keyed to one another so that comparable passages could be juxtaposed and examined. The Folio is a volume of more than 900 pages which exists in 230 copies, and the quarto editions (there are from one to six individual editions for each play for which there is a quarto version) range in number of extant copies from one, the unique copy of the First Quarto of *Titus Andronicus*, to about two dozen. A complete record of the whole set of early texts would thus run to several hundred thousand pages. As a beginning, the Shakespeare Electronic Archive will include in its first phase a complete set of page images in both corrected and uncorrected states for the First Folio, and all copies of *Hamlet* Q1 (1603—two extant copies) and Q2 (1604/5—seven extant copies).

The selection of corrected and uncorrected states of the Folio is only possible because of the existence of more than eighty copies in one library, the Folger, and the monumental printing history of the edition undertaken by Charlton Hinman in the 1950s and 1960s. Using a specially designed optical collator, Hinman examined more than 50 individual copies of the First Folio character by character in order to catalog variants, to discover the order in which the copies were printed, and to learn as much as possible about the habits of proofreaders and compositors and other matters affecting the printing history and text of the Folio.[23] The identification of variant states also allowed him to produce a new kind of photographic fascimile, an 'ideal' representation of the edition, in which one exemplar of all 'corrected' pages was reproduced.[24] Since no copy contains all corrected states, the Hinman fascimile was made by selecting pages from over forty individual copies.

For the digital fascimiles in the Shakespeare Electronic Archive, Peter W. M. Blayney has reviewed all of Hinman's selections, and in some cases revised choices in the light of his own research or of published scholarship since Hinman. In addition, our collection includes all *uncorrected* as well as corrected states. This is an important addition not only for the sake of modelling as fully as possible the successive states of pages, but because, as Hinman himself established, the 'corrections' to the Folio were often miscorrections or cosmetic improvements without consulting copy, and, therefore, take us no nearer to the underlying textual sources than the corrected states. Hinman had to decide between corrected and uncorrected states (and perhaps chose wrongly according to his own account of the printing history) because their inclusion would have added a great deal of bulk to an already large volume, and because the problem of sequence could not be gracefully solved within the confines of a large printed book. Hinman does print several variant pages of special interest in an appendix, but in that location they cannot easily be compared to the alternative states which appear in the normal page sequence. If he had chosen to interleave variant pages, the sequence would have been interrupted; if he had chosen to include these pages in additional columns, the size of the volume would have had to be doubled.

Each fascimile image in the Shakespeare Electronic Archive is linked to the corresponding page of the Oxford Electronic Edition (1989) as well as to the electronic transcription of the texts of the early editions themselves published by the Oxford Text Archive (OTA). In the case of *Hamlet*, the transcriptions prepared by Bernice Kliman and Paul Bertram for their *Three Text Hamlet*[25] will also be included. While the OTA texts and the *Three Text Hamlet*, being transcriptions, offer precise correlations to the page images, the Oxford Electronic Edition, like any modern critical edition, provides a far less exact mapping—spellings are modernized, readings are drawn, necessarily, from only one early edition when these differ. Nevertheless, the inclusion of a modern edition is extremely important to the design for several reasons—it helps us to connect the experience of *reading* Shakespeare in a familiar, contemporary form, with the experience of examining the digitized documents, it makes it possible to study the relationship between the early texts and a contemporary edition, and it provides a way to search the early texts 'in modern spelling'. Since spelling was not standardized in Shakespeare's time, many common words appear in half a dozen or more spellings, and a modern reader may not be able to guess them ('doe' for 'do' may be easy to find, but it is only one of many possibilities; and for some words spellings cannot be guessed, e.g. 'Scilens' for 'Silence' in *Henry IV, Part 2*). A search on the Oxford Electronic Edition can lead one to the corresponding page images in quarto and folio and provides, as well, a link to the old spelling OTA transcriptions. The Oxford Electronic Edition was chosen as the first contemporary text to include because, while controversial, it offers a better mapping to the Folio text than other electronic versions, and because, where it omits quarto readings—as in key passages of *Hamlet*—it often supplies them in a list of 'additional passages' at the end of each play.

In a typical session, a user might begin by searching for a word or passage in the Oxford Edition (though the facsimiles themselves, or the art files or films might also be chosen as a place to start). From that passage in the electronic text, a menu offers choices among linked materials, arranged in hierarchies—the initial choice might be among art files, film versions, and Folio and quarto page images. In the case of *Hamlet* there is a further choice among particular quarto copies, and for the Folio among variant states when these exist. In our most developed prototype, several windows can be opened at the same time, moved and juxtaposed, and these windows can display relevant material in different media—for a particular speech, for example, one might wish to compare variant versions in quarto and folio—or perhaps variants within a single edition—with interpretations of the speech in art or film.

The facsimile images are made available in several sizes or resolutions (see Figures 4 and 5), so that the image can be magnified on the screen—at the highest level of magnification, drawn from the 18MB '16base' files of photoCD, details are magnified several times beyond actual size, while for ordinary reading one-third of a column of Folio text or a whole quarto page fills an average monitor.

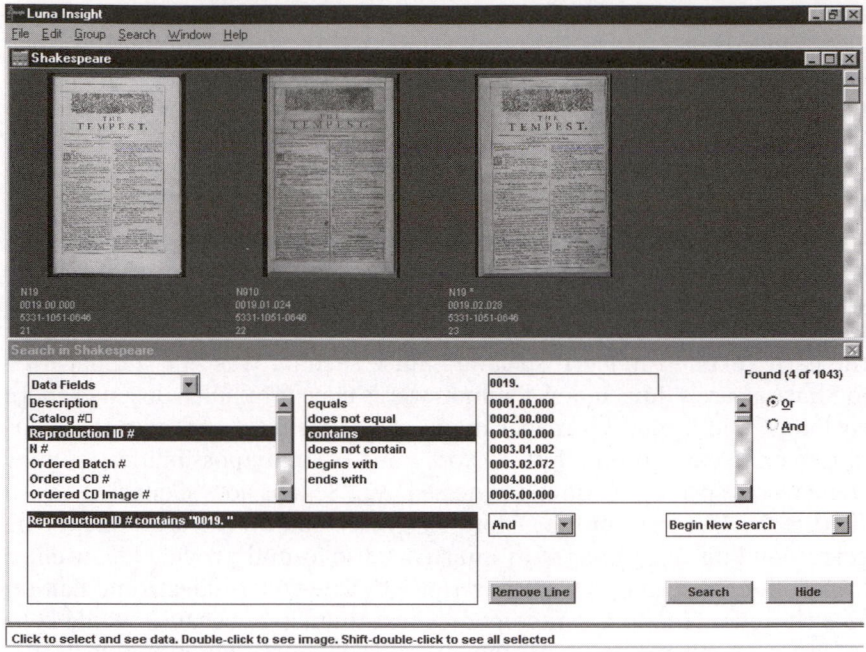

F<small>IG</small>. 4. In this prototype CD-ROM using Luna Imaging's *Insight* software, the user can search a database of images for all First Folio variants of the first page of *The Tempest* (Sig. A1ʳ). Here, three of the four variants have been transferred to an image workspace.

As one moves from the Oxford Edition to OTA transcriptions, to juxta-positions of facsimile images of corresponding passages, and from there, perhaps, to examination of the variants within a single edition, displayed in high magnification, several kinds of transitions are occurring that blend 'reading' as we are used to thinking of it, and other kinds of attention that might be thought of as specialist or scholarly. *Reading* text shades into the *comparing* of variant texts and the *examination* of documents in digital form, and selection among these options is made by the user. In contrast to the modern critical edition in print, in which the main text is a distillation of the evidence, and only one of many that are possible, the *documentary hypertext* presents images of the evidence itself, and does so in a dynamic structure that makes it possible to toggle rapidly between alternate states so that not merely the fact and the content of a variation can be noted, but the *effect* of alternatives can be experienced in the context of the text in which it appears. Such an integration of variant and context can, of course, be approached in some measure using a modern printed edition: one can consult the textual notes for a given line, locate the word or lemma

Fig. 5. Details of Sig. A1ʳ (Folger copies 7, 24, 28) are compared in movable windows.

for which there is a variant, read that variant, and, keeping it in mind, return to the main text and mentally insert the variant into the context of the passage being read. Yet few students and even scholars do this! For the most part, knowledge of variation, even the highly selected knowledge presented in the textual notes of a typical edition, is theoretical, rather than active.

The digital facsimile represents a clear advance over the presentation of variation in the modern collected edition and also over previous efforts to present the evidence provided by the early editions in the medium of print. These fall into two categories, facsimiles and parallel text editions, though the most complex, the *Complete King Lear* edited by Michael Warren,[26] combines facsimile and parallel presentation, and its principles, not fully realized in the medium of print-on-paper, served as a direct inspiration for the digital facsimile collection we have designed. Michael Warren has since joined the Shakespeare Electronic Archive team as an active collaborator.

Facsimile reproduction of Shakespeare text begins in the eighteenth century, in the medium of pen and ink, when defective copies of the First Folio were often 'completed' by the insertion of pen facsimiles of missing

 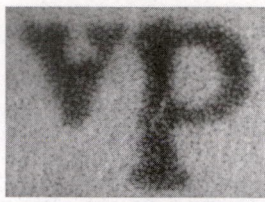 

FIG. 6. *Hamlet* 1603, Sig. C1ʳ 'And lifted vp his head to motion'. *Left*: 1825 type facsimile (*The First Edition of the Tragedy of Hamlet*, London: Payne and Foss, 1825). Note use of turned small capital A. *Middle*: 1951 collotype facsimile '*Hamlet*': *First Quarto, 1603* (*Shakespeare Quartos in Collotype Facsimile*, No. 7), ed. W. W. Greg (London: Shakespeare Association, 1951). Collotype reproduces the heavy inking in the 'v' ambiguously. *Right*: 1880 photofacsimile *Shakespere's 'Hamlet'; The First Quarto: A Facsimile in Photo-Lithography* (London: W. Griggs, 1880). The technique used in this example reproduces letterforms in black and white only, with no gradations.

pages of text, and also of the engraved Martin Droeshut portrait of Shakespeare which was often missing from individual copies.[27] In 1807[28] and again in 1862–4,[29] *type facsimiles* of the entire book were produced. These are more than transcriptions of text, for in them an effort was made to reproduce the layout of the page, including box rules and centre rules, the appearance of the type, and even obvious errors. Indeed, some type facsimiles, such as the 1825 facsimile of the then recently discovered *Hamlet* First Quarto, attempt to reproduce such details as inking spaces, broken letters, and inadvertent use of 'turned' letters, so that, for example, if the text contains a turned 'n' where a 'u' should be, the type facsimile sets a turned 'n', even though the difference between the two letterforms is confined to the length of the serifs (see Figure 6).[30] Beginning in 1861, Edward Ashbee produced an extensive set of lithographed quarto facsimiles, tracing every letterform by hand,[31] and in 1866 the first photolithographed facsimile of the First Folio was produced by Howard Staunton.[32] Indeed, the Folio was one of the very first books to be reproduced by photolithography. Since 1864, the entire Folio has been reproduced a number of times by several methods—unlined offset, screened offset, photozincography, collotype: in 1902 by Sidney Lee,[33] in 1909 by Methuen and Co., in 1954 by Helge Kokeritz,[34] and in 1968 by Charlton Hinman. The Hinman facsimile, discussed earlier, represents one culmination of the effort to represent the edition—or any edition of any book—in photographic form.

Like facsimiles, parallel text editions have a long history. Samuel Timmins published facing page transcriptions of the Devonshire copies of *Hamlet* Q1 and Q2 in 1860,[35] and a comprehensive series of 'quarto plays' with facing folio texts was published between 1888 and 1906 as *The Bankside*

Shakespeare.[36] In the case of *Hamlet*, which has three significant early texts, the facing page format was strained: the Bankside prints Q1 and the Folio as the first in its series, and a separate volume, published later, prints the Second Quarto in parallel with *Die Bestrafte Brüdermord*, a seventeenth-century German version of the Hamlet story of uncertain relation to Shakespeare's play. In 1891 Wilhelm Viëtor published several parallel texts including a three-text Hamlet with facing pages for Q1 and Q2 with F printed at the bottom of each page.[37] Kliman and Bertram's *Three Text Hamlet* of 1991 prints all three texts in columns at each opening, with a fourth column for 'Q1 transpositions'. This is a better solution, but produces a volume which is much wider than high and difficult to handle. In addition, all of the parallel text editions on paper produce blank spaces —sometimes extending over whole pages in one version or the other— when one of the texts lacks material found in the other, or when such material appears in the other text but not in the same order. Reading such texts, therefore can be a somewhat fragmentary experience.

In 1989 Michael J. Warren produced the *Complete King Lear*, a facsimile that attempts to solve the problem of reconciling parallel and sequential representations, and takes the solution perhaps as far as the medium of ink-on-paper will permit. In contrast to traditional editors, Warren's aim was to present the evidence in all its complexity:

The book demonstrates the problem of the term *King Lear*. *King Lear* here is not a single play presented in sanitized form, domesticated, processed for easy consumption. Rather *King Lear* is the convenient term for the evidence from the seventeenth century for the theatrical and literary phenomenon known by that name. (p. vii)

Photographic facsimile was chosen as a medium because it 'retained not just the look and feel of the originals, but their uncertainties also' (p. vii). *The Complete King Lear* is actually four discreet publications, unified by being presented in a slip case. The first of these is a parallel text of four columns, in which the Folio and First Quarto (1608) texts of the play are juxtaposed in the two columns of each opening nearest the spine. The parallel texts have, like almost all parallel Shakespeare texts, gaps—white spaces where there is not quarto material that directly corresponds to the Folio, or vice versa. Unlike most parallel text editions, however, the blocks of text are photofacsimiles of each text, cut and pasted so that they are parallel. The term 'cut page parallel facsimile' has been adopted for this style of presentation. The outer columns contain uncorrected press variants of each text. The four-column cut page facsimile that results provides the 'completeness' of representation that Warren sought—both texts and their variants are photographically reproduced and presented in parallel. Though extremely useful for detailed comparisons, the book is difficult to read because of the fragmenting effect of reading a page consisting of alternating rectangles of collotype greyscale facsimile and white spaces. This varies from page to page, of course, but for some pages the effect is extreme.

In order to remedy this, to provide an alternative way of aligning texts, and to accommodate the Second Quarto, Warren also provides facsimile texts of F1, Q1 and Q2 (1619) in fascicles of unbound page images. Using these, the reader can read each text in its own sequence without the fragmentation effect, or can customize the alignment of any two or all three texts by placing them next to one another in a workspace. These procedures, too, have their awkwardness as well as their value—not the least of which is the vulnerability to damage of unbound pages.

Of the many lessons of *The Complete King Lear* perhaps the most immediate is this—that in order to represent the complete history of a book, it is necessary to disassemble the book to permit kinds of juxtapositions—I would say kinds of *readings* of the expanded text and of the artefact itself—that are not possible in the single sequence of pages in a bound volume. Such disassembly may be actual—when books are disbound for study or reproduction (as they seldom are today)—or it may be photographic, or digital.

Another lesson of Warren's work is that access to the history of a variant text must not be only analytic but holistic or reintegrative as well—we must be able to shift from looking at pieces or parts in conjunction to looking at or reading the whole, since the object of study is a literary/dramatic work that has a fixed, indicated—some would say 'linear'—sequence.

Again, it is apparent that digital forms can mediate more effectively between analytic and syncretic presentations. In electronic facsimile, display of the text can be tailored to the user's needs and preferences at a given moment. Any text can be read alone on the screen, any text can be placed in one column and another arranged in parallel to it, or, in a manner similar to the 'unbound' pages of Warren's *Complete King Lear*, digital facsimile pages can be juxtaposed in separate scrolling windows. The computer allows us to make the kinds of comparisons most appropriate for our present needs, and to switch back to sequential reading of one text at any time. The user will thus have substantial control over the display of the text.

Digital presentation will also be more accessible than *The Complete King Lear* while retaining its determination to present documentary evidence in all its specificity. If well designed, electronic texts can reduce the apparent distance between simply 'reading the play' and access to complex textual evidence that must, in a publication such as *The Complete King Lear*, seem the province of specialists simply because of its unconventional and awkward formats. Even the best designed interface will not, of course, eliminate the need for introduction to the issues involved in understanding the textual history of Shakespeare's plays, nor will it eliminate the disparity between scholarly and general use—but it can make even the beginning student aware of a range of possibilities, and serve as a reminder that all Shakespeare texts are based on documentary evidence.

The types of objects that appear on the screen of the Shakespeare Electronic Archive are typical of contemporary computer environments: text that can be read, images, animations, video and other representations or pictures, and dynamic tools for moving among them are all familiar objects in applications of many kinds. As in the general case, text or images can themselves be configured as tools—a click on an image or passage of highlighted text can call up another text or image, can 'bring us' to another place in the simulated environment. In the case of the documentary hypertext formed by modern text, transcription, and facsimile, the fluid and interpenetrating character of *texts, tools,* and *representations* is particularly striking because the character-based texts and facsimiles are versions of one another: one abstract, edited and 'ideal', removed from the materiality and history of its origin; the other documentary and highly particularized—a representation of a specific page of a specific copy of an early edition, located in a specific library. In the case of the Folger collection, each page is identified by copy number and state, so that the user is aware, for example, that there are one, two, three, or four variant states of that particular page, and that the one being examined has been photographed from Folger copy #68, #6, or any of the other 40 Folger copies from which the full set is drawn.

A facsimile text is one of the subtler manifestations of a represented world beyond the computer screen, or beyond the 'text'. It is text, in an obvious sense, but it is also a digital photograph. It signals its difference from electronic text in the narrower sense by its colour, texture, and shading, and by the appearance of its old-fashioned and often damaged letterforms; in the images in our collection, edges and gutter and a glimpse of other pages and cover make obvious the fact that it is a photograph of a page of an opened book. Unlike most photographs, it shows a surface that is flat or only slightly curved, rather than a perspectival space. So the dynamic movement from text to page image is a muted, specialized example of the way in which electronic text can seem to evoke a real world, bringing a part of that world to the screen, or, to use an equally common metaphor, permit travel to a distant location—in this case the Folger Library, the British Library, or the University Library of Wrocław— in a simulated space.

For many uses, transcriptions of early editions in ASCII text will be nearly as useful as page images, while for others, such as the examination of particular letterforms, or for checking readings, or for distinguishing among possible causes of distortion in individual readings—broken letters, damage to the page, etc.—the full colour, high resolution images are needed. However, even when the digital image is not strictly required by the nature of the information being sought, the experience of using it differs from that of reading electronic text. There is a 'reality effect' that is produced by the appearance of the digital photograph that can stimulate the imagination in ways that the ASCII text cannot; there is the connection with the specificity and materiality of the processes that produced the text, and a higher degree of awareness of the location of such evidence in specific libraries. In addition, there is another effect, caused not merely by the photographic reproduction of a page of a real book, but by its evocation in response to the user's selection. When representations of materials that are rare or unique appear on screen, there is an effect that strikes some as surrogate travel in the simulated space, and others as the movement of objects or their simulacra to the screen. These are two forms of telepresence or the sense of the presence of remote represented objects.

An electronic research environment can thus present objects that are more and less textual, more and less documentary, along an axis of gradation from 'flat' ASCII characters, to formatted text, to black and white representations of the text columns of facsimiles isolated from context to full colour page images situated in a realistic space. For different uses, and different levels of use, various options may be appropriate. In a current MIT project based on the archives of the late Harold 'Doc' Edgerton, the inventor of stroboscopic photography, the notes, letters, apparatus, and other artefacts in the collection are accessible in a simulated space that models the space of the laboratory. In some specific applications, it might well be appropriate to evoke, to a greater degree than we currently do, the actual space of the libraries in which the originals of our digital copies are kept. Whether and to what extent this is done, however, it is important that the potential for doing it exists—like the space 'beyond the frame' in cinematic representation, electronic documents can be connected with a wider and more fully visualized environment. In fact, the ability we currently have to reframe or 'crop' digital images of documents gives, to a limited degree, control over the extent to which digitized text appears as text, cut off from context, or as document existing in a real space beyond the screen.

The potential for contextualization and connection made possible by the fact that the computer screen is something like the page of a book and something like a movie screen or the frame of a painting is important because the world represented on the screen of the computer is often thought of as bounded or cut off from the real world. This sense is, I believe, derived from the traditions and aesthetics of such arts as perspectival painting and classic film, in which a self-contained, realistically portrayed world is visible through the 'window' of the canvas or screen. The computer screen is different: representations share space with text and with a variety of dynamic controls on the screen—and, of course, depending on design, text, or image can themselves function as active controls, 'hot spots' or buttons in a hypertext structure. The dynamic, transformative quality of the composite environment of the computer screen makes against passive immersion in illusionist space.

In fact, what makes an electronic research environment powerful is the *oscillation* between abstraction and realistic representation. The range of options—in this case from plain text to rich colour reproductions—is under the control of the user. Because our relationship to these options is not fixed, it is possible not only to select the most useful presentation of information, but also to find quickly the limits of the information presented. Magnification of images is a good example of this principle: like photographic images, the information provided by digital images is of course limited by the resolution of their constituent elements, in this case not the grain of a photographic emulsion, but the pixels of the electronic image. In a typical image processing program, it is possible to find the limits of the digital representation by 'zooming in' or magnifying the image so that the pixels of which it is composed are visible. A similar operation *could* be applied to photographs, but using a magnifying glass to look at a photographic image is uncommon among non-professionals. In this and other ways, differences in medium and in the expectations we have of each medium affect differences in how we perceive a photograph and the image on a computer screen. As William Mitchell has argued,[38] the protean nature of the digital image and the ease with which it can be altered give it a different 'truth' status from that long claimed by photography. We view the digital image more sceptically, and understand it as one representation of reality among many that are possible. If this is so, such scepticism and the provisional nature of the truth claimed by the digital image are of potential benefit in constructing research and teaching environments, for oscillation between trust and scepticism, immersion and reflection is a necessary part of scholarly enquiry.

I will conclude this discussion of digital facsimile texts with an example from our work in progress that illustrates the potential importance of even the tiniest details recoverable from a high resolution digital image as well as their limits.

While distortion or damage to individual letterforms in particular copies of an edition affects far fewer readings than the differences between editions caused by revision or the transmission of the text, it can be crucial to the meaning of a passage, or even the play as a whole. One example of alleged damage to a single character is the controversial variant in the text of *The Tempest* that reads, in most copies 'So rare a wondered father

> *Fer.* Let me liue here euer,
> So rare a wondred Father, and a wife
> Makes this place Paradiſe.

> *Fer.* Let me liue here euer,
> So rare a wondred Father, and a wife
> Makes this place Paradiſe.

Fɪɢ. 7. Sig. B2ʳ, lines 1785–7. Folger copies 68 (top) and 73 (bottom).

and a wise makes this place Paradise'. In 1978 Jean Addison Roberts found six Folger copies in which the cross-bar of what appeared to be an 'f' was in the process of breaking off, suggesting that the line originally read: 'So rare a wondered father and a *wife* makes this place Paradise.'[39] (See Figure 7.) Regarding 'wife' as the original reading yields a very different speech, with implications for the play as a whole. For *The Tempest* is a play in which there is only one female character, and in which Prospero's own wife is hardly mentioned. The standard reading 'wise' reinforces this pattern, for in it Ferdinand, even while celebrating his own betrothal to Miranda, thinks only of the wisdom of her father. The new reading quickly became part of the debate about gender and sexuality in the play and in the Shakespeare canon as a whole. 'Wife' was a reading, as Stephen Orgel put it, 'whose time had come', and he included it in the text of the Oxford edition in 1986.[40] In the early stages of planning the digital Folio collection I used this variant in our first prototype, creating digital images of the line from several of the Folger copies Roberts cited in her article. As discussions with Peter Blayney proceeded concerning whether to photograph all accidental variants or merely all typographical variants in the Folio, I used the Roberts 'variant' as an example, and we examined it on the screen of my laptop computer (see Figure 8). Blayney

Fɪɢ. 8. Detail, Folger copies 68, 73, 2.

was sceptical that the alleged damage was really there—something that appeared to be the cross-bar of an 'f' did appear in the magnified images, but Blayney doubted that the physical construction of the type would permit such an accident—though something similar might occur in other letterforms in which serifs and other fine details were more vulnerable. We decided that individual examination of every Folger copy of every page for which a variant reading had been claimed by anyone should be undertaken, with the aim of distinguishing variant typesetting from accidental damage and other non-intentional differences. In the case of the 'wife/ wise' crux Blayney used a microscope to make the distinction. His conclusions support the traditional reading, but both states of the page will be included in the collection.

This return to the documents took place under special circumstances, of course, but it offers a model for how we might think of a digital research environment, and how we might design the 'expanded text' so that the passage from text to document extends from the computer screen to the library. The boundaries of the 'expanded text' are more shifting and elusive than those of the bound volume of a collected edition. Internally, the shifting of boundaries means that information is presented in many forms, and includes versions and variants in all media and from all periods of a work's history. But the external boundaries of the documentary multimedia hypertext are permeable as well, and at their outer limit lead back to real objects, and to the specific locations, in the 'real world' in which Shakespeare materials are preserved, interpreted, and used—back, that is, to the library, the theatre, and the classroom.

NOTES

1. Kenneth S. Rothwell and Annabelle Henkin Melzer, *Shakespeare on Screen: An International Filmography and Videography* (New York: Neal-Schuman, 1990).
2. Luke McKernan and Olwen Terris, *Walking Shadows: Shakespeare in the National Film and Television Archives* (London: British Film Institute, 1994).
3. 'A Living Variorum: Plans for an International Globe Centre Museum', unpublished manuscript.
4. Principal funding for the work of the Shakespeare Electronic Archive has been provided by grants from the National Endowment for the Humanities and the Andrew W. Mellon Foundation.
5. Philip Brockbank, 'Towards a Mobile Text', in Ian Small and Marcus Walsh (eds.), *The Theory and Practice of Text Editing: Essays in Honour of James T. Bolton* (Cambridge: Cambridge University Press, 1991), pp. 90–106; *Macbeth* [CD-ROM], ed. A. R. Braunmuller, Voyager Company Software (Irvington, NY: Voyager, 1994).

6. Though in common usage an electronic text file can be referred to as a 'document', I distinguish here between character-based electronic texts of all kinds and electronic reproductions of documents created through digital imaging of primary records—books, manuscripts, film, and other artefacts.

7. 'The Shakespeare Interactive Archive: New Directions in Electronic Scholarship on Text and Performance', in Edward Barrett and Marie Redmond (eds.), *Contextual Media* (Cambridge, Mass.: MIT Press, 1995), p. 124.

8. *Wired*, 1.5 (1993).

9. *Complete Works*, ed. Stanley Wells and Gary Taylor (Oxford: Oxford University Press, 1986); Stanley Wells and Gary Taylor, with John Jowett and William Montgomery, *William Shakespeare: A Textual Companion* (Oxford: Oxford University Press, 1987).

10. Photographic, type facsimile, and edited texts of these revisions appear with brief discussion and bibliography in *The Riverside Shakespeare*, ed. G. Blakemore Evans (Boston: Houghton Mifflin, 1974), pp. 1683–1700.

11. Sig. πA2^r (Title-page). Facsimile in *The Norton Facsimile: The First Folio of Shakespeare*, ed. Charlton Hinman (New York: W. W. Norton, 1968), p. 3.

12. *The Works of Shakespeare* (London: Tonson, 1723–5).

13. Sig. ff6^r, *Norton Facsimile*, p. 823, lines 600–1.

14. Sig. C4^v, facsimile in *Shakespeare's Plays in Quarto*, ed. Michael J. B. Allen and Kenneth Muir (Berkeley: University of California Press, 1981), p. 797.

15. Sigs. D4^v, H2^v–H3^r, facsimiles in *Shakespeare's Plays in Quarto*, pp. 592 and 606.

16. E. A. J. Honigmann, *The Stability of Shakespeare's Text* (Lincoln: University of Nebraska Press, 1965); Michael J. Warren, 'Quarto and Folio *King Lear* and the Interpretation of Albany and Edgar', in David Bevington and Jay L. Halio (eds.), *Shakespeare, Pattern of Excelling Nature* (Newark: University of Delaware Press, 1978); Steven Urkowitz, *Shakespeare's Revision of 'King Lear'* (Princeton: Princeton University Press, 1980); *The Division of the Kingdom: Shakespeare's Two Versions of 'King Lear'*, ed. Gary Taylor and Michael Warren (Oxford: Clarendon Press, 1983).

17. Michel Foucault, 'What is an Author?', in Josué V. Harari (ed.), *Textual Strategies: Perspectives in Post-Structuralist Criticism* (Ithaca, NY: Cornell University Press, 1979), pp. 141–60.

18. Barbara Hodgdon, 'Splish Splash and the Other: Lepage's Intercultural *Dream Machine*', *Essays in Theatre / Études Théâtrales*, 12: 1 (1993), 29–39.

19. George P. Landow, *Hypertext: The Convergence of Contemporary Critical Theory and Technology* (Baltimore: Johns Hopkins University Press, 1992), p. 56. Landow's formulations—e.g. 'hypertext offers the possibility of presenting a text as a dispersed field of variants and not as a falsely unitary entity' (loc. cit.)—suggest a 'convergence' of hypertext and new directions in the editing of Renaissance texts, such as those taken by Michael Warren, Wells and Taylor, and others.

20. See my essay 'Olivier, Hamlet, and Freud', *Cinema Journal*, 26: 4 (1987), 22–48 and refs.

21. Philip C. McGuire, *Speechless Dialect: Shakespeare's Open Silences* (Berkeley: University of California Press, 1985).

22. See Robert Coover, 'The End of Books', *New York Times Book Review*, 21 June 1992, 1, 11, 24–5; and Sven Birkerts, *The Gutenberg Elegies: The Fate of Reading in an Electronic Age* (New York: Ballantine Books, 1994).

23. Charlton Hinman, *The Printing and Proofreading of the First Folio of Shakespeare* (2 vols.; Oxford: Oxford University Press, 1963).

24. *Norton Facsimile*. See n. 11 above.

25. *Three Text Hamlet*, ed. Bernice Kliman and Paul Bertram (New York: AMS Press, 1991).

26. *The Complete 'King Lear', 1608–1623*, ed. Michael J. Warren (Berkeley: University of California Press, 1989). Subsequent references have been included in the text.

27. *The First Folio of Shakespeare*, ed. Peter W. M. Blayney (Washington, DC: Folger, 1991), pp. 36–8.

28. London: E. and J. Wright.

29. This facsimile, prepared by Lionel Booth, was published in three formats— a single volume in both actual size and slightly reduced versions, and as a three-volume set.

30. *The First Edition of the Tragedy of Hamlet* (London: Payne and Foss, 1825).

31. Ashbee's quartos were issued in separate volumes beginning in 1861 and as a 48-volume set in 1871.

32. London: Day and Son.

33. Oxford: Oxford University Press.

34. New Haven: Yale University Press.

35. London: S. Low.

36. *The Bankside Shakespeare*, ed. Appleton Morgan (New York: Shakespeare Society, 1888–1906).

37. *Shakespeare Reprints* (3 vols.; Marburg: Elwert, 1891).

38. William Mitchell, *The Reconfigured Eye: Visual Truth in the Post-Photographic Era* (Cambridge, Mass.: MIT Press, 1992).

39. Jeanne Addison Roberts, ' "Wife" or "Wise"—*The Tempest* line 1786', *Studies in Bibliography*, 31 (1978), 205–8.

40. *The Tempest*, ed. Stephen Orgel (Oxford and New York: Oxford University Press, 1986), iv. i. 123–4, and note.

9
Coda: Is It Morphin Time?

DAVID GREETHAM

Whenever the Mighty Morphin Power Rangers get into real trouble (surrounded by slimy, amorphous, self-replicating creatures), like Byrhtnoth at Maldon or Henry V at Harfleur, they have a battle cry that strengthens them in adversity: 'It's morphin time!' Once the ritual phrase has been uttered, the five teenagers become—like Clark Kent changing into Superman in his telephone booth—a different order of being; they transcend their crudely human physical limitations to become, what else? 'Superheroes'. The incantation is thus a form of wish-fulfilment: wouldn't it be convenient if we could fly and beam ourselves biomorphically from one location to another, overcoming the merely temporal and logistic and the single-state to become demigods and shapeshifters? Morphing of the self as an exemplum of the law of the preservation of energy. Trickster's transmogrifications in the folklore of Native Americans; Wagner's *Tarnhelm* (the wearing of which can turn a dwarf into a dragon or a toad, and give the weak and timorous Gunther at least the *appearance* of being the heroic Siegfried); Zeus as swan or cloud or bull to advance his amorous predilections: all of these are part of this powerful cultural testimony to the omnipresence of morphing wish-fulfilment. If only we were like the gods, if only we had some technical device (like the *Tarnhelm*) to make morphing the *normal* and *ordinary* state of nature rather than only a consummation devoutly to be wished. The question for a 'coda' to a collection on the electronic text is thus whether we might be close to achieving that new norm, whether the brave new world of biomorphs and cybernetics (and at the more modest level considered by this volume, digitized textuality) has begun to change the temporal and logistic contours of identity so that, just as the agency of the human subject may be called into question as a biographical, biological, and coherently historical figure under postmodernism, so may the textual productions of a newly digitized sensibility. To put it bluntly: is digitized morphing different in kind, in phenomenology, in ontology, from previous forms of textual morph? What does digitization do to the sensibilities of the morph-producer and the morph-consumer? Are we now Victor Frankenstein without the technical (or moral) limitations of his time, or have we just donned this year's new fashion in *Tarnhelms*?

For some messianic enthusiasts, there can be no doubt that morphing is NOW. In awe at the 'technodazzle' of *Terminator 2* and Michael Jackson's $4 million, 11-minute 'music film', *Black or White*, Mark Dery can pronounce: 'I have seen the future and it is morphed.'[1] But morphing is not just immortality, it is change itself, including the mutability and corruption that ordains the death of the self. In other words, morphing as a general biological phenomenon *is* already a condition of nature, according to this law of the preservation of energy. Publius Ovidius Naso knew this, as the opening lines of his *Metamorphoses* show.

> Now I shall tell of things that change, new being
> Out of old: since you, O Gods, created
> Mutable arts and gifts, give me the voice
> To tell the shifting story of the world
> From its beginning to the present hour

(In Horace Gregory's translation)

Ovid's 'present hour' might not have entertained digitization, but since his story is that of creation and mutability, not just as a *metaphor* but as the very nature of things, it is fitting that our own closing benediction in this volume on the electronic text ask for divine or at least technological guidance on the nature of the morph in this, *our* present hour: perhaps a *deus ex pentium*.

Ovid's family name, it has been supposed, arose from a morph, that bending out of the flatness of the norm that produces the warp of *caricature*. For Ovid, the warp was nasal: Naso-Nose-Nixon and his ski-sloped, familiar because barely recognizable, characteristic feature, as in the well-known series of Scarfe cartoons of that ever-extending proboscis. Now through digitization and a deft recalibration of the characteristic features of the subject we wish to emphasize, we can all become caricaturists electronically, and thus set in motion 'new being out of old'. Ovid as precursor is thus more creative for us, more hopeful, than the warping melancholy of his own precursor, Lucretius, whose *de Natura Rerum* emphasizes not the startling anecdote and the miraculous morph of the *Metamorphoses* but rather the mutability of things under the law of the indestructibility of matter as grimly manifest in the mortality of form: 'For whenever a thing changes and quits its proper limits, at once this change of state is the death of that which was before.' Spenser's platonist attempt in the *Mutabilitie Cantos* to find the necessary reciprocity between mutability and permanence, between recycling of form and the continuity of matter as *energeia*, is perhaps an epistemological half-way house between Lucretius and $e = mc^2$, and the Ovidian style of morphing I am going to

play on in this essay (the Derridean *jeu*, encompassing our cultural universe from Velázquez-cum-Francis Bacon to 2 Live Crew, and from the
Jewish journal, *Forward*, to Simon and Garfunkel) will always be only a
partial escape, a flight of fancy, from the *memento mori* that is the presid-
ing deity of all morphing: the skull beneath the skin (see Figures 1a–1c).

We may discover that the current digitization of the morph, while technically and conceptually a fulfilment of much of what both Ovid, Lucretius,
and even Spenser were reaching for, gives us only the illusion of sup-
pressing the linearity of time. The digitized morph can give the morphist
enormous power to adjust and calibrate the interstitial states within (and
beyond) the opening and closing frames of a morph 'storyboard'; and
digital morphing is, moreover, the most culturally ubiquitous (in movies,
popular music and music videos, graphic arts, print and television advertisements) of electronic textuality familiar to, and accessible by, the general public. Even people who have never operated a computer—and for
whom the mysteries of SGML and HTML, the World Wide Web and the
Internet are *terra incognita*—are comfortable with the phenomenology of
digital morphing, for the artefacts of our contemporary life surround
them with its results in popular culture. Does this general cultural acceptance of the digital morph reflect the general postmodernist anxieties over
identity, boundaries, and teleology? Is it different in kind as well as complexity from the morphing described and practised by Ovid, Lucretius, and
Spenser? How do the technical requirements and specific construction of
the digital morph interact with the apparent formlessness and liminal
freedom that digitization appears to confer? These are very large questions, and they cannot be fully resolved in a short exploratory essay; but
they are questions fundamental to our cultural as well as technical understanding of the morphing phenomenon, and I hope at least to illustrate
some of the ways in which the questions can be posed—in various media
and in various disciplines.[2]

These are clearly very serious matters, and they respond to my central thesis that the current digitized morph cannot be considered in isola-
tion from its non-digital predecessors, for digitization is only one stage in
the evolution and signification of (meta)morphing. And these concerns
are, in any case, mother's milk to most textual theorists, from Zenodotus
of Samothrace and the Alexandrian librarians to Jerome McGann, his
Rossetti Archive, and his essay, 'Rationale of Hypertext', printed in this
volume. As McGann's title suggests, his deployment of electronic textuality is to redefine and develop both W. W. Greg's and G. Thomas Tanselle's
precursor 'rationales' (the 'Rationale of Copytext' and *A Rationale of Textual Criticism*, respectively[3]). Where Greg offered a temporary resting-place
in the relentless morphing of texts by suggesting that we might strive for
a sort of pragmatic ideality of form based on a cross-referential conflation

(a)

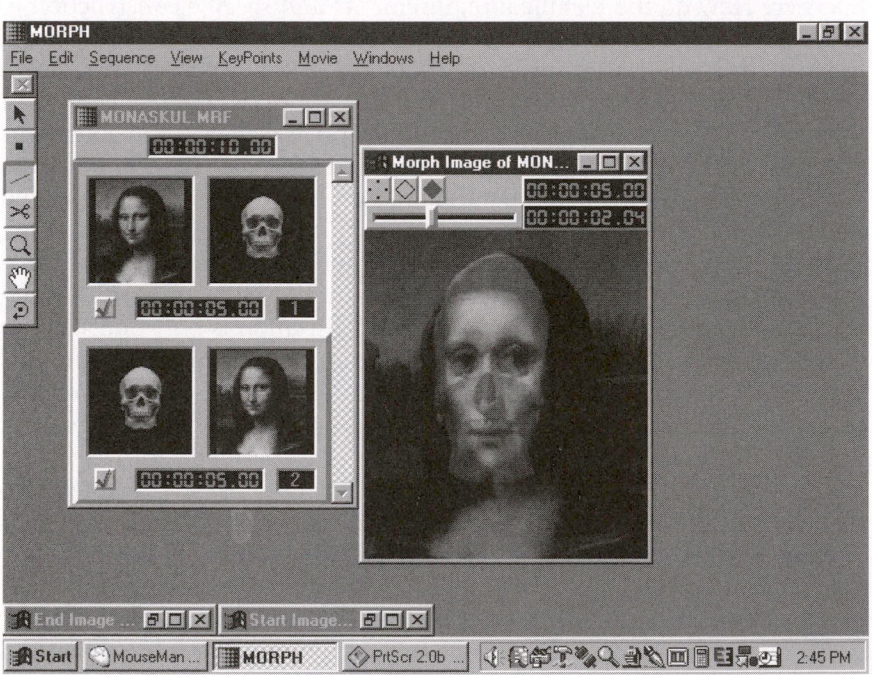

(b)

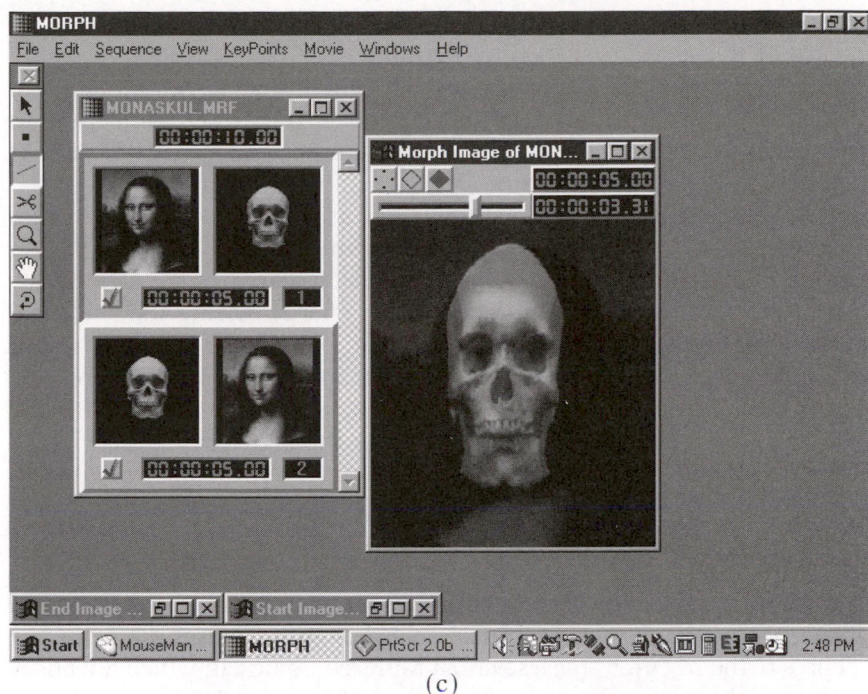

(c)

Fig. 1(a–c). Digital morph of *portrait/skull*, with opening and closing frames of storyboard and intermediate states.

of the *substance* and *accidence* of a text; and where Tanselle held out the lure of stasis, of the 'inhuman tranquility' that would overcome 'the hazards of the physical' (*Rationale*, p. 93); McGann celebrates the instability and unlinearity of the electronic text, its inevitable calling into question of our positivist expectations for proof, demonstrability, and closure, as a 'means to secure freedom from the analytic limits of hard-copy text' (p. 23). I have elsewhere argued that the breakdown of the great modernist narrative of textual teleology which had been formulated under the auspices of the 'principle of thrift' that Foucault delineated as the classic *author*[4] is but one instance of the general postmodernist failure and fracture of the *grands récits*:[5] a fragmentation (or, if you will, a *pixellation*) that Jean-François Lyotard has declared to be the resident genius of the postmodern.[6] Marxism, Whiggism, Christianity, Nationality, Textuality: none of these centres will hold, and it is in the margins of discourse, in the interstitial and the interlinear and the digressive, that our cultural conversations now take place. And I have also argued that the pattern in the carpet that is text as textile (the two words are etymologically parallel) makes citationality—the presence of one text within another and the intertextual viral invasions of what Hillis Miller has playfully described as *guest* and *host*[7] (again, etymologically identical forms, morphed into opposites)—but the *de Natura Rerum* of textuality, electronic or otherwise.

I have thus seen the history of textual debate very largely in terms of a struggle between text as *textile* (woven, indeterminate, cross-referential) and text as *textus*, text as *the Scriptures*, that 'authority' for which Platonists like Tanselle yearn as an escape from the morphing corruptions of the secular.[8] Hypertext, and digitized textuality as a whole, I would contend, must therefore be seen as part of an epistemic history of two thousand years and more, in which the morph has been feared as the sign of our corruptible nature and/or embraced as the energy driving the citational ethic of the (inter)text. Similarly, my present play in the fields of morphing—through the algorithmic typology of the spatial, the linear, the recursive, and the receptional—is just one aspect of my fascination with the *incursive* power of the embedded citation in the body of the text.

The viral metaphor may be quite appropriate, but the appropriateness and aptitude of morphing to represent the *Zeitgeist* can lead to some heady claims, as when:

1. Mark Dery's enthusiasm for the morph as cultural icon (see above) is just a part of his history of the morphology of morphing from the cyborgs of the research space scientist Manfred Clynes, in which advances in biological engineering have 'dramatized the permeability of the membrane separating organism and mechanism',[9] through Coca-Cola's spots on the theme of 'I'd Like to Buy the World a Coke' and Benetton's 'faux-multicultural "United Colors of Benetton"', with side glances at the so-called 'cloaca concept' of the movie sequel *Aliens* (in which 'the mensche machine's pathological fear of the glutinous feminine goo that will gum up its gears . . . is given ironic spin by the fact that the masculinist protagonist is a woman'[10] and Klaus Theweleit's *Male Fantasies*, the anthology of Nazi *Freikorps* writings in which the hardened male body 'becomes a mechanism for eluding the dreaded liquid and "feminine" emotions associated with it';[11] and

2. when Donna Haraway, author of *Simians, Cyborgs and Women: The Reinvention of Nature*, declares that 'We are all cyborgs'[12] and advocates a subversive use of cybernetic technology to overcome the 'traditions of "Western" science and politics';[13] and

3. most pertinently for this essay and this collection, when Sherry Turkle, in her web site at MIT <http://www.mit.edu:8001/afs/athena.mit.edu/user/s/t/sturkle/www/PowerRanger.html> endorses the morph of Foucault's prognosis for identity under postmodernism by opening her site with Foucault morphing into a Power Ranger (see Figure 2). Whether or not the five teenagers of the Mighty Morphin Power Rangers realize they are but emblems of Foucault's claim that power is a 'multiplicity of

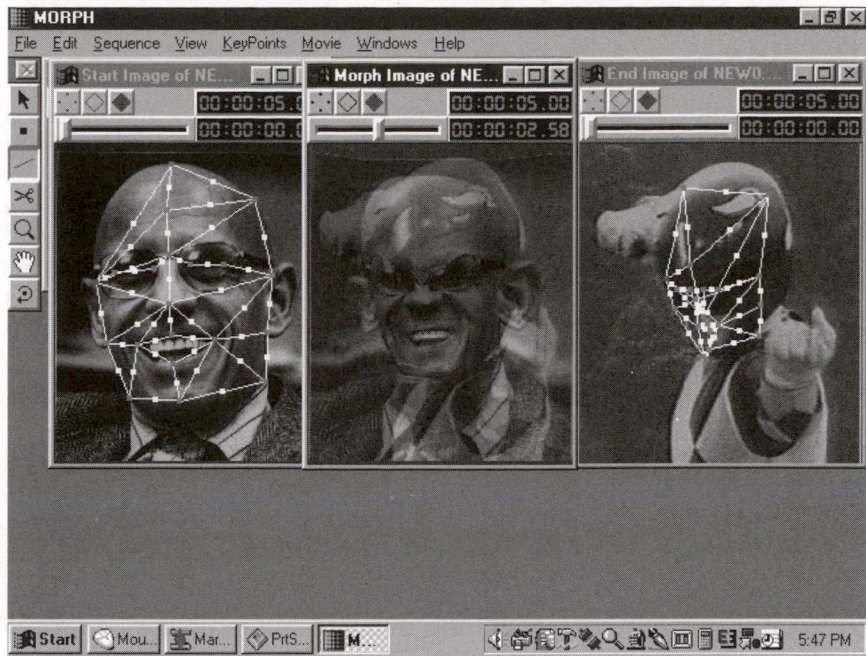

FIG. 2. Morph of intermediate state between Foucault and Power Ranger, based on, but not replicating, opening morph movie at Turkle website.

force relations' (as quoted in the Turkle site), each gaining support from the other, Turkle's morph of Foucault (which I emulate electronically but do not 'quote') is part of a polemical, and in her case, feminist resituation of computer aesthetic and power relations. Opposing what she calls 'scientific', masculinist, early 'hard' computing (for example, in the rigidity of DOS-based command structures) by a flexible, transitional, and liberating feminist aesthetic of the continuous postmodernist morph, Turkle has turned the Net, and specifically the graphics-based Web, into a cultural site for celebrating a 'non-hierarchical' fluid composition, cognition, and reception.[14]

While I recognize incursive fluidity as a useful, indeed 'powerful' trope for a feminist sensibility (and have celebrated this fluidity in some of my theoretical writings on textuality and editing[15]), I share Edward Rothstein's suspicion that Turkle's political and epistemological agenda for the morph of Foucault with Power Rangers may be yet another 'romance' of 'pomo',[16] and I will argue that such technoculture critics as Dery, Miller, Haraway, and Turkle have been too parochial in both their synchronic and diachronic contemplation of the morph. I am not going to act as technoLuddite in this volume, but part of the function of this essay as a *coda* is to show, *per exempla*, how the pixellation of the morph is just one stage in its own history of transformations (or what Randy McLeod playfully respells as '*trance*-formations')[17] in textual morphology; and as a technophile, I will demonstrate that the ontology of the morph is just as determined, linear, programmatic and, well, 'masculinist' as earlier forms of production, even though its phenomenology—the way we experience those *trance*-formations—may seem fluid, flexible, and 'feminist'.

I have promised a Derridean *jeu* and an Ovidian series of 'startling' examples, so I will now cast off the philosophical-political *moralitas* and turn to the *exempla*. Like the Pardoner (via a textual morph—what textual critics would usually regard as a variant or a corruption), 'my theme is oon and alway ever was / *radix textorum est morbiditas*':[18] my own morphed texts in this essay will move from the *spatial* representation of the morph in textual history to the *linear* (and therefore usually chronological) to the *loop* of the *recursive* text, the basic tripartite tabulation of algorithmic logic—with an extension into the *receptional* morph. The exhibits will take us from the development of Gothic script out of Carolingian to the changing Chicago skyline to the ontological and legal function of parody as a powerful token of morphing and the simulacrum (or *fac-simile*[19]) in rap music to the morphing profile of the textual receptor: reader, auditor, observer, conceived individually and collectively as a databank of variant responses to a singular text. All the morphs, spatial, linear, recursive, and receptional, are built on a narrative 'storyboard' of beginning and ending images, sometimes with a storyboard 'loop' that completes the cycle and begins it over again. Sometimes the two ends, and even the intermediate states, of the storyboard, may be experienced at a single glance (this is so in the spatial morphs), even when they represent diachronic evolution; but in all cases, the digitized version of morphing is no longer just an act of nature: it is a result of textual intervention by the morphist, a co-equal *Prime Mover* (literally), and of a laying out of strictly determined synchronic or diachronic collaterals, as this *mrp* file of a fairly straight-forward morph shows (see Figures 3a and 3b).

1. I begin with spatial morphs, some digitized and some begging for digitization, and take palaeography as a first exhibit: the morph, conceived as a device of historical mensuration, lay at the heart of the positivist project of *Altertumswissenschaft*, the 'science of ancient times' that was largely sponsored as a body of research by the historicism of Valla and his discrimination between the 'authentic' and the 'fake', and by the attempts of Mabillon and the Maurists to arrange orthographic morphs into a predictive 'morphology' that would eventually result in the 'laws' for change in historical linguistics (see Figure 4).[20] This desire for order, a 'literal' (i.e.

letter by letter) ordinal configuration of the morph, was a *sine qua non* for positivist history, as this neat entablature of the 'development' of Gothic out of Carolingian all-too-tidily demonstrates. As we shall see later when we confront the less predictable (and more dangerous) recursive forms of the morph, this desire for neatness has no space for the successful simulacrum, or what I have referred to as the 'recycling of scripts'[21] (Carolingian as a supposed reconstitution of roman, humanist as a refurbishing of Carolingian, twentieth-century italic as a return of humanist, and so on), but the basic model will serve. It gives direction and momentum to the morph in a spatial representation, just as the gradual morphing from Hebrew to Latin alphabets for the Jewish journal, *Forward* (as the journal changed from Yiddish to English), incorporates the chronological progression within a singular spatial layout (see Figure 5). In a God-like purview over the interlaced stages of change and corruption, we see the morph and its history writ large and whole in both palaeography and in, say, the symptomatic Cubist flattening of perspective and motion, where multiple viewpoints and diachronic actions are rendered simultaneously in two-dimensional space. Such variance in both synchronic and diachronic modes does not have to be produced digitally, of course, but the fine calibration through multiple states can be more exactly achieved in a digital format, as in Donald Knuth's *Metafont* program (see Figure 6), where the gradual stylistic changes between old-style typography and modern can be calibrated through minute adjustments on the interstitial stages between the two ends of the morphing storyboard. This digitized series of reformulated images is, of course, ahistorical, in that we should not suppose that every letter-form on the storyboard actually existed; but it is the non-historical, undocumentable 'artifice' of the morph storyboard that gives it its unique phenomenological function: apparent seamlessness constructed out of infinitesimally small calibrations.

2. From spatial morphs, or the diachronic observed as synchronic, I turn to linear morphs, usually on a chronological continuum. In these examples, the morphist first determines the opening and closing images (and multiple interstitial positions) in complex, multi-stage morphs (see Figure 7), then decides which elements of those images are to be the graphic (or auditory) anchors around which the morphing will be mapped, then plots out such parameters as speed, compression, pixellation, and graphic radiation, before 'producing' the morph movie and modifying its direction, looping, and size. Such contemporary movies as *Willow*, *Terminator 2*, *Indiana Jones and the Last Crusade*, and *Sleepwalkers* have used digitized morphing along the storyboard as a basic narrative ingredient. But long before formal digitization, the movies were quick to realize the potential for frame-by-frame reconstitution of shape, form, and thus identity. The 1932 Fredric March version of *Dr. Jekyll and Mr. Hyde*, for example, while

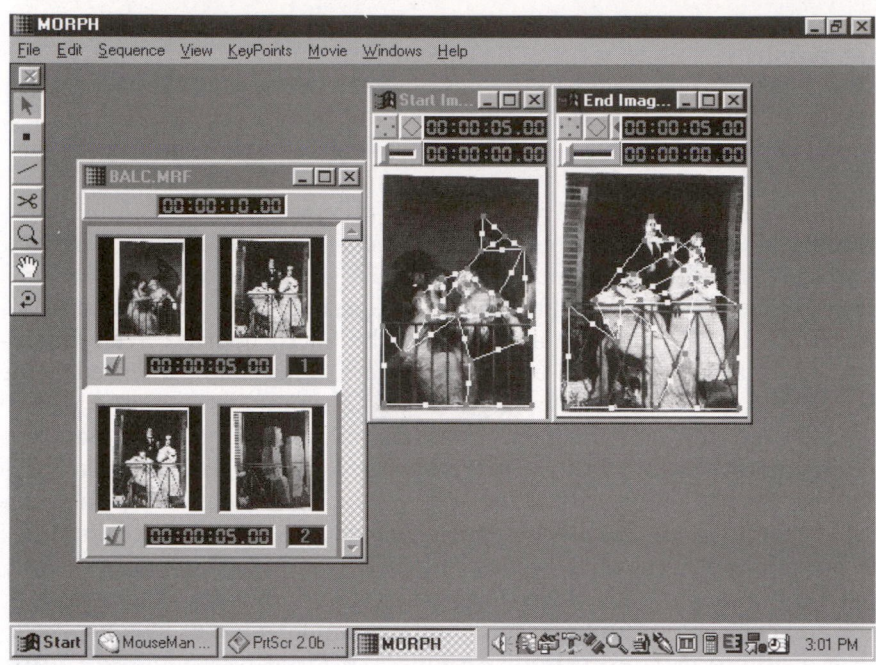

(a)

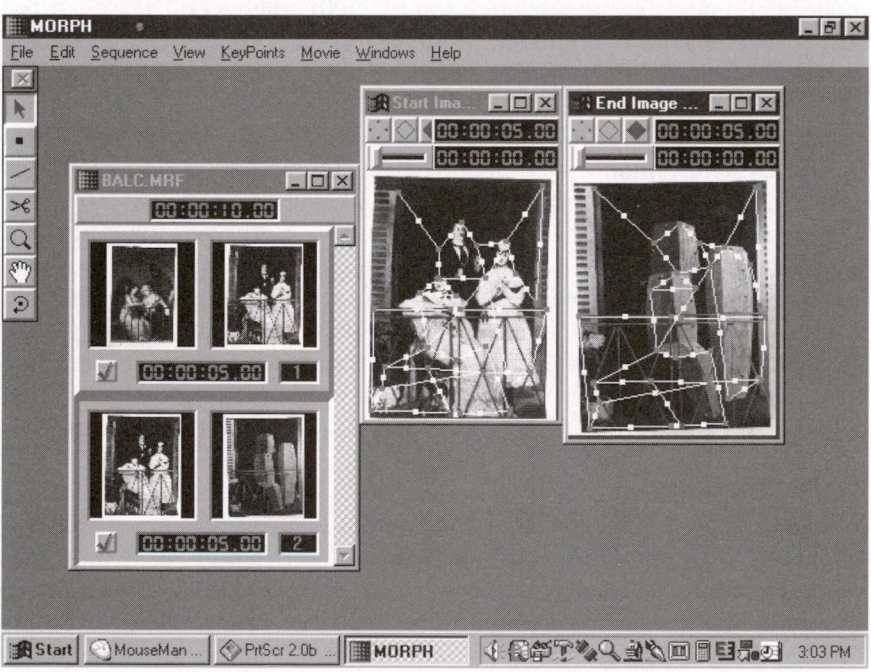

(b)

technically rather clumsy, seized on the morph as the perfect visual embodiment of the shifting identity between the two parts of the protagonist's personality. Similarly, pre-digital 'stop-frame' live action children's movies —where each movement of a figure has to be photographed separately and then strung together in a complete storyboard to form the total action —have been a major influence on the phenomenology of fully digitized 'animation' and have not been entirely superseded by the digitized equivalents of the same 'stop action' technique, as in *Toy Story*. Indeed, the digitized construction of intermediate states in such genres as parody (of which digitized morphing is a primary example) may even occlude or subvert the conceptual 'gap' that the parodist is relying upon between the target image and the parodic extension, as in this mixed-state digitized frame between Manet's *Le Déjeuner sur l'herbe* and a contemporary (updated) parody, with the intimacy of the woods and nudity in Manet replaced by screaming traffic and a beleaguered group of urban picnickers (see Figure 8). Digitization, while instructive in showing the gradual morphing achieved by the parodist, may ironically reduce the conceptual value of the parody by removing the necessary disjunctive gap between target and parody. Similarly, a digitization between two actual historical states, as in this storyboard and interstitial frame of the changes in the Chicago skyline over several decades (see Figure 9), may be both amusing and graphically instructive as a seamless morph movie, but because the actual

Fɪɢ. 3(a–b). Complex Morph storyboard, showing selection of key points and keylines in a two-sequence morph on three states. Note that once a keypoint has been selected in the opening frame of each level of a storyboard, the morphist must then make a subjective decision on what will be the appropriate analogous keypoint on the closing frame of that level (i.e. the initial digital pairing of the two keypoints is based purely on the positions of individual pixels in the graphic frame, and it is the morphist who must then drag the corresponding keypoint to the pixel that best represents the *formal or ontological* equivalence in the morph narrative being constructed). Other technical and critical decisions made by the morphist that will have direct effects on *every frame* of the total morph movie include the setting of *time codes*, the *image resolution* (in dpi), the *image resizing*, the *chroma-keying* (adjustment of colour wheel), the *zoom ratio*, the setting of *interpolation points* (transformation-control points along each keyline), degrees of *rotation*, the selection of *crossfade* protocols, the *compression ratio*, the relation between quality of *animation-image* and *animation motion* (in inverse proportion), the *frames per second* (8 is standard low-end for computer animations, 30 for NTSC [US] and 25 [European] video), and the *pixel depth* (i.e. the number of colours in the transition image), which will depend on the technical capacities of the playback device (8-bit, 24-bit). All of this demonstrates that, while the resulting morph may look like 'free play' or 'feminist fluidity', it is in fact the construct of a very complex series of technical and critical decisions made by the morphist.

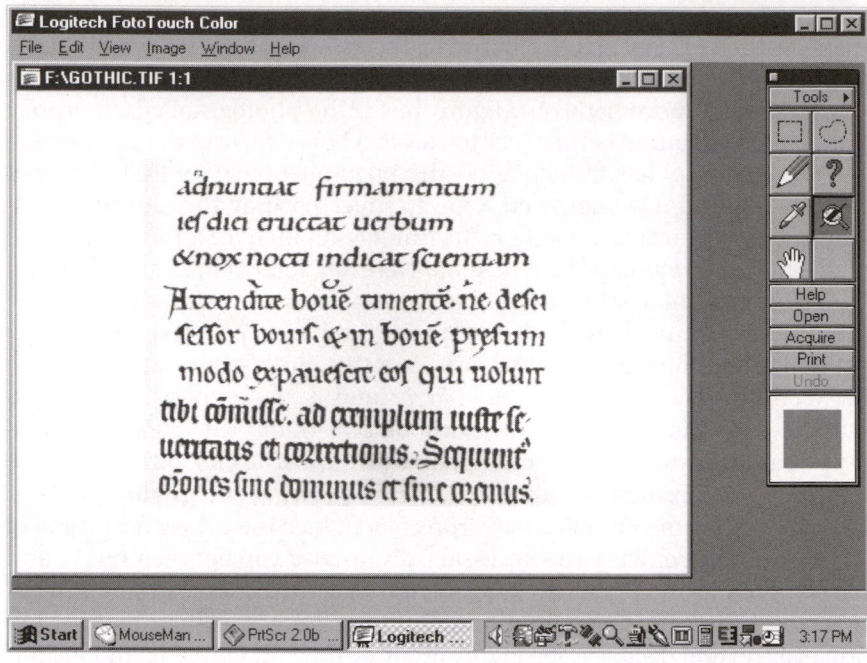

Fig. 4. A spatial (synchronic) morph displaying linear (diachronic) formal changes in palaeography between Carolingian and Gothic. Note that each of these actual documentary states could be digitized as the opening and/or closing frames of a morph storyboard, to produce intermediate states that do not reflect actual documents or actual scripts.

architectural changes of form took place in major disjunctive leaps (tearing down one building and putting up another), the interstitial frames will not only be ahistorical—texts that never were—but will also literally 'distort' the shape-shifting phenomenology of the total architectural changes. On the other hand, constructing a digitized morph movie of a painting used as a graphic 'target' and its later 'version' (again, an essentially parodic exercise, since it results in caricatured states that were never actually produced by either artist) may clarify and illuminate the formal liberties that the belated artist may have taken, as in this intermediate frame representing a non-extant state between Velázquez's 'original' *Portrait of Pope Innocent X* and Bacon's later deconstruction of it in his *Study after Velasquez's Portrait of Pope Innocent X*—a digitally produced state that is not the 'property' of either Velázquez or Bacon but a hybrid 'in the style of' some completely fictitious intermediate artist sharing and combining formal attributes of the two artists (see Figure 10). As we will see later,

FIG. 5. *Forward* magazine spatial morphing of a chronological process, from Hebrew characters in the original Yiddish version to the Latin alphabet in the English-language version. (Reproduced by courtesy of *Forward* magazine.)

such linear extensions of an original are ultimately to be seen within the generally 'recursive' or 'looping' effect of Bacon's *œuvre*.

While it is easy to see the basic ontological permutations in the visual mode of the linear morph—within the conventions of 'text' conceived as any object of study that embodies a *textile*, cross-referential function—these relations along a linear morph have, to my mind, been most convincingly and eloquently set out for all media in Justice David Souter's opinion in the US Supreme Court's decision in the famous parody case concerning the Roy Orbison song 'Pretty Woman' and the 2 Live Crew rap parody, where Souter noted that the relations between 'target' (opening of

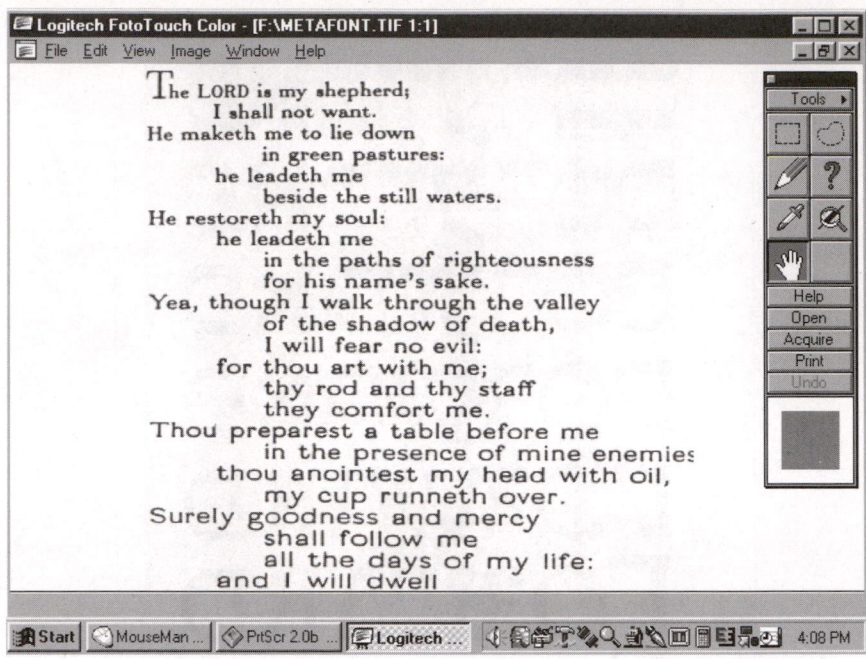

F<small>IG</small>. 6. Spatial morph displaying linear formal changes: Knuth's *Metafont*, showing the digital calibration between old-style and modern typography.

the storyboard) and 'parodic' stretching in the closing image of the story-board must have a measurable 'critical element' (but note, not an element that is susceptible to 'evaluating its quality'). As Souter acknowledges,

Parody's humor, or in any event its comment, necessarily springs from recognizable allusion to its object through *distorted* imitation [emphasis added]. Its art lies in the tension between a known original and its parodic twin. When parody takes aim at a particular work, the parody must be able to conjure up at least enough of that original to make the object of its critical wit recognizable [through] quotation of the original's most distinctive or memorable features, which the parodist can be sure the audience will know. . . . the heart is what most readily conjures up the song for parody, and it is the heart at which the parody takes aim.[22]

In reversing the decision of the Circuit Court and in finding for 2 Live Crew's parodic version of Roy Orbison's song,[23] Souter made an important conceptual distinction between what he called the 'duplicative' and the 'transformative' nature of the copy, that is between the *fac*-simile or simulacrum and the morph:[24] 'This distinction between the potentially remediable displacement and unremediable disparagement is reflected in the rule that there is no protectable derivative market for criticism.' This

FIG. 7. Complex multi-level storyboards, in added sequences that may then be looped back to the original frame of first-level storyboard, creating a recursive morph. Note that all the technical and critical decisions listed in Figure 3 will have to be made for *each level* of the multi-sequenced morph. In this case, since there are four states to be recursively morphed (so that the final image of level four can be linked back to the opening image of level one in the continuous playing of the morph movie), there are five levels of storyboard, and opening and closing frames for each one. Only the first three levels and the opening and closing frames of the first level are shown here. The other two levels of the storyboard can be scrolled up as needed. There is no theoretical limit to the number of levels, only the RAM and storage of the equipment (and the patience of the morphist).

sophisticated argument—especially as it emphasizes the parodic formal and cultural distancing ('unremediable disparagement')—is a perfect rationale for the digitized morph, conceived as a series of 'disparagements' based on a 'critical' element that re-forms the 'characteristic . . . heart' of the opening storyboard frame. Moreover, the argument that parody, as exemplified technically by the fine calibrations of the digitized morph, is not an infringement of copyright under US law, frees the parodist/morphist from any claims of proprietorship that might otherwise be made by the 'target' of the morph/parody. And Souter's insistence that the 'germ of

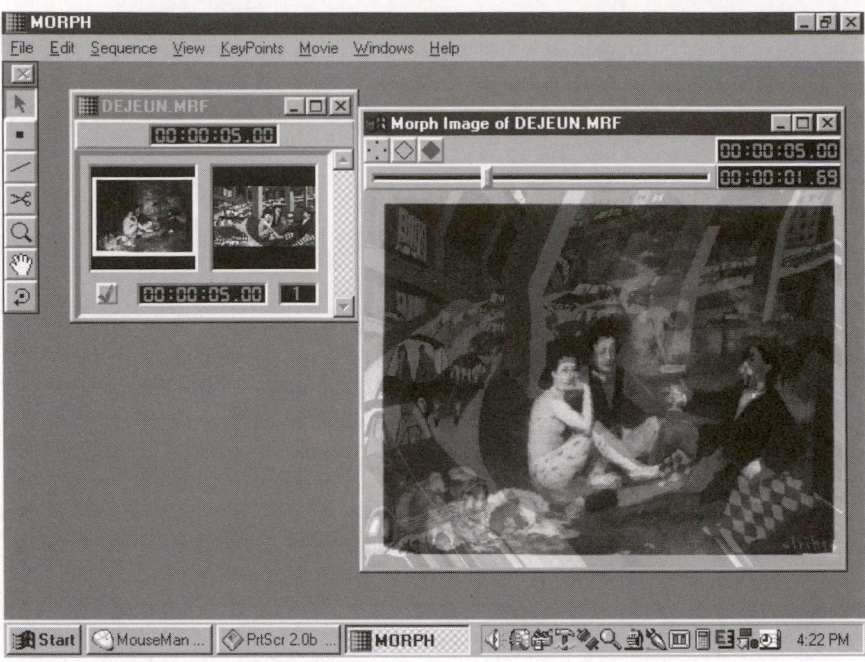

FIG. 8. Intermediate digitized state in parody, reducing the parodic disjunct but displaying a graphic overlap or 'see-through' of the specific frame. Note that varying states of the formal distance between 'target' and 'parody' can be produced by moving the time-scale slide to different positions within the total morph movie and then morphing to that point in the sequence.

parody lies in the definition of the Greek, parodeia . . . a song sung alongside another' and that the audience must be able to gauge the distance between the original and the parody will, as we shall see, be a perfect link with the concluding 'reception' part of this essay.

Perhaps the most pervasive form of the linear morph is in the musical variation, where, after laying down an 'opening frame' for the aural 'storyboard', the composer proceeds to push against the perceptible limits of this frame by a series of narrative warps away from it. The challenge for the composer is to play with enough variability to give a sense of development and thus narrative line, while at the same time always keeping enough of the template that has been established in the opening frame (the theme) phenomenologically and conceptually active in the auditor's consciousness. This formal requirement is most severely challenged in, for example, digital sampling[25] and in the jazz improvisation, which are both virtually impossible to map in a non-aural medium like this essay (at least, without embedded MIDI files). But we can see a simplified, and at the

F<small>IG</small>. 9. Chicago skyline storyboard and ahistorical intermediate state, showing formal 'distortion' produced by morphing to a non-extant interstitial slide-point on the time-scale.

same time, a culturally conditioned version of the problem in the opening and closing processionals of Britten's church opera *Curlew River*, where the plainchant 'Te lucis ante terminum', cited more or less 'straight' in the opening processional, is morphed into a Balinesque, 'orientalized', melismatic, gamelan version *of the same musical line* in the closing processional.[26] It is comparatively easy to trace the intermediate narrative frames of the *Curlew River* morph, for we can establish that Britten was heavily influenced by his visit to Japan and Bali as he was composing the opera. The morph is both intentional and culturally definable, two of the qualities that Souter claimed should be present in the successful playing of one 'song sung alongside another'. Similarly, the permutations, inversions, and paired linear morphing that are the fundamental formulations of both 'identity' and 'meaning' in the Wagnerian *Leitmotif* system, can graphically as well as aurally illustrate the ironic distance that Souter saw as perceptually necessary in the successful functioning of the *parodeia*, as witness the mirror-like ironic pairing of the *Nature/Erda/Earth* (rising, positive) and *Götterdämmerung* (falling, negative) motifs from *Der Ring des Nibelungen* (see Figure 11).

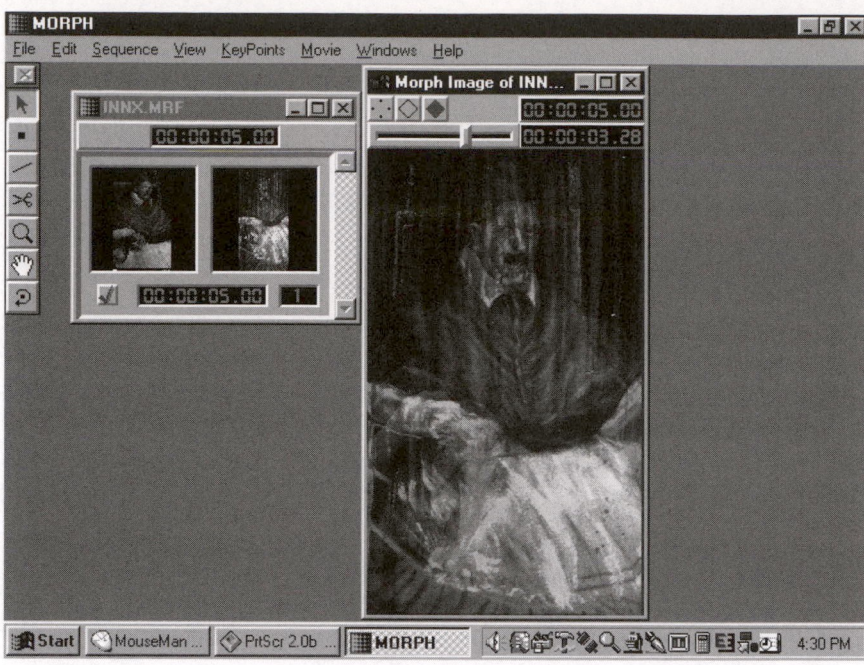

Fig. 10. Non-extant, parodic, digitized state between Velázquez and Bacon, 'in the style' of an artist who is formally an amalgam of the two.

3. From the linear I turn to the recursive, those lines of 'disparagement' and ironic distance that eventually fold back up to the original frame of the storyboard. Here, Justice Souter's distinction between disparagement and displacement will no longer serve as an epistemological or even a procedural model, for the recursive morph's invaginations.[27] Its turning inside out to become a *Doppelgänger* of its original re-forms the linear into a circle, and one that questions the boundaries of identity even more problematically than Foucault becoming a Power Ranger. *Terminator 2* provides the most chilling examples of the recursive morph, when the Terminator morphs from its base, 'romantic' identity into a replication (and therefore *simultaneous* duplication) of another identity: in one scene, the Terminator rises out of a linoleum floor and takes on the shape of a prison guard, so that the 'authentic' guard gazes uncomprehendingly on his own simulacrum and is then killed by the Terminator. In formal terms, the guard thus murders 'himself'. In a later scene, the Terminator takes on both voice and shape of the mother-figure, so that her son is confronted by two apparently identical 'mothers' and has to decide, in a critical moment which must rely more on 'intuition' than sensory perception, which is the 'authentic' and which the morphed 'simulacrum'—as stark and disturbing and

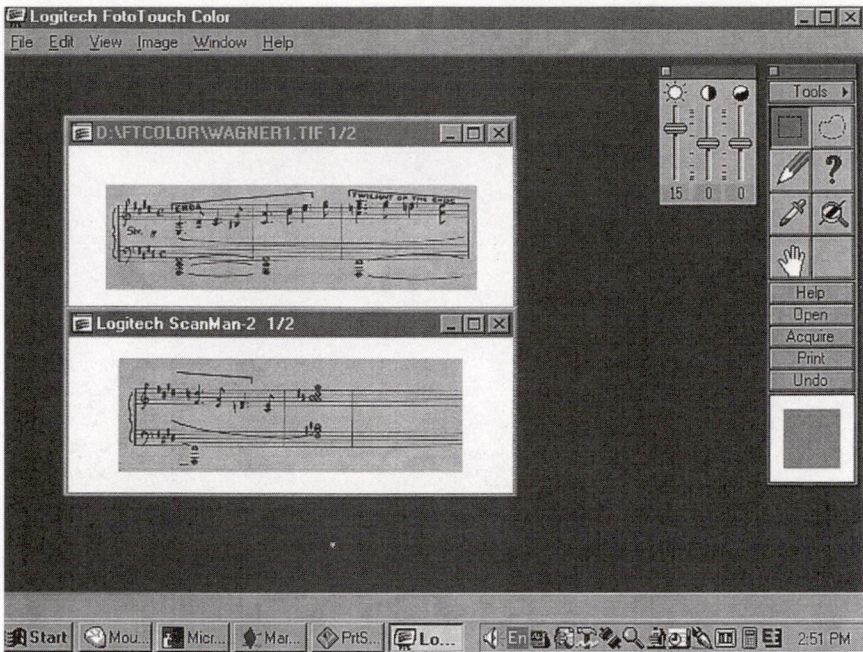

FIG. 11. Wagner, *Nature/Erda* and *Gotterdämmerung* motifs as paired morphs of each other: spatial (in score) and linear (in aural medium). Note that, in other, more complex parts of the score, Wagner not only morphs these two motifs together but also morphs one motif into others through intermediate slide-points on the aural scale. For example, Deryck Cooke (*An Introduction to* Der Ring des Nibelungen, Decca Records, 1968, pp. 8, 13) demonstrates the 'embryonic', 'intermediate', 'definitive', states of the *Ring* motif as well as the relations between the 'harmonic basis' and 'outline' states of the same motif to produce, for instance, the 'scheming' motif (from the 'outline') and the 'resentment' motif out of the 'diminished triad' version of the harmonic basis of the *Ring*. As in the spatial morph of Figure 4, all of these extant aural morphs could, of course, be digitized to produce non-extant yet more intermediate and extended states.

threatening a playing out of the anxieties of the 'Are you my mother?' theme as we are ever likely to encounter: the morphing Terminator abandons the 'romantic' precepts of his sense of self and invades and *replicates* the self of another, while that 'other' is simultaneously present.

But we can observe the recursive morph even in spatial media, when seen as a sequence, in, say, the intertextual relations within an artist's *œuvre*, and through digitization, in the parodic 'disparagement' of the actual compositions of an artist into the production of morphed extensions of the 'style' that do not represent any work actually created by the artist.

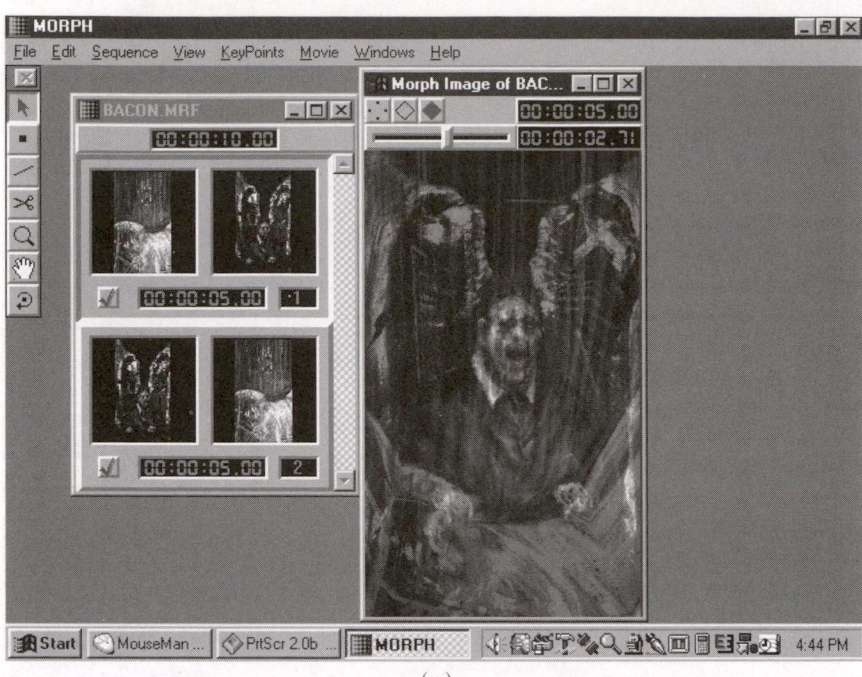

(a)

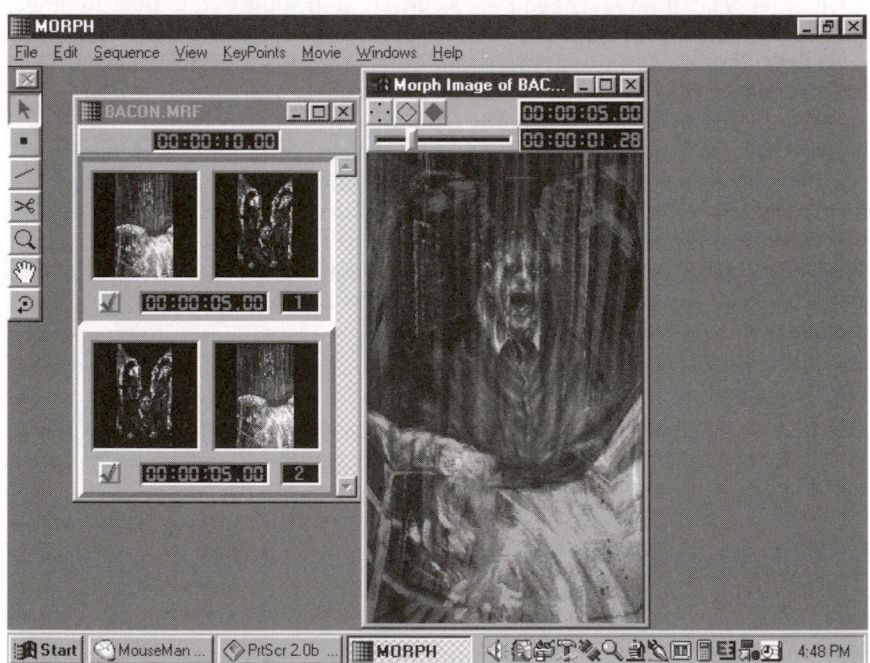

(b)

As I suggested earlier, the digitized, non-extant, and non-proprietary intermediate state between Velázquez and Bacon's *Study* should not only be seen as a straightforward linear morph, but within the recursive (re)formations of Bacon's *œuvre*. This similarly non-extant digitized state reflecting certain stylistic formulations that may cumulatively distil a 'Baconian' vision without ever representing an actual painting (see Figure 12)—especially if played as 'loop' morph movie—illustrates this recursive tendency and overlapping of formal and ontological boundaries in Bacon's work, and any one of these non-extant frames could be digitally morphed to other similarly recursive aspects of Bacon's production. In so doing, we would be constructing a 'parodic' rendering of Bacon, but not necessarily of a specific work: the individual paintings would cumulatively become a complex of recursive form, in which digitization would further obscure the boundaries of a work even more than is already done in Bacon's actual canon.

4. The spatial, linear, and recursive morphs have all assumed a fairly stable reception history, as does Justice Souter's declaration that the audience must *recognize* the original. But one of the major problems confronting the textual scholar is that the audience for a work is not stable, that it morphs both in space and time. In fact, some textuists (Ralph Hanna, Ian Small come to mind) have argued that the editorial desire for 'plenitude' in annotating the perceived allusions in 'difficult' texts should be resisted, and that an editor should take care *not* to provide for a modern audience more information than the originating author might have intended.[28] I have major problems with such appeals to a deliberately obfuscating or opaque intentionalism, but I do find the calibration of differing levels of referential awareness in different audiences to be a particularly valuable tool in the analysis of morphs. To put it as directly as may be: if a later or other audience than that envisaged by the morphist does not recognize the gap between the morphed conclusion and the original, in a visual or aural storyboard, can we still say that a morph has in fact taken place? Berg's reported claim that, in writing the last part of his *Violin Concerto*, he did not know the Bach chorale 'Es ist genug' from Cantata 60, *O Ewigkeit, du Donnerwort II*, despite the universal critical assumption that the last part of the concerto quotes directly and then produces variations on the Bach theme, obviously calls into question the transparency of authorial intention in morphing (or, of course, in a mendacious or faulty or misreported recollection).

Fɪɢ. 12(a–b). Digitized emblem of a recursive Baconian style. The morph emulates the artist's recursive mode in his *œuvre* by producing a state that is paradoxically both an electronic *distillation* and at the same time an *extension* of the stylistic manner of Bacon: that is, this slide-point on the morph does not exist and is not the 'property' of the artist, even though it displays, in caricatured form, the 'properties' of the artist's style.

At the conference on digital resources in the humanities at which the first version of this essay was presented, I conducted an experiment in receptional morphing by giving the audience a copy of the lyrics of Simon and Garfunkel's 1960s song, 'A Simple Desultory Philippic (Or How I Was Robert McNamara'd into Submission)', which consist almost entirely of specific cultural references (Norman Mailer, Maxwell Taylor, Ayn Rand, Phil Spector, Lou Adler, Barry Sadler, Lenny Bruce, etc., mostly in verbal formations) and then asking the audience to check off those references for which they might now need a 'gloss'. This information was then calibrated against the personal and demographic profile that the respondents *chose* to provide as 'potentially significant' in graphing the morphed responses (age, gender, nationality, native language, politic leaning, education, field, etc.). I was thus able graphically to illustrate the gap that a morphed historical context and demography had created, especially in the light of the 'new' meaning of the verb, 'to McNamara' (to be contrite for one's earlier actions) after the publication of McNamara's Vietnam memoirs ('We were wrong, terribly wrong') and after the satirical extension of 'Doing the McNamara' in the *New Yorker*'s attaching a similar changed meaning to such figures as Quaddafi, Hitler, and Ayatollah Khomeini, all of whom, like McNamara, confessed to past sins and claimed that, if given the chance, they would do it all differently. Simon and Garfunkel's verb, 'to McNamara', associated specifically with 'submission' and political control, had become a new verb in a different chronological and political climate.

Inevitably, this survey of spatial, linear, recursive, and receptional morphing has fallen into the trap of seeing morphs under every bush. But for a volume on electronic texts, I think the morph is a particularly apt figure, because it is both figure and ground, tenor and vehicle, metaphor and substance. As I hope I have demonstrated, my brief for the morph is greater and yet more modest than the utopian or dystopian romances of some other commentators. For example, Turkle's claim for the feminist fluidity of the morph concentrates primarily on the phenomenology of the morphed result and its seeming instability; it ignores (or at least prefers to pass over) the fact that this apparent instability is based on a careful, in fact extremely tedious, plotting of storyboards, correspondent pixellation, intermediate points, compression ratios, frames per second, video transfers, and so on. As Don McKenzie remarked to me in email correspondence while I was composing this essay, recalling his experiences in observing and participating in the Michael Jackson *Black or White* music video, 'I was struck by the technical processes and found greater interest in the continuity so many of them showed with traditional skills required in the more traditional media (e.g. the supreme importance of register in printing, especially colour printing, and in plotting the detailed stages of morphing).'[29] Quite so. The morphist operator is confronted with a battery of critical and technical choices that will collectively determine the characteristics of the apparently seamless morph observed and/or manipulated by the viewer. The finer the register and the more detailed the investment of pixellation control, the more seamless will be the transformation from Foucault to Power Ranger or from Velázquez to Bacon and Bacon-ism. And there may be times (for example, if one concentrates primarily on the opening and closing images of the morph storyboard) when it is the very shock of the disjunct between the two rather than transparency and fluidity of change that needs to be emphasized. Ironically, caricature and parody may become less, not more cognitively effective as a result of the intervening frames of the complete morph movie.

So my sense of the morph is both much more and much less than some of those utopian 'romances' of digitization I cited earlier: that the morph is not just our future but our past and present too, and it inhabits phenomenologically not just the diachronic but also the synchronic axis—space as well as time. The morph is thus not something *added to* our human condition by technology, and specifically by digitization, but is already deeply embedded in both our hopes (our progressional, ameliorative mode) and our fears (our acknowledgement of mutability and 'nature corrumpable'): as Hamlet expostulates to the skull of Yorick, 'Now get you to my lady's table, and tell her, let her paint an inch thick, to this favour she must come. Make her laugh at that' (v. i), just as the digitized human face and skull that was my presiding deity at the conference presentation had already shown. But because the warp of the morph enables the continued recursive return of the living human from the skull, Hamlet is also right on target in his deft but cynical demonstration of how 'the noble dust of Alexander [may] stop a bung-hole' (v. i) or how 'a king may go a progress through the guts of a beggar' (IV. iii). E does indeed equal mc^2. Like Wordsworth's Lucy, 'rolled round in earth's diurnal course, | With rocks, and stones, and trees,' Alexander in the bung-hole and the king in the beggar interrogate the very boundaries of identity: where does Lucy stop and the rocks and stones begin?

Spenser's figure of Nature in the *Mutabilitie Cantos* tries to answer this question by recalibrating the balance of Foucauldian 'power relations' between change and stasis. Replying to Mutability, Nature declares:

> I well consider all that ye haue sayd,
> And find that all things stedfastnes doe hate
> And changed be: yet being rightly wayd
> They are not changed from their first estate;
> But by their change their being doe dilate:
> And turning to themselves at length againe,
> Doe worke their own perfection so by fate:
> Then ouer them Change doth not rule and raigne;
> But they raigne ouer change, and doe their states maintaine.

(Mutabilitie Cantos, VII. 58)

This formulation may adequately describe the recursive morph (dilating, via *Change*, to its 'perfect' or 'maintained' state), but it is hardly much comfort in contemplating the spatial, linear, or receptional morph. Indeed, Spenser the narrator recognizes this inadequacy, for after Nature's disappearance, he 'bethinks . . . on that speech whyleare' and, in the appropriately 'vnperfite' Canto VIII, longs for that Platonic 'stedfast rest of all things firmely stayd', in fact the same 'stasis' that Tanselle had wished for texts.

But no matter how the matter is resolved morally, philosophically, or ontologically, morphin is recognized by Lucretius, Ovid, Spenser, and Tanselle, in their different ways, as an inevitable condition of nature. Given this long human experience of, and wrestling with, the condition of the morph, then it is surely not surprising to discover that the power of modern technological morphing, by digital pixellation and audio mixing, to emblematize this condition—both in its ontology and its phenomenology —is a special pertinent 'resource' for the humanities and a particularly valuable epistemological tool in exploring the multiform states of the electronic text in various media, and perhaps a perfect descriptor of our postmodernist anxieties over boundary and identity. But it is only that: a 're-source' for digitization of the morph and a 'tool' for testing the limits of electronic textuality. Like the electron microscope or the ultrasound scanner or the radio telescope, morphing may allow us entry into a field of micro- and macroscopic observation that was technically impossible in earlier times. But just as Douglas Hofstadter has reminded us that ultrasound scanning does not provide 'reality' but only a morphed *medium* of perception that we take for reality (sound waves converted into the visible spectrum),[30] so our apparent mastery of pixellation is as much a function of our will and our desire as it is of our empiricism. The thing that allows Hamlet to morph Alexander is, what else, Coleridgean 'Imagination'[31] and good, stolid Horatio predictably feels that ' 'twere to consider too curiously, to consider so' [v. i]. Have I considered 'too curiously' in finding, creating, and showing the digitized morphs of painting, film, architecture, fiction, advertising, music, and so on? I hope so. Digital morphing *is* a stretch, sometimes quite literally so, but in stretching it provides a renewed sense of the intertwined warp and weft of a text, and how it may be done and undone. I cannot yet fully endorse the Mighty Morphin Power Rangers' confidence in their battle cry for transmutation, but I can at least ask: 'Is it morphin time?'

NOTES

I am grateful for the co-operation of Gryphon Software in allowing storyboards and individual frames generated by the program *Morph* to be used through this essay. Further information about the technical aspects of this morphing can be obtained at Gryphon's Web Site <http://www.gryphon. software.com> The research for this essay was sponsored in part by a grant from the Research Foundation of the City University of New York.

1. Mark Dery, 'Cyberculture', *South Atlantic Quarterly*, 91: 3 (Summer 1992), 501. I am grateful to my colleague, Gerhard Joseph, for having brought this article to my attention.

2. The philosophical and technical issues are examined, in the very digital medium which prompts them, in my ongoing study, *Morphologies*, to be available on the Web, on CD-ROM, and in a supplementary critical monograph.

3. W. W. Greg, 'The Rationale of Copy-Text', *Studies in Bibliography*, 3 (1950–1), 19–36; G. Thomas Tanselle, *A Rationale of Textual Criticism* (Philadelphia: University of Pennsylvania Press, 1989).

4. Michel Foucault, 'What is an Author?', in Paul Rabinow (ed.), *The Foucault Reader* (New York: Pantheon, 1984), p. 118.

5. See, for example, my 'Editorial and Critical Theory: From Modernism to Postmodernism', in George Bornstein and Ralph Williams (eds.), *Palimpsest* (Ann Arbor: University of Michigan Press, 1993), pp. 9–28; the 'Forms of the Text' chapter of *Theories of the Text* (Oxford: Clarendon Press, 1996); and 'Textual Forensics', *PMLA*, 111 (1996), 32–51.

6. Jean-François Lyotard, *The Postmodern Condition: A Report on Knowledge*, trans. Geoff Bennington and Brian Massumi (Minneapolis: University of Minnesota Press, 1984), esp. pp. xxiii, 31–7.

7. J. Hillis Miller, 'The Critic as Host', in Harold Bloom *et al.* (eds.), *Deconstruction and Criticism* (New York: Continuum, 1979), pp. 217–53.

8. For example, 'Textual Scholarship', in Joseph Gibaldi (ed.), *Introduction to Scholarship in the Modern Languages and Literatures* (New York: MLA, 1992); and the 'Ontology' chapter of *Theories of the Text*.

9. Manfred Clynes, as quoted in David F. Channell, *The Valid Machine: A Study of Technology and Organic Life* (New York: Oxford University Press, 1991), p. 129; and cited in Dery, 'Cyberculture', 502–3.

10. Ibid., p. 505; cf. Mark Crispin Miller, *Boxed in: The Culture of TV* (Evanston, Ill.: Northwestern University Press, 1989), pp. 306–7.

11. Klaus Theleweit, *Male Fantasies*, quoted in Dery, 'Cyberculture', pp. 504–5.

12. Donna Haraway, 'A Manifesto for Cyborgs', 1985, quoted in Dery, 'Cyberculture', p. 504.

13. Donna Haraway, *Simians, Cyborgs and Women: The Reinvention of Nature* (New York: Routledge, 1991), p. 150.

14. Sherry Turkle, *Life on the Screen: Identity in the Age of the Internet* (New York: Simon and Schuster, 1995). See also her *The Second Self: Computers and the Human Spirit* (New York: Simon and Schuster, 1984).

15. See the 'Gender' chapter of *Theories of the Text* (and references therein) and 'The Manifestation and Accommodation of Theory in Textual Editing', in Philip Cohen (ed.), *Devils and Angels: Textual Editing and Literary Theory* (Charlottesville: University of Virginia Press, 1991), pp. 78–102, esp. 78–9, 93–4. See also Brenda R. Silver, 'Textual Criticism as Feminist Practice: Or, Who's Afraid of Virginia Woolf, Part II', in George Bornstein (ed.), *Representing*

Modernist Texts: Editing as Interpretation (Ann Arbor: University of Michigan Press, 1991); and Silver's 'Whose Room of Orlando's Own? The Politics of Adaptation', in D. C. Greetham (ed.), *The Margins of the Text* (Ann Arbor: University of Michigan Press, 1997).

16. Edward Rothstein, 'Technology: If Life on the Web Is Postmodern, Maybe Foucault Really Was a Power Ranger', *New York Times*, 1 Apr. 1996, D3.

17. Randall McLeod, 'From *Trance-formations* in the Text of *Orlando Furioso*', in Dave Oliphant and Robin Bradford (eds.), *New Directions in Textual Studies* (Austin: Harry Ransom Humanities Research Center/University of Texas Press, 1990), pp. 60–109.

18. The 'trance-formation' of the quotation is, of course, from, 'My theme is alway oon, and ever was | *Radix malorum est cupiditas*' (Chaucer, *Canterbury Tales*, VI (C) 333–5).

19. See Joseph Grigely on the textual ontology of the 'fac-simile' ('The Textual Event', in Cohen (ed.), *Devils and Angels*, pp. 167–94, esp. 174–5, repr. in his *Textualterity: Art, Theory, and Textual Criticism* (Ann Arbor: University of Michigan Press, 1995)) and my response in the 'Ontology' chapter of *Theories of the Text*, esp. pp. 31–5.

20. On the textual problem of the fake and forgery, see Grigely (n. 19); and Mark Jones (ed.), *Fake? The Art of Deception* (Berkeley: University of California Press, 1990), esp. Nicholas Barker, 'Textual Forgery', pp. 22–7; and my ™*Copy/ Right©* (forthcoming on Web site and CD-ROM) and the 'Ontology' chapter of *Theories of the Text*. On the role of the palaeographical work of Mabillon and the Maurists as it relates to a theory of historical linearity, see the 'History' chapter of *Theories*, esp. pp. 69–71.

21. See the 'Palaeography' chapter of my *Textual Scholarship: An Introduction* (New York: Garland, 1992, 1994), esp. pp. 172–3; and the 'History' chapter of *Theories of the Text*, esp. pp. 64–7.

22. Supreme Court of the United States, No. 92–1292; *Luther R. Campbell aka Luke Skywalker, et al.* v. *Acuff-Rose Music, Inc.* on a writ of a certiorari to the United States Court of Appeals for the Sixth Circuit, 7 Mar. 1994. All subsequent citations are from this decision.

23. The first couple of lines of the lyrics of the 2 Live Crew version of Orbison and William Dees' 'Pretty Woman' are virtually identical to the target of the parody. And even when the rap version then substitutes 'Big Hairy Woman you need to shave that stuff' for Orbison's 'Pretty Woman, won't you pardon me,' and then morphs still further into 'Bald headed woman', 'Two timin' woman' etc. (with a significant recursive return to 'pretty woman' in the last line), there is a notable absence of the pornographic, violent, 'gangsta rap' qualities that had previously brought notoriety to the group. The specific morphing parody (including the musical riffs as well) thus falls squarely within Souter's requirements of 'recognizability' and the 'transformative'. There is a canonical joke being played here, as well, for the album on which the 2 Live Crew parody appears (*As Clean as They Wanna Be*) is itself a parody, by diminution and acceptable acculturation, of their earlier *As Bad as They Wanna Be*, which was full of the violence and sexual aggression that

is absent from the parodic 'Pretty Woman'. The main quality connecting the two albums is the misogyny and anti-romanticism that is, as Souter observes, a cultural antidote to the squeaky-clean, sentimentalized vision of sexuality promoted in the original Orbison version.

24. See, for example, Jean Baudrillard, *Simulacra and Simulation*, trans. Sheila Faria Glaser (Ann Arbor: University of Michigan Press, 1995), esp. 'The Precession of Simulacra' and 'Simulacra and Science Fiction'.

25. David Sanjek, ' "Don't Have to DJ No More": Sampling and the "Autonomous" Creator', *Intellectual Property and the Construction of Authorship*. Special Issue of *Cardozo Arts and Entertainment Law Journal*, 10: 2 (1992), 607–24.

26. Britten's morph from 'direct' quotation of the tradition of the spare, masculinist, linear form of Gregorian chant illustrates the nineteenth-century re-formation of the history of Western Chant as a rejection of the perceived 'oriental', 'feminine', origins of Old Roman chant and the codification of a 'masculinist', 'linear', non-recursive tonal Gregorian form that more conveniently historicized the position of German post-Beethoven music as a fulfilment of the Western Tradition. Thus, Britten's subsequent 'orientalization' of 'Te lucis' is itself a recursive morph (perhaps unconsciously) into the pre-Gregorian tradition. See Leo Treitler, 'The Politics of Reception: Tailoring the Present as Fulfillment of a Desired Past', *Journal of the Royal Musicological Association*, 116 (1992), 280–98, for a brilliantly argued critique of this putative (but historically and formally inaccurate) morph from the feminist oriental to the masculinist Western.

27. On the concept of Derridean 'invagination' and its textual/bibliographical function, see Derrida, 'Living On. Border Lines', trans. James Hulbert, in Bloom *et al.* (eds.), *Deconstruction and Criticism*, pp. 75–176, and my '[Textual] Criticism and Deconstruction', *Studies in Bibliography*, 44 (1991), 1–30.

28. See Ralph Hanna, 'Annotating *Piers Plowman*', *Text*, 6 (1993), 153–63; and 'Annotation as Social Practice', in Stephen Barney (ed.), *Annotation and Its Texts* (Oxford: Oxford University Press, 1991); Ian Small, 'The Editor as Annotator as Ideal Reader', in Small and Walsh (eds.), *The Theory and Practice of Text-Editing* (Cambridge: Cambridge University Press, 1991), pp. 186–209.

29. D. F. McKenzie, email message, 7 June 1996.

30. Douglas Hofstadter, 'On Computers, Creativity, Credit, Brain Mechanisms, and the Turing Test', in *Fluid Concepts and Creative Analogies: Computer Models of the Fundamental Mechanisms of Thought* (New York: Basic Books, 1995), p. 482. Hofstadter uses ultrasound scanning of the fetus to argue that 'any boundary between "direct observation" and "inference" is a subjective matter' (p. 488); that is, we have become culturally conditioned to believe we actually 'see' the fetus, whereas in fact it is only the existence of fast computer hardware capable of reconstituting the scattered sound waves that allows the apparent but not real 'direct observation'. This distinction between observation and interference is an apt figure for the phenomenology of the creation and experience of any stage of the morph movie. See my elaboration of Hofstadter's thesis as it relates to textual editing in 'The Telephone

Directory and Dr. Seuss: Scholarly Editing after *Feist* v. *Rural Telephone*', *Studies in the Literary Imagination*, Special Issue on Editing the Imagination, ed. Tom Quirk, 29 (1996), 53–74.

31. 'The poet, described in ideal perfection, brings the whole soul of man into activity. . . . He diffuses a tone and spirit of unity, that blends, and (as it were) *fuses* each into each, by that synthetic and magical power, to which I would exclusively appropriate the name of Imagination' (Coleridge, *Biographia Literaria*, ch. 14).

SELECT BIBLIOGRAPHY

ALTHUSSER, LOUIS, 'Ideology and Ideological State Apparatuses (Notes towards an Investigation)', in *Lenin and Philosophy and Other Essays*, trans. Ben Brewster (New York: Monthly Review Press, 1971).

American Civil Liberties Union, 'ACLU Freedom Network' homepage, <URL: http://www.aclu.org/>

American Library Association, Resource Book for Banned Book Week 1986, <URL: http://rainbow.rmii.com/~grymntl/bos/banned.html>

ANDERSON, BENEDICT, *Imagined Communities: Reflections on the Origin and Spread of Nationalism* (London: Verso, 1983).

ATKINSON, ROSS, 'Networks, Hypertext, and Academic Information Services: Some Longer Range Implications', *College and Research Libraries*, 54: 3 (May 1993), 199–215.

BARNARD, DAVID T., *et al.*, 'SGML-Based Markup for Literary Texts: Two Problems and Some Solutions', *Computers and the Humanities*, 22 (1988), 265–76.

BARNEY, STEPHEN A. (ed.), *Annotation and Its Texts* (New York: Oxford University Press, 1991).

BARTHES, ROLAND, *The Pleasure of the Text* (New York: Hill and Wang, 1975).

—— *Image–Music–Text*, trans. Stephen Heath (London: Fontana, 1977).

—— *Barthes: Selected Writings*, ed. Susan Sontag (London: Fontana, 1982).

BATTESTIN, MARTIN C., 'A Rationale of Literary Annotation: The Example of Fielding's Novels', *Studies in Bibliography*, 34 (1981), 1–22.

BAUDRILLARD, JEAN, *Simulacra and Simulation* (Ann Arbor: University of Michigan Press, 1995).

BENNETT, PAULA, 'By a Mouth that Cannot Speak: Spectral Presence in Emily Dickinson's Letters', *Emily Dickinson Journal*, 1 (1992), 76–99.

BENSKIN, MICHAEL, 'The Hands of the Kildare Poems Manuscript', *Irish University Review*, 20 (1990), 163–93.

Beowulf: An Edition with Manuscript Spacing Notation and Graphotactic Analyses, ed. R. D. Stevick (New York: Garland, 1975).

BERK, EMILY, and DEVLIN, JOSEPH (eds.), *Hypertext/Hypermedia Handbook* (New York: Internet Publications, McGraw Hill, 1991).

BHABHA, HOMI K., 'Dissemination: Time, Narrative, and the Margins of the Modern Nation', in Homi K. Bhabha (ed.), *Nation and Narration* (London: Routledge, 1990).

BIRKERTS, SVEN, *The Gutenberg Elegies: The Fate of Reading in an Electronic Age* (New York: Ballantine Books, 1994).

—— 'The Book as Emblem: The Besieged Stronghold?', *Journal of Scholarly Publishing*, 26: 1 (Oct. 1994), 3–8.

BLAKE, N. F., and ROBINSON, P. M. W. (eds.), *The Canterbury Tales Project: Occasional Papers*, 1 (Oxford: Office for Humanities Communication Publications, 1993).

BLOOM, HAROLD, *et al.* (eds.), *Deconstruction and Criticism* (New York: Continuum, 1979).

BOLTER, JAY DAVID, *Writing Space: The Computer, Hypertext, and the History of Writing* (Hillsdale, NJ: Lawrence Erlbaum Associates, 1991).

BROCKBANK, PHILIP, 'Towards a Mobile Text', in Small and Walsh (eds.), *Theory and Practice of Text Editing*.

BUELL, LAWRENCE, 'American Literary Emergence as a Postcolonial Phenomenon', *American Literary History*, 4 (1992), 411–42.

BURNS, ROBERT, *The Poems and Songs of Robert Burns*, ed. James Kinsley (Oxford: Clarendon Press, 1968).

CHANNELL, DAVID F., *The Valid Machine: A Study of Technology and Organic Life* (New York: Oxford University Press, 1991).

CHAUCER, GEOFFREY, *The Canterbury Tales. Geoffrey Chaucer. A Facsimile and Transcription of the Hengwrt Manuscript, with Variants from the Ellesmere Manuscript*, ed. Paul G. Ruggiers (Norman: University of Oklahoma Press, 1979).

—— *The Legend of Good Women*, ed. George Kane and Janet Cowen (East Lansing, Mich.: Colleagues Press, 1995).

—— *The Wife of Bath's Prologue on CD-ROM*, ed. P. M. W. Robinson (Cambridge: Cambridge University Press, 1996).

CHERNAIK, WARREN, DAVIS, CAROLINE, and DEEGAN, MARILYN (eds.), *The Politics of the Electronic Text* (Oxford: Office for Humanities Communication Publications, 1993).

CLAIR, COLIN, *A History of European Printing* (London: Academic Press, 1976).

COHEN, PHILIP (ed.), *Devils and Angels: Textual Editing and Literary Theory* (Charlottesville: University of Virginia Press, 1991).

CONNER, PATRICK W., 'Hypertext in the Last Days of the Book', *Bulletin of the John Rylands University Library of Manchester*, 74 (1992), 7–24.

COOMBS, JAMES S., RENEAR, ALLEN H., and DEROSE, STEVEN J., 'Markup Systems and the Future of Scholarly Text Processing', *Communications of the Association for Computing Machinery*, 30: 11 (1987), 933–47.

COOVER, ROBERT, 'The End of Books', *New York Times Book Review*, 21 June 1992, 1, 11, 24–5.

COPE, VIRGINIA H., *Mark Twain's Huckleberry Finn: Text, Illustrations, and Early Reviews*, <URL: http://etext.lib.virginia.edu/twain/huckfinn.html>

COULMAS, FLORIAN, *The Writing Systems of the World* (Oxford: Blackwell, 1989).

Critical Issues in African American Life and Culture (Listserv Discussion Group) <AFROAM-L@HARVARDA.HARVARD.EDU>; archives: <URL: http//www. afrinet.net/~hallh/afrotalk/afrosep95/0434.html>

DEEGAN, MARILYN, LEE, STUART, and TIMBRELL, NICOLA, *An Introduction to Multimedia for Academic Use* (Oxford: Oxford University Computing Services, 1996).

DELANY, PAUL, and LANDOW, GEORGE P. (eds.), *Hypermedia and Literary Studies* (Cambridge, Mass. and London: MIT Press, 1991).

—— —— (eds.), *The Digital Word: Text-Based Computing in the Humanities* (Cambridge, Mass. and London: MIT Press, 1993).

DEROSE, STEVEN J., *et al.*, 'What is Text, Really?', *Journal of Computing in Higher Education*, 1: 2 (1990), 3–26.

—— 'Biblical Studies and Hypertext', in Delany and Landow (eds.), *Hypermedia and Literary Studies*.

DERRIDA, JACQUES, 'Living On. Border Lines', in Bloom *et al.* (eds.), *Deconstruction and Criticism*.

—— *Positions*, trans. Alan Bass (Chicago: University of Chicago Press, 1981).

—— 'This Is Not an Oral Footnote', in Barney (ed.), *Annotation and Its Texts*.

DERY, MARK, 'Cyberculture', *South Atlantic Quarterly*, 91: 3 (1992), 501–23.

DICKINSON, EMILY, *The Manuscript Books of Emily Dickinson*, ed. R. W. Franklin (2 vols.; Cambridge, Mass.: Belknap Press, Harvard University Press, 1981).

DONALDSON, PETER S., 'Olivier, Hamlet, and Freud', *Cinema Journal*, 26: 4 (1987), 22–48.

—— 'The Shakespeare Interactive Archive: New Directions in Electronic Scholarship on Text and Performance', in Edward Barrett and Marie Redmond (eds.), *Contextual Media* (Cambridge, Mass.: MIT Press, 1995).

ENGELBART, D. C., 'A Conceptual Framework for the Augmentation of Man's Intellect', in P. Howerton (ed.), *Vistas in Information Handling*, 1 (Washington, DC: Spartan Books, 1963).

FEBVRE, LUCIEN, and MARTIN, HENRI-JEAN, *The Coming of the Book: The Impact of Printing 1450–1800* (New York: Verso, 1976).

FISH, STANLEY, *Is There a Text in This Class? The Authority of Interpretive Communities* (Cambridge, Mass. and London: Harvard University Press, 1980).

FIX, H., 'Production and Usage of a Machine-Readable Manuscript: A Report on the Saarbrücken Version of *Grágás Konungsbók*', in A. Gilmour-Bryson (ed.), *Computer Applications to Medieval Studies* (Kalamazoo: Western Michigan University, 1984).

FORTIER, PAUL, and the TEI Literature Working Group, 'The TEI Guidelines (version 1.1 10/90): A Critique' (1995). Available from the TEI listserv server, TEI-L, as document AI3W5 DOC.

FOUCAULT, MICHEL, 'What is an Author?', in Josué V. Harari (ed.), *Textual Strategies: Perspectives in Post-Structuralist Criticism* (Ithaca, NY: Cornell University Press, 1979).

GENETTE, GÉRARD, *Palimpsestes: La Littérature au second degré* (Paris: Seuil, 1982).

—— 'Structuralism and Literary Criticism', in *Figures of Literary Discourse*, trans. A. Sheridan (New York: Columbia University Press, 1982).

GOLDFARB, CHARLES, 'A Generalized Approach to Document Markup', in *Proceedings of the ACM SIGPLAN-SIGOA Symposium on Text Manipulation* (New York: ACM, 1981), pp. 68–73.

—— *The SGML Handbook* (Oxford: Oxford University Press, 1990).

DE GRAZIA, MARGRETA, *Shakespeare Verbatim* (Oxford: Clarendon Press, 1991).

GREETHAM, D. C., '[Textual] Criticism and Deconstruction', *Studies in Bibliography*, 44 (1991), 1–30.

—— *Textual Scholarship: An Introduction* (New York and London: Garland, 1992).

—— 'Editorial and Critical Theory: From Modernism to Postmodernism', in George Bornstein and Ralph Williams (eds.), *Palimpsest* (Ann Arbor: University of Michigan Press, 1993).

—— 'Textual Forensics', *Proceedings of the Modern Language Association of America*, 111 (1996), 32–51.

—— *Theories of the Text* (Oxford: Clarendon Press, 1997).

GREG, W. W., 'The Rational of Copy-Text', *Studies in Bibliography*, 3 (1950–1), 19–36.

GRIGELY, JOSEPH, *Textualterity: Art, Theory, and Textual Criticism* (Ann Arbor: University of Michigan Press, 1995).

GRUSIN, RICHARD, 'What Is an Electronic Author? Theory and the Technological Fallacy', in Robert Markley (ed.), *Virtual Realities and Their Discontents* (Baltimore and London: Johns Hopkins University Press, 1996).

HANNA, RALPH, III, *The Ellesmere Manuscript of Chaucer's* Canterbury Tales: *A Working Facsimile* (Cambridge: D. S. Brewer, 1989).

—— 'Annotation as Social Practice', in Barney (ed.), *Annotation and Its Texts*.

—— 'Annotating *Piers Plowman*', *Text*, 6 (1993), 153–63.

HARAWAY, DONNA, *Simians, Cyborgs, and Women: The Reinvention of Nature* (New York: Routledge, 1991).

HEMINGWAY, ERNEST, *Green Hills of Africa* (New York: Scribner, 1935).

HEWITT, DAVID, *et al.* (eds.), *The Edinburgh Edition of the Waverley Novels: A Guide for Editors* (Aberdeen: EEWN, 1996).

HINMAN, CHARLTON, *The Printing and Proofreading of the First Folio of Shakespeare* (2 vols.; Oxford: Oxford University Press, 1963).

HODGDON, BARBARA, 'Splish Splash and the Other: Lepage's Intercultural *Dream Machine*', *Essays in Theatre/Études Théâtrales*, 12: 1 (1993), 29–39.

HOFSTADTER, DOUGLAS, *Fluid Concepts and Creative Analogies: Computer Models of the Fundamental Mechanisms of Thought* (New York: Basic Books, 1995).

HOLLAND, JEANNE, 'Scraps, Stamps, and Cutouts: Emily Dickinson's Domestic Technologies of Publication', in O'Brien O'Keeffe and Ezell (eds.), *Cultural Artifacts and the Production of Meaning*.

HONIGMANN, E. A. J., *The Stability of Shakespeare's Text* (Lincoln: University of Nebraska Press, 1965).

HOWE, SUSAN, 'These Flames and Generosities of the Heart: Emily Dickinson and the Illogic of Sumptuary Values', *Sulfur*, 28 (Spring 1991), 134–55.

The Huck Finn Homepage <URL: http://etext.virginia.edu/railton/huckfinn/huchompg.html>

HUITFELDT, CLAUS, *MECS—A Multi-Element Code System*, Working Papers from the Wittgenstein Archives, No. 3 (University of Bergen, 1993).

—— 'Multi-Dimensional Texts in a One-Dimensional Medium', *Computers and the Humanities*, 28 (1994), 235–41.

International Organization for Standardization (ISO), *Information Processing—Text and Office Systems—Standard Generalized Markup Language (SGML)*, ISO8879-1986 (International Organization for Standardization (ISO), 1986).

JACK, IAN, 'Novels and those "Necessary Evils": Annotating the Brontës', *Essays in Criticism*, 32 (1982), 321–37.

JAMESON, FREDERIC, *The Political Unconscious: Narrative as a Socially Symbolic Act* (Ithaca, NY: Cornell University Press, 1981).

JED, STEPHANIE H., *Chaste Thinking: The Rape of Lucretia and the Birth of Humanism* (Bloomington and Indianapolis: Indiana University Press, 1989).

JENNY, LAURENT, 'The Strategy of Form', trans. R. Carter, in Tzvetan Todorov (ed.), *French Literary Theory Today* (Cambridge: Cambridge University Press, 1982).

JOHANNESSEN, K., and NORDENSTAM, T. (eds.), *Culture and Value: Philosophy and the Cultural Sciences* (Austrian Ludwig Wittgenstein Society, 1995).

JOHNSON, SAMUEL, 'Preface' to *The Plays of William Shakespeare* (1765), in *Johnson on Shakespeare*, The Yale Edition of the Works of Samuel Johnson, vol. vii (New Haven and London: Yale University Press, 1968).

JONES, KATHRYN, 'Candidates Seek Votes On Line But Largely Avoid Internet Issues', Cybertimes Section, *New York Times*, 12 Mar. 1996, <URL: http://www.nytimes.com/>

JONES, MARK (ed.), *Fake? The Art of Deception* (Berkeley: University of California Press, 1990).

KANE, GEORGE, 'John M. Manly and Edith Rickert', in Paul G. Ruggiers (ed.), *Editing Chaucer: The Great Tradition* (Norman, Okla.: Pilgrim Books, 1984).

KENNER, HUGH, *The Mechanic Muse* (Oxford: Oxford University Press, 1987).

KIERNAN, K., 'Digital Image Processing and the *Beowulf* Manuscript', *Literary and Linguistic Computing*, 6 (1991), 20–7.

KRISTEVA, JULIA, *Séméiotiké* (Paris: Seuil, 1969).

—— *La Révolution du langage poétique* (Paris: Seuil, 1974).

—— *The Kristeva Reader*, ed. Toril Moi, trans. Seán Hand, *et al.* (Oxford: Blackwell, 1986).

—— *Language—the Unknown: An Initiation into Linguistics*, trans. Anne M. Menke (New York: Columbia University Press, 1989).

The Lancashire Domesday, ed. A. Williams and G. H. Martin (London: Alecto Historical Editions, 1991).

LANCASHIRE, IAN, *Humanities Computing Yearbook, 1989–90* (Oxford: Oxford University Press, 1991).

LANDOW, GEORGE P., *Hypertext: The Convergence of Contemporary Critical Theory and Technology* (Baltimore and London: Johns Hopkins University Press, 1992) [and see items under Delany, Paul].

LANHAM, RICHARD A., *The Electronic Word: Democracy, Technology, and the Arts* (Chicago: University of Chicago Press, 1993).

LIU, ALAN, 'Local Transcendence: Cultural Criticism, Postmodernism, and the Romanticism of Detail', *Representations*, 32 (1990), 75–113.

LOWRY, M., *The World of Aldus Manutius* (Oxford: Blackwell, 1979).

LYOTARD, JEAN-FRANÇOIS, *The Postmodern Condition: A Report on Knowledge*, trans. Geoff Bennington and Brian Massumi (Minneapolis: University of Minnesota Press, 1984).

McGANN, JEROME J., *A Critique of Modern Textual Criticism* (Chicago: University of Chicago Press, 1983).

—— *The Textual Condition* (Princeton: Princeton University Press, 1991).

—— 'What is Critical Editing?', *Text*, 5 (1991), 15–30.

—— 'Emily Dickinson's Visible Language', *Emily Dickinson Journal*, 2 (1993), 40–57.

—— 'Composition as Explanation', in O'Brien O'Keeffe and Ezell (eds.), *Cultural Artifacts and the Production of Meaning*.

McGUIRE, PHILIP C., *Speechless Dialect: Shakespeare's Open Silences* (Berkeley: University of California Press, 1985).

McKenzie, D. F., *Bibliography and the Sociology of Texts*, The Panizzi Lectures (London: British Library Publications, 1986).

McKernan, Luke, and Terris, Olwen, *Walking Shadows: Shakespeare in the National Film and Television Archives* (London: British Film Institute, 1994).

McLeod, Randall, 'From *Trance-formations* in the Text of *Orlando Furioso*', in Dave Oliphant and Robin Bradford (eds.), *New Directions in Textual Studies* (Austin: Harry Ransom Humanities Research Center/University of Texas Press, 1990).

Manly, J. M., and Rickert, E., *The Text of 'The Canterbury Tales'* (8 vols.; Chicago: Chicago University Press, 1940).

Mayali, Laurent, 'For a Political Economy of Annotation', in Barney (ed.), *Annotation and Its Texts*.

Memmi, Albert, *The Colonizer and the Colonized*, tr. Howard Greenfeld (New York: Orion Press, 1965).

Miller, J. Hillis, 'The Critic as Host', in Bloom *et al.* (eds.), *Deconstruction and Criticism*.

—— *Illustration: Essays in Art and Culture* (Cambridge, Mass.: Harvard University Press, 1992).

Miller, Mark Crispin, *Boxed in: The Culture of TV* (Evanston, Ill.: Northwestern University Press, 1989).

Mitchell, William, *The Reconfigured Eye: Visual Truth in the Post-Photographic Era* (Cambridge, Mass.: MIT Press, 1992).

Möðruvallabók, ed. A. Van Arkel (Leiden: E. J. Brill, 1987).

Nelson, Theodore, *Literary Machines* (Sausalito, Calif.: Mindful, 1990).

Nyíri, J. C., 'Electronic Networking and the Unity of Knowledge', in Stephanie Kenna and Seamus Ross (eds.), *Networking in the Humanities: Papers in Honour of Michael Smethurst for his Sixtieth Birthday* (London: Bowker-Saur, 1995).

O'Brien O'Keeffe, Katherine, and Ezell, Margaret J. (eds.), *Cultural Artifacts and the Production of Meaning: The Page, the Image, and the Body* (Ann Arbor: University of Michigan Press, 1994).

Parkes, M. B., and Doyle, A. I., 'The Production of Copies of the *Canterbury Tales*', in M. B. Parkes (ed.), *Scribes, Scripts, and Readers: Studies in the Communication, Presentation, and Dissemination of Medieval Texts* (London and Rio Grande: Hambledon Press, 1991), pp. 210–48 (originally published in M. B. Parkes and A. G. Watson (eds.), *Medieval Scribes, Manuscripts, and Libraries* (1978)).

Pichler, Alois, 'Transcriptions, Texts, and Interpretations', in Johannessen and Nordenstam (eds.), *Culture and Value*.

—— 'Advantages of a Machine-Readable Version of Wittgenstein's Nachlass', in Johannessen and Nordenstam (eds.), *Culture and Value*.

Ramsey, R. Vance, 'The Hengwrt and Ellesmere Manuscripts of the *Canterbury Tales*: Different Scribes', *Studies in Bibliography*, 35 (1982), 133–54.

—— 'Paleography and Scribes of Shared Training', *Studies in the Age of Chaucer*, 8 (1986), 107–44.

Reid, Brian, 'A High-Level Approach to Computer Document Formatting', in *Proceedings of the Seventh Annual ACM Symposium on Programming Languages* (New York: ACM, 1980), pp. 24–30.

RENEAR, ALLEN, 'Representing Text on the Computer: Lessons for and from Philosophy', *Bulletin of the John Rylands University Library of Manchester*, 74 (1992), 221–48.

—— 'Theory and Practice: The Textbase Methodology of the Brown Women Writers Project', *SCMLA, The Journal of the South Central Division of the Modern Language Association*, 11: 3 (1994), 99–117.

—— 'Practical Ontology: The Case of Written Communication', in Johannessen and Nordenstam (eds.), *Culture and Value*.

—— DURAND, DAVID, and MYLONAS, ELLI, 'Refining our Notion of What Text Really Is', in Susan Hockey and Nancy Ide (eds.), *Research in Humanities Computing*, 4 (Oxford: Clarendon Press, 1996).

REYNOLDS, L. D., and WILSON, N. G., *Scribes and Scholars*, 3rd edn. (Oxford: Oxford University Press, 1991).

ROBERTS, JEANNE ADDISON, ' "Wife" or "Wise"—*The Tempest* line 1786', *Studies in Bibliography*, 31 (1978), 205–8.

ROBINSON, P. M. W., 'An Approach to the Manuscripts of the Wife of Bath's Prologue', in Ian Lancashire (ed.), *Computer-based Chaucer Studies* (Toronto: University of Toronto Press, 1993).

—— *The Digitization of Primary Textual Sources* (Oxford: Office for Humanities Communication Publications, 1993).

—— '*Collate*: A Program for Interactive Collation of Large Textual Traditions', in Susan Hockey and Nancy Ide (eds.), *Research in Humanities Computing*, 3 (Oxford: Clarendon Press, 1994).

—— *The Transcription of Primary Textual Sources Using SGML* (Oxford: Office for Humanities Communication Publications, 1994).

—— *Collate: A Program for Interactive Collation of Large Manuscript Traditions*, Version 2.1 (Milton Keynes: International Institute for Electronic Library Research, 1996).

—— 'Computer-Assisted Stemmatic Analysis and "Best-Text" Historical Editing', in M. van Mulken and P. van Reenen (eds.), *Studies in Stemmatology* (Amsterdam: John Benjamins, 1996).

—— and O'HARA, R. J., 'Cladistic Analysis of an Old Norse Manuscript Tradition', in Susan Hockey and Nancy Ide (eds.), *Research in Humanities Computing*, 4 (Oxford: Clarendon Press, 1996).

ROTHSTEIN, EDWARD, 'Technology: If Life on the Web Is Postmodern, Maybe Foucault Really Was a Power Ranger', *New York Times*, 1 Apr. 1993.

ROTHWELL, KENNETH S., and MELZER, ANNABELLE HENKIN, *Shakespeare on Screen: An International Filmography and Videography* (New York: Neal-Schuman, 1990).

ROUSE, M. A., and ROUSE, R. H., *Authentic Witnesses: Approaches to Medieval Texts and Manuscripts* (Notre Dame, Ind.: University of Notre Dame Press, 1991).

RUGGIERS, PAUL G. (ed.), *Editing Chaucer: The Great Tradition* (Norman, Okla.: Pilgrim Books, 1984).

SAID, EDWARD W., *Culture and Imperialism* (New York: Alfred A. Knopf, 1993).

SANJEK, DAVID, ' "Don't Have to DJ No More": Sampling and the "Autonomous" Creator', *Intellectual Property and the Construction of Authorship*, Special Issue of *Cardozo Arts and Entertainment Law Journal*, 10: 2 (1992), 607–24.

SCHOR, NAOMI, *Reading in Detail: Aesthetics and the Feminine* (New York and London: Routledge, 1987).

SHAKESPEARE, WILLIAM, *The Norton Facsimile: The First Folio of Shakespeare*, ed. Charlton Hinman (New York: W. W. Norton, 1968).

—— *The Riverside Shakespeare*, ed. G. Blakemore Evans (Boston: Houghton Mifflin, 1974).

—— *Shakespeare's Plays in Quarto*, ed. Michael J. B. Allen and Kenneth Muir (Berkeley: University of California Press, 1981).

—— *The Division of the Kingdom: Shakespeare's Two Versions of 'King Lear'*, ed. Gary Taylor and Michael Warren (Oxford: Clarendon Press, 1983).

—— *Complete Works*, ed. Gary Taylor and Stanley Wells (Oxford: Oxford University Press, 1986).

—— *The Tempest*, ed. Stephen Orgel (Oxford and New York: Oxford University Press, 1986).

—— *The Complete 'King Lear', 1608–1623*, ed. Michael J. Warren (Berkeley: University of California Press, 1989).

—— *Three Text Hamlet*, ed. Bernice Kliman and Paul Bertram (New York: AMS Press, 1991).

—— *The First Folio of Shakespeare*, ed. Peter W. M. Blayney (Washington, DC: Folger, 1991).

—— *Macbeth* [CD-ROM], ed. A. R. Braunmuller, Voyager Company Software (Irvington, NY: Voyager, 1994).

SHILLINGSBURG, PETER L., *Scholarly Editing in the Computer Age: Theory and Practice* (Athens and London: University of Georgia Press, 1986).

SILVER, BRENDA R., 'Textual Criticism as Feminist Practice: Or, Who's Afraid of Virginia Woolf, Part II', in George Bornstein (ed.), *Representing Modernist Texts: Editing as Interpretation* (Ann Arbor: University of Michigan Press, 1991).

—— 'Whose Room of Orlando's Own? The Politics of Adaptation', in D. C. Greetham (ed.), *The Margins of the Text* (Ann Arbor: University of Michigan Press, 1997).

SMALL, IAN, 'The Editor as Annotator as Ideal Reader', in Small and Walsh (eds.), *Theory and Practice of Text-Editing*.

—— 'Text-editing and the Computer: Facts and Values', in Chernaik, Davis, and Deegan (eds.), *Politics of the Electronic Text*.

—— and WALSH, MARCUS (eds.), *The Theory and Practice of Text Editing: Essays in Honour of James T. Bolton* (Cambridge: Cambridge University Press, 1991).

SMILEY, JANE, 'Say it ain't so, Huck: Second Thoughts on Mark Twain's "Masterpiece"', *Harper's Magazine*, 292 (Jan. 1996).

SPERBERG-McQUEEN, C. MICHAEL, 'Text in the Electronic Age: Textual Study and Text Encoding, with Examples from Medieval Texts', *Literary and Linguistic Computing*, 6: 1 (1991), 34–46.

—— and BURNARD, LOU (eds.), *Guidelines for Electronic Text Encoding and Interchange* (Chicago and Oxford: TEI, 1994).

STEINER, GEORGE, *Real Presences: Is There Anything in What We Say?* (London: Faber and Faber, 1989).

STERLING, BRUCE, 'Internet', *Magazine of Fantasy and Science Fiction*, Science Column no. 5 (Feb. 1993).

SUTHERLAND, KATHRYN, 'A Guide through the Labyrinth: Dickens's *Little Dorrit* as Hypertext', *Literary and Linguistic Computing*, 5 (1990), 305–9.

—— 'Challenging Assumptions: Women Writers and New Technology', in Chernaik, Davis, and Deegan (eds.), *Politics of the Electronic Text*.

—— 'Waiting for Connections: Hypertexts, Multiplots, and the Engaged Reader', in Susan Hockey and Nancy Ide (eds.), *Research in Humanities Computing*, 3 (Oxford: Clarendon Press, 1994).

—— 'Looking and Knowing: Textual Encounters of a Postponed Kind', in Warren Chernaik, Marilyn Deegan, and Andrew Gibson (eds.), *Beyond the Book: Theory, Culture, and the Politics of Cyberspace* (Oxford: Office for Humanities Communication Publications, 1996).

SWOFFORD, D. L., *PAUP: Phylogenetic Analysis Using Parsimony*. Macintosh Version 3.0r. Computer program distributed by the Illinois Natural History Survey (Champaign, Ill., 1991).

TANSELLE, G. THOMAS, *A Rational of Textual Criticism* (Philadelphia: University of Pennsylvania Press, 1989).

TREITLER, LEO, 'The Politics of Reception: Tailoring the Present as Fulfillment of a Desired Past', *Journal of the Royal Musicological Association*, 116 (1992), 280–98.

TURKLE, SHERRY, *The Second Self: Computers and the Human Spirit* (New York: Simon and Schuster, 1984).

—— *Life on the Screen: Identity in the Age of the Internet* (New York: Simon and Schuster, 1995).

TWAIN, MARK, 'A Defense of General Funston', *North American Review*, 174 (May 1902). <URL: http://web.syr.edu/~fjzwick/twain_html/deffunst.html>, in Jim Zwick (ed.), *Anti-Imperialism in the United States, 1898–1935*, <URL: http://web.syr.edu/~fjzwick/ ail98–35.html>

—— 'In Defense of Maxim Gorki', *New York Sun, Tribune, World* (1906), cited from *Mark Twain Quotations* <URL: http://www.tarleton.edu/activities/pages/facultypages/schmidt/Mark_Twain.html>

—— *Adventures of Huckleberry Finn*, ed. Walter Blair and Victor Fischer, in *The Works of Mark Twain*, vol. viii (Berkeley: University of California Press, 1988).

URKOWITZ, STEVEN, *Shakespeare's Revision of 'King Lear'* (Princeton: Princeton University Press, 1980).

VOLOSHINOV, V. N., *Marxism and the Philosophy of Language*, trans. Ladislav Matejka and I. R. Titunik (New York: Seminar Press, Inc., 1973).

WALL, STEPHEN, 'Annotated English Novels?', *Essays in Criticism*, 32 (1982), 1–8.

WARREN, MICHAEL J., 'Quarto and Folio *King Lear* and the Interpretation of Albany and Edgar', in David Bevington and Jay L. Halio (eds.), *Shakespeares, Pattern of Excelling Nature* (Newark: University of Delaware Press, 1978).

WELLS, STANLEY, TAYLOR, GARY, *et al.*, *William Shakespeare: A Textual Companion* (Oxford: Oxford University Press, 1987).

WHITE, HAYDEN, *The Content of the Form: Narrative Discourse and Historical Representation* (London: Johns Hopkins University Press, 1987).

WILLIAMS, RAYMOND, *Marxism and Literature* (Oxford: Oxford University Press, 1977).

WIMSATT, W. K., *The Verbal Icon: Studies in the Meaning of Poetry* (Lexington: University of Kentucky Press, 1954).

WOODMANSEE, MARTHA, and JASZI, PETER (eds.), *The Construction of Authorship: Textual Appropriation in Law and Literature* (Durham, NC: Duke University Press, 1994).

WOODS, KEITH, ' "NIGGER": A Case Study in Using a Racial Epithet', Poynter Institute for Media Studies, Nov. 1995,
    <URL: http://www.poynter.org/poynter/ec1195a.html>
—— 'An Essay on a Wickedly Powerful Word', ibid.,
    <URL: http://www.poynter.org/poynter/ec1195b.html>

INDEX